CULLEN BUNN   JONAS SCHARF   ALEX GUIMARÃES

VOLUME ONE

Published by

BOOM!
STUDIOS

BASILISK Vol. 1, December 2021. Published by BOOM! Studios, a division of Boom
Entertainment, Inc. Basilisk is ™ & © 2021 Cullen Bunn & Jonas Scharf. Originally published in
single magazine form as BASILISK No. 1 - 4. ™ & © 2021 Cullen Bunn & Jonas Scharf. All rights
reserved. BOOM! Studios™ and the BOOM! Studios logo are trademarks of Boom Entertainment,
Inc., registered in various countries and categories. All characters, events, and institutions depicted
herein are fictional. Any similarity between any of the names, characters, persons, events, and/or institutions in this publication to
actual names, characters, and persons, whether living or dead, events, and/or institutions is unintended and purely coincidental.
BOOM! Studios does not read or accept unsolicited submissions of ideas, stories, or artwork.

BOOM! Studios, 5670 Wilshire Boulevard, Suite 400, Los Angeles, CA, 90036-5679. Printed in China. First Printing.

Standard Edition:
ISBN: 978-1-68415-748-8, eISBN: 978-1-64668-326-0

BOOM! Studios Exclusive Edition:
ISBN: 978-1-68415-830-0

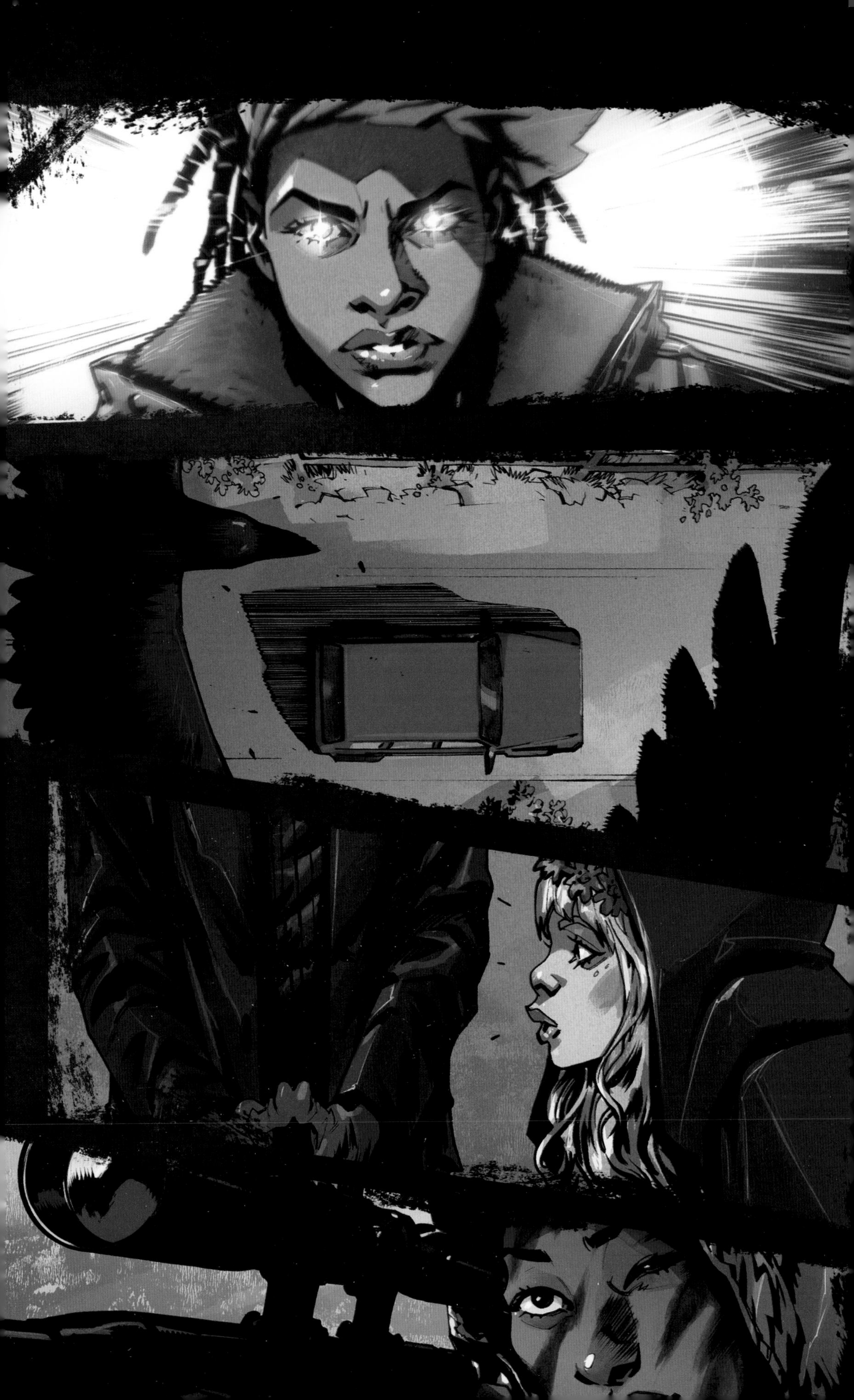

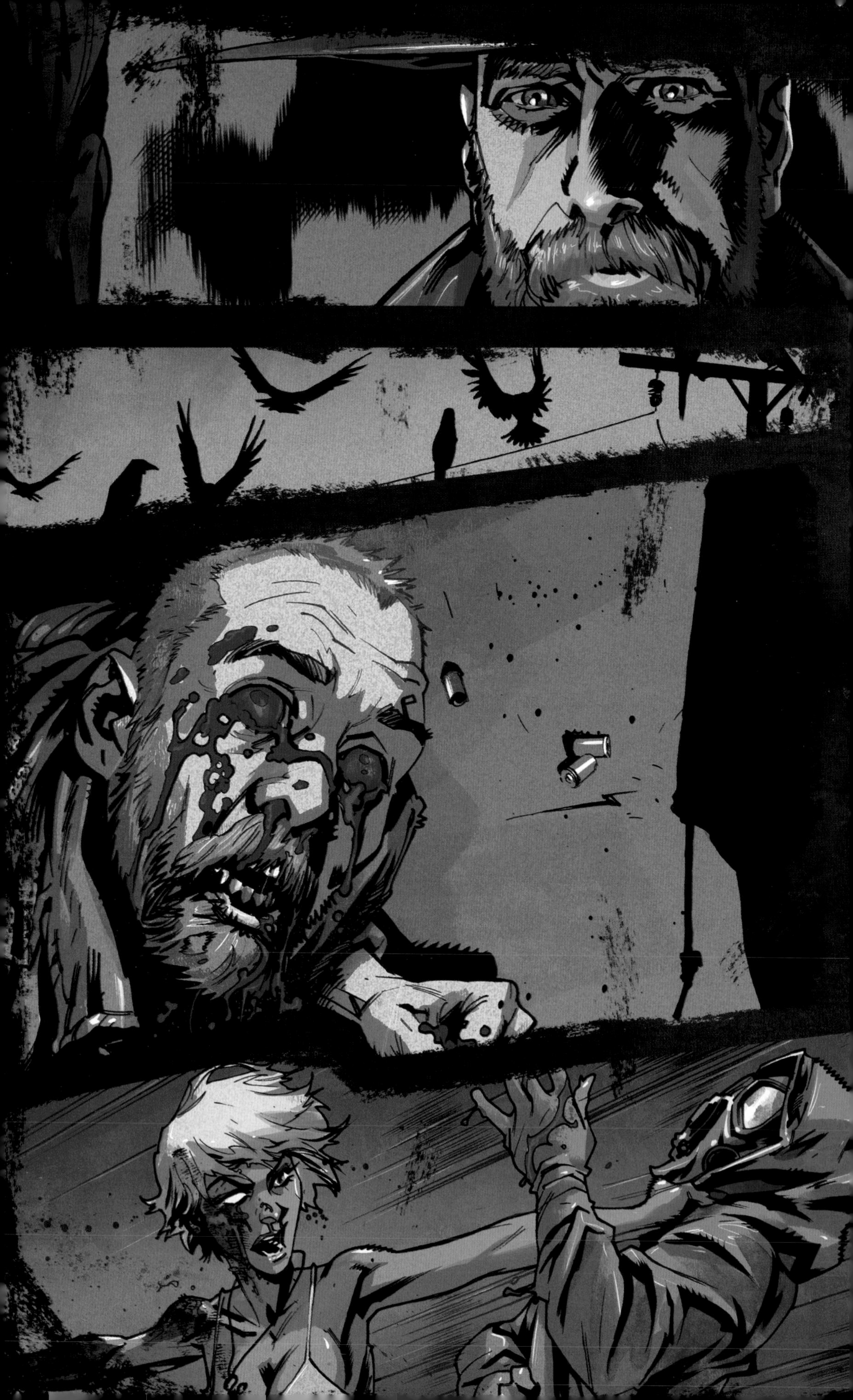

Written by
CULLEN BUNN

Illustrated by
JONAS SCHARF

Colored by
ALEX GUIMARÃES

Lettered by
ED DUKESHIRE

Cover by
JONAS SCHARF

BOOM! Studios Exclusive Cover by
JAHNOY LINDSAY

Series Designer
GRACE PARK

Collection Designer
CHELSEA ROBERTS

Assistant Editor
RAMIRO PORTNOY

Associate Editor
JONATHAN MANNING

Editor
ERIC HARBURN

BASILISK Created by
CULLEN BUNN & JONAS SCHARF

CHAPTER ONE

DOWN FROM
THE MOUNTAINS

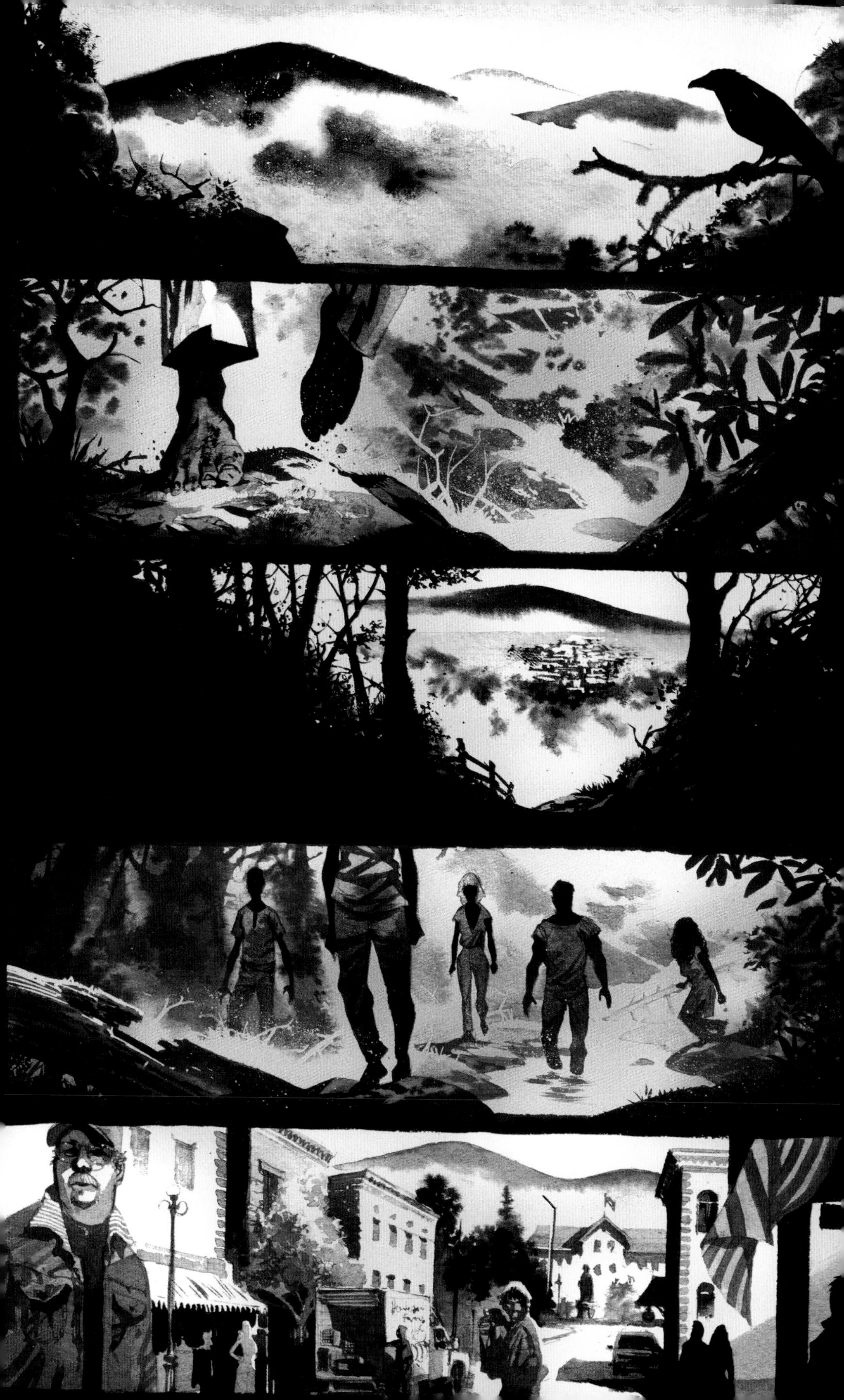

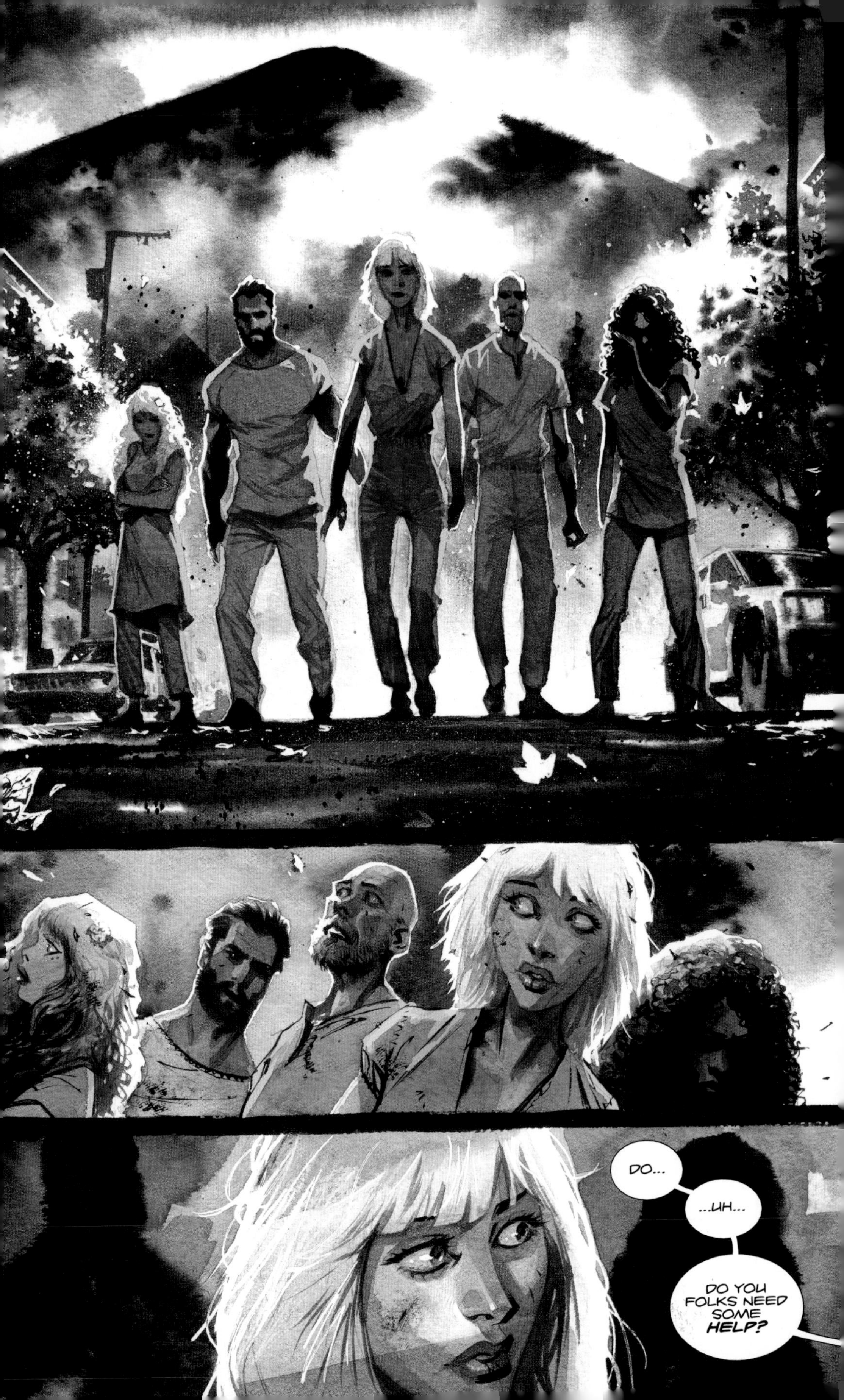
DO...
...UH...
DO YOU FOLKS NEED SOME HELP?

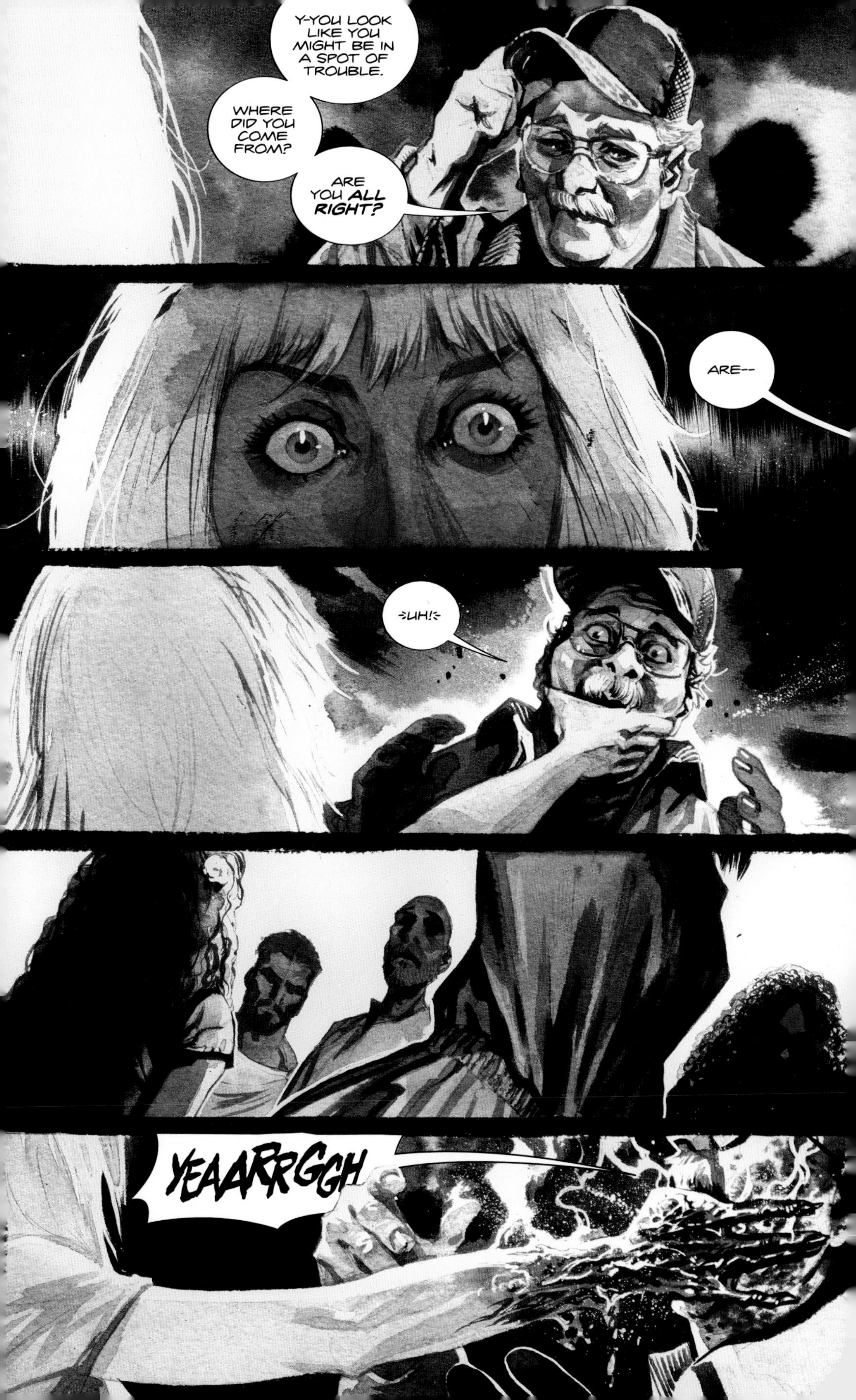
Y-YOU LOOK LIKE YOU MIGHT BE IN A SPOT OF TROUBLE.
WHERE DID YOU COME FROM?
ARE YOU **ALL RIGHT?**
ARE--
UH!
YEAARRGGH

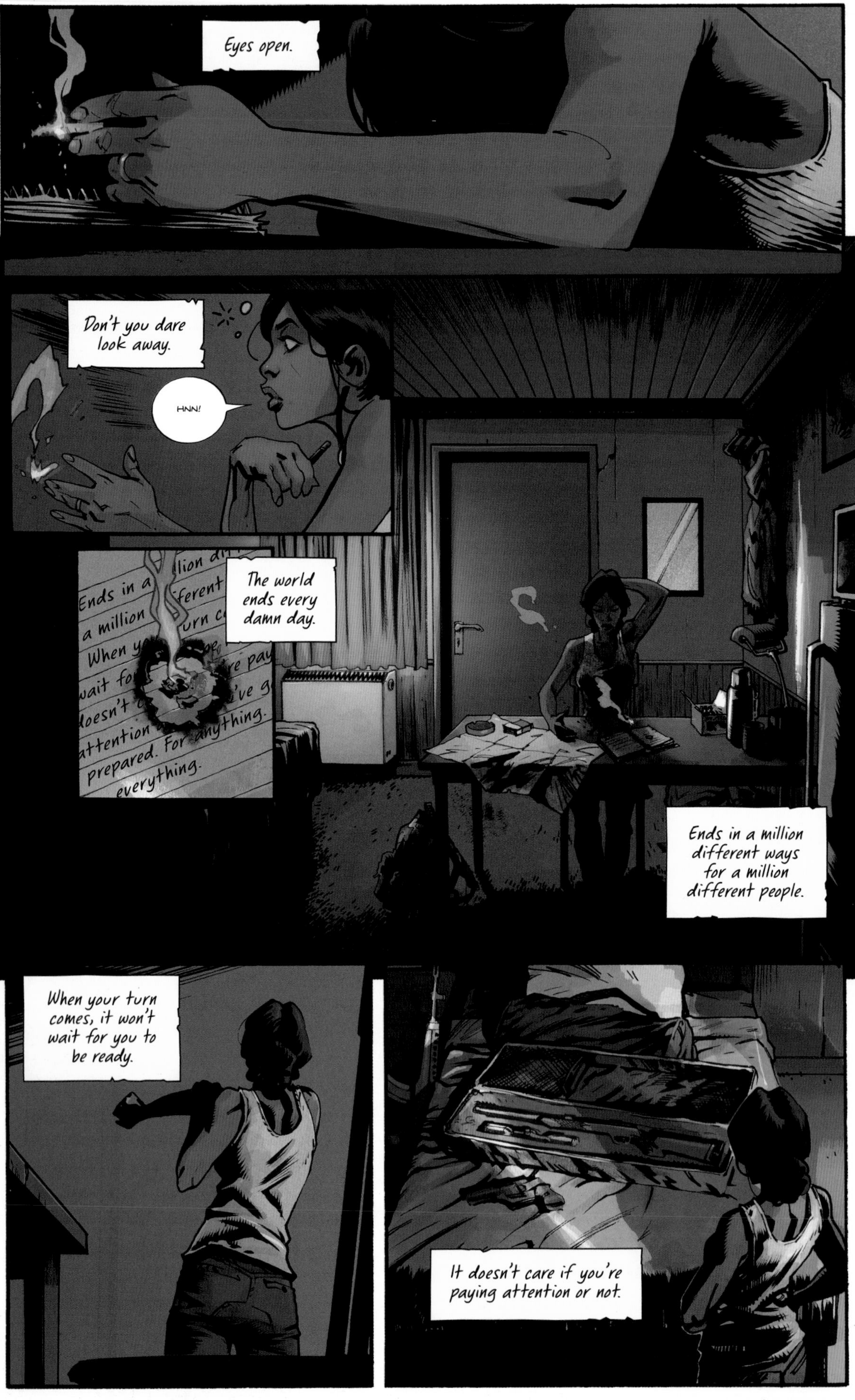
Eyes open.
Don't you dare look away.
HNN!
The world ends every damn day.
prepared. For anything.
everything.
Ends in a million different ways for a million different people.
When your turn comes, it won't wait for you to be ready.
It doesn't care if you're paying attention or not.

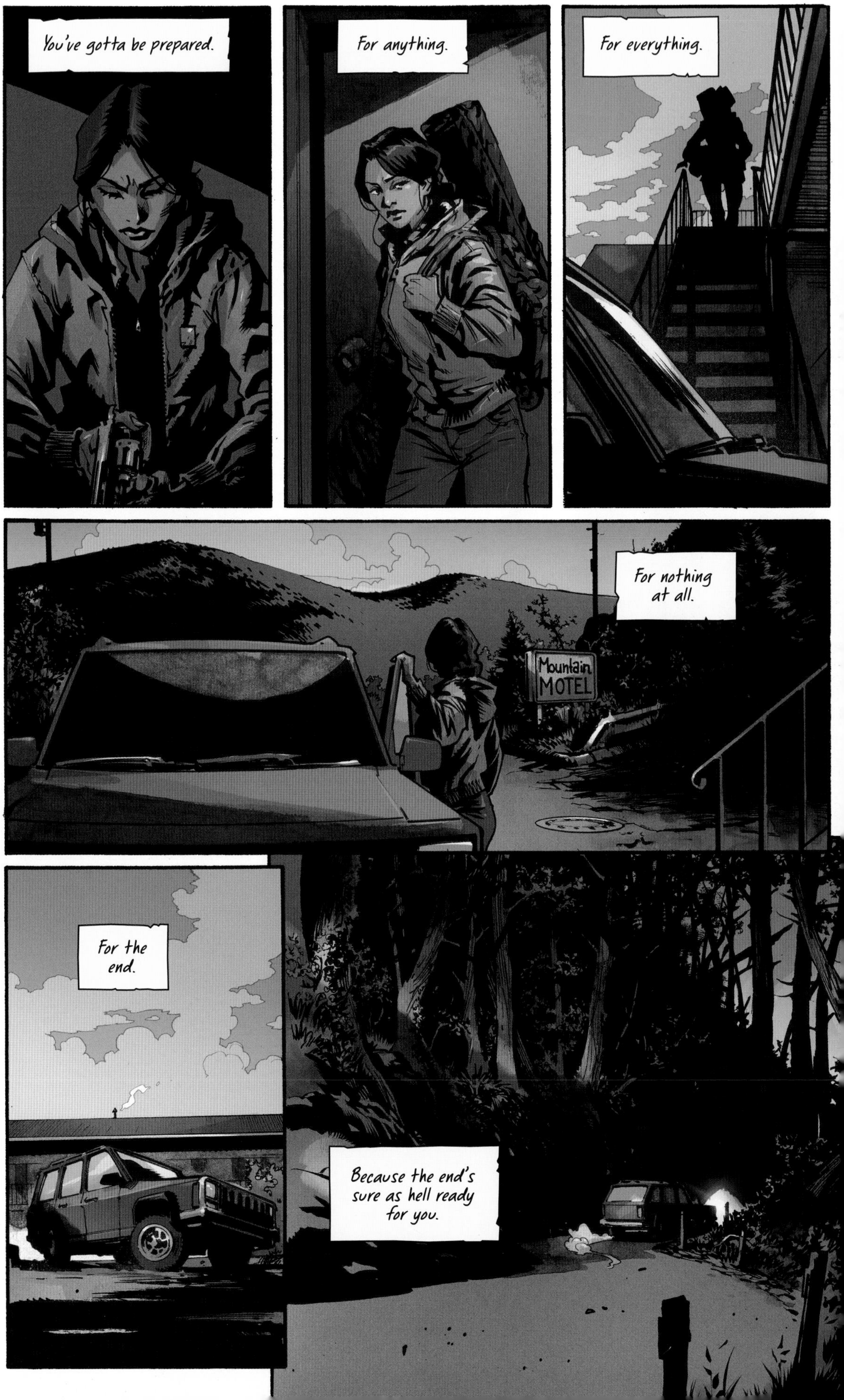

You've gotta be prepared.
For anything.
For everything.
For nothing at all.
Mountain MOTEL
For the end.
Because the end's sure as hell ready for you.

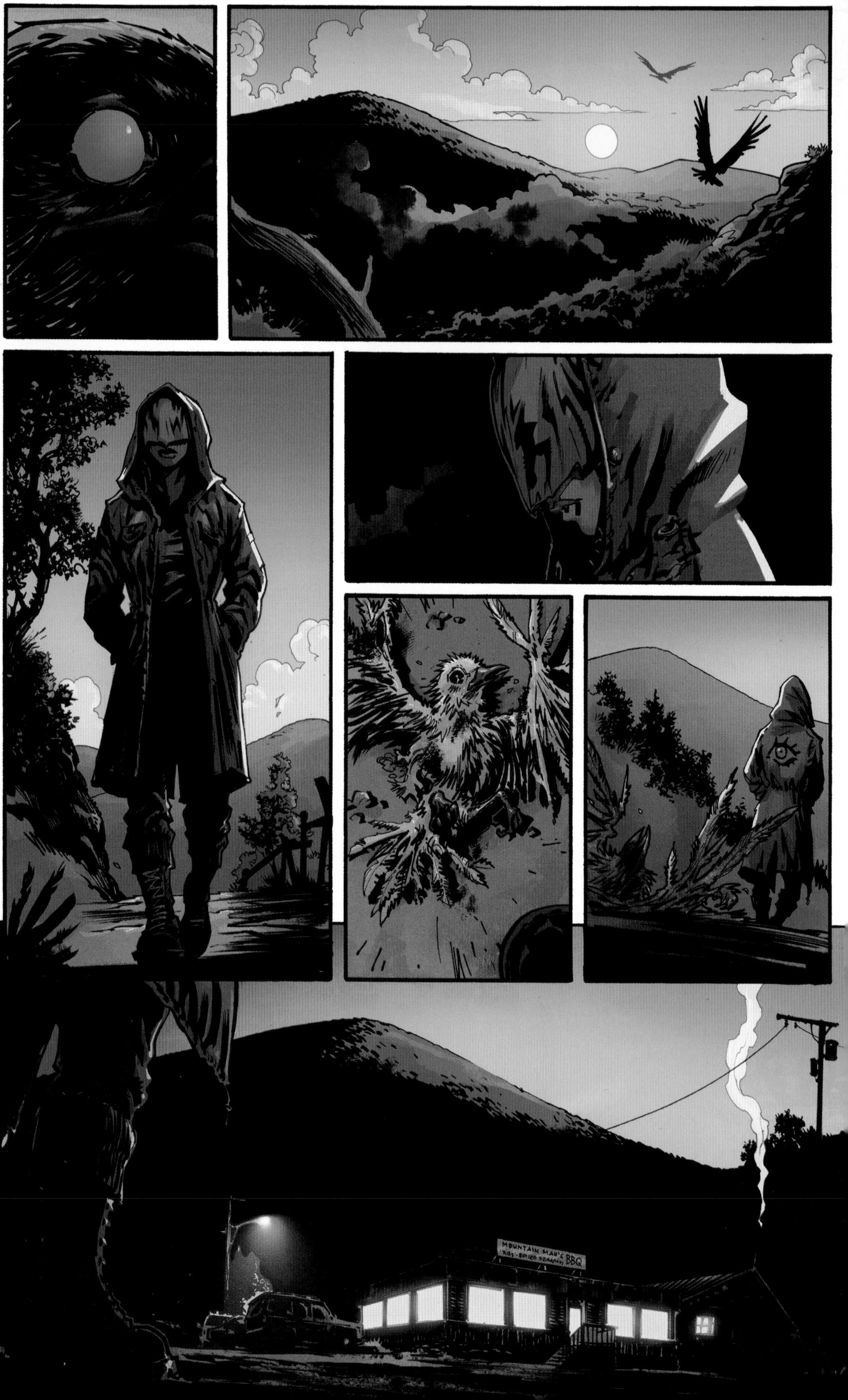
MOUNTAIN MAN'S BBQ
RIBS • BOILED PEANUTS

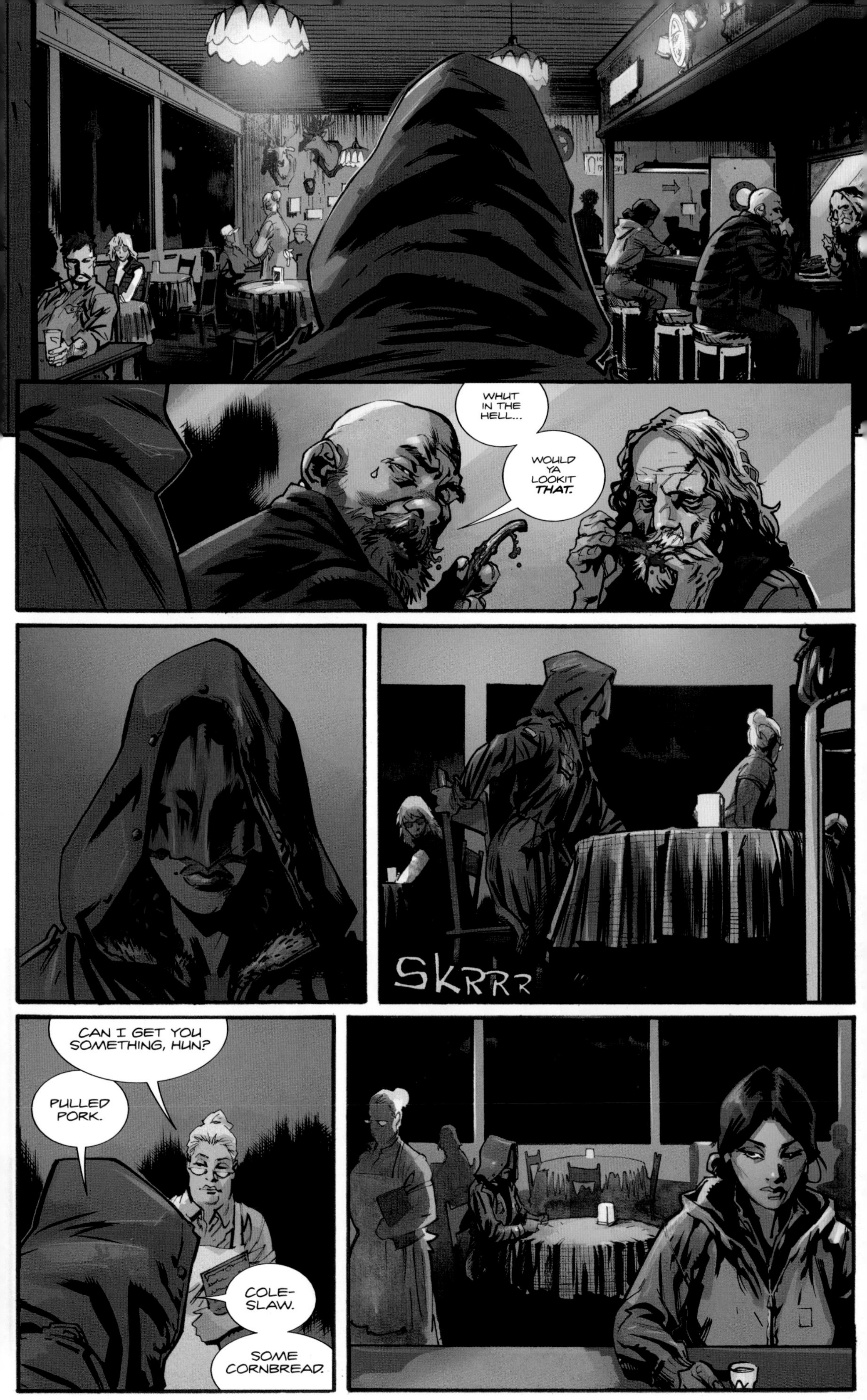
WHUT IN THE HELL...
WOULD YA LOOKIT *THAT.*
SKRRR
CAN I GET YOU SOMETHING, HUN?
PULLED PORK.
COLE-SLAW.
SOME CORNBREAD.

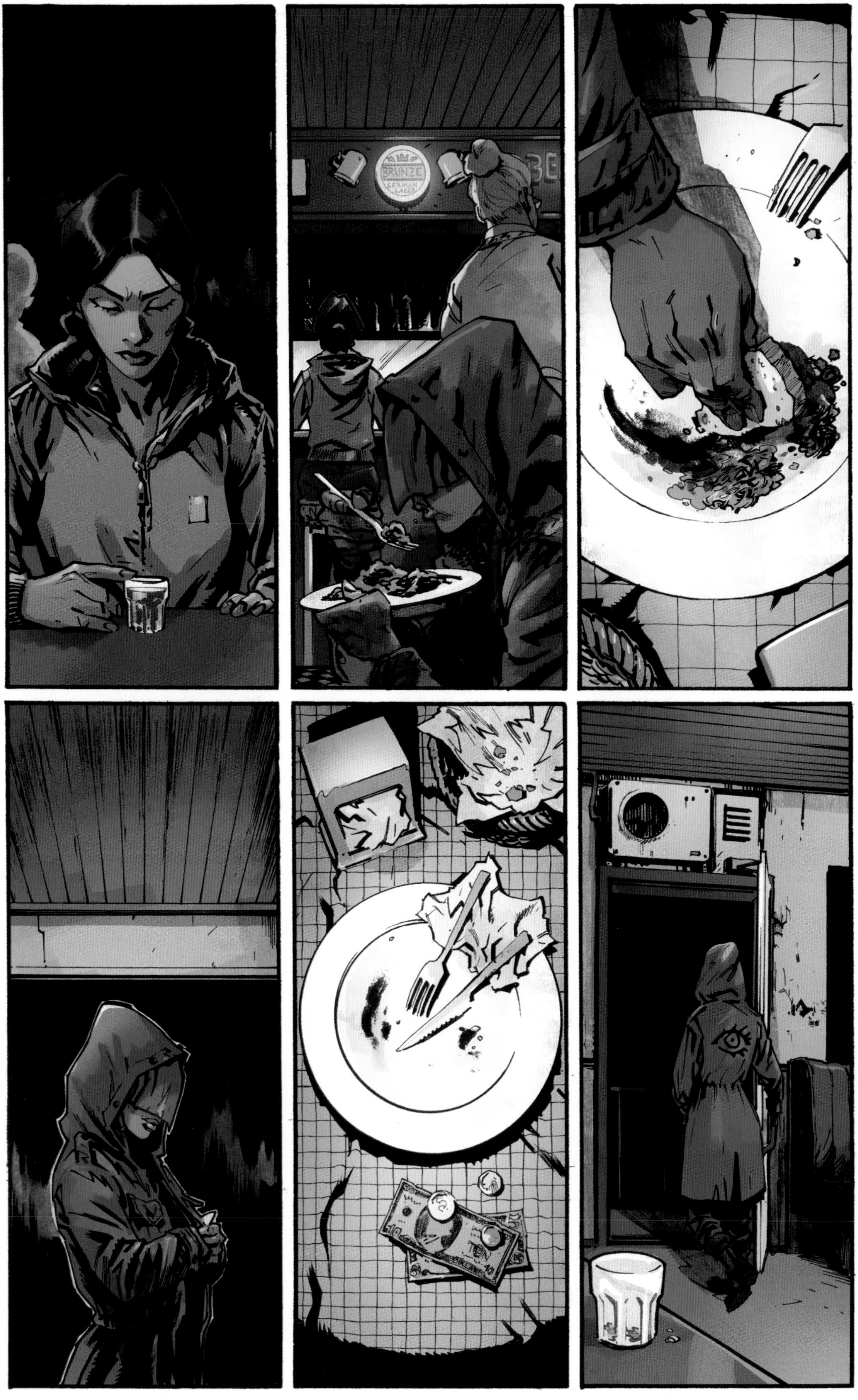
BRUNZE
GERMAN LAGER
TEN

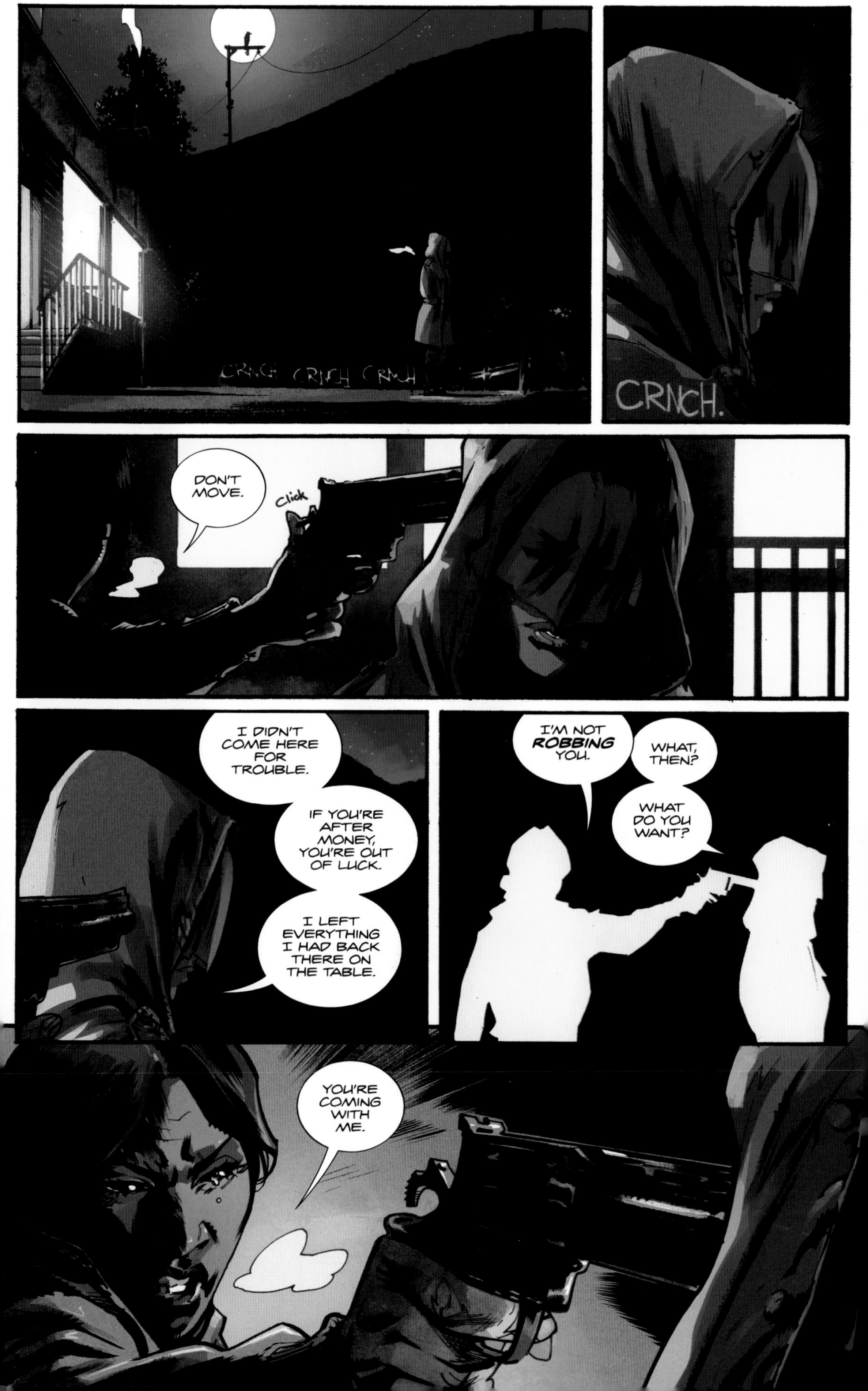
CRNCH CRNCH CRNCH
CRNCH.
DON'T MOVE.
Click
I DIDN'T COME HERE FOR TROUBLE.
IF YOU'RE AFTER MONEY, YOU'RE OUT OF LUCK.
I LEFT EVERYTHING I HAD BACK THERE ON THE TABLE.
I'M NOT **ROBBING** YOU.
WHAT, THEN?
WHAT DO YOU WANT?
YOU'RE COMING WITH ME.

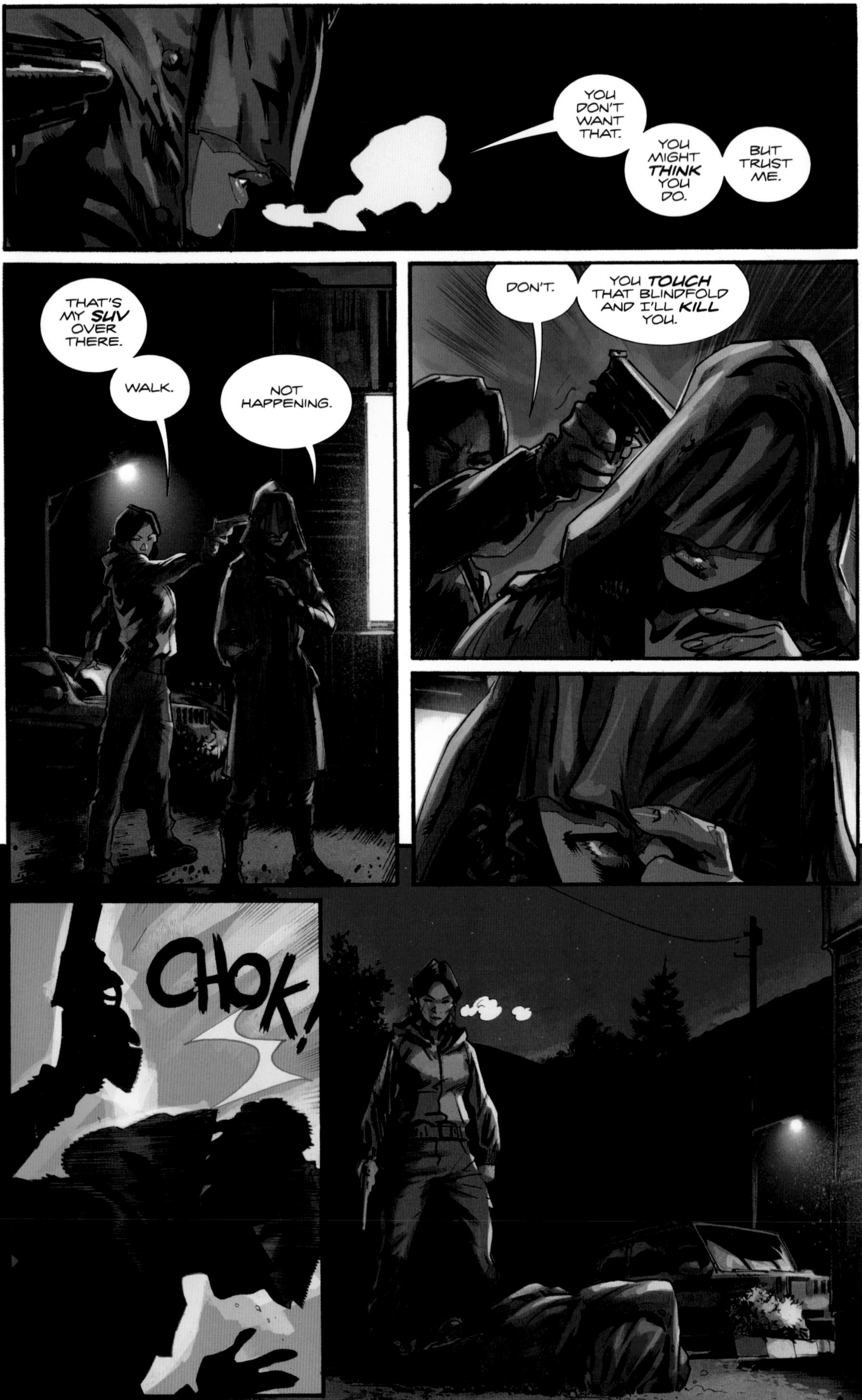
YOU DON'T WANT THAT.
YOU MIGHT THINK YOU DO.
BUT TRUST ME.
THAT'S MY SUV OVER THERE.
WALK.
NOT HAPPENING.
DON'T.
YOU TOUCH THAT BLINDFOLD AND I'LL KILL YOU.
CHOK!

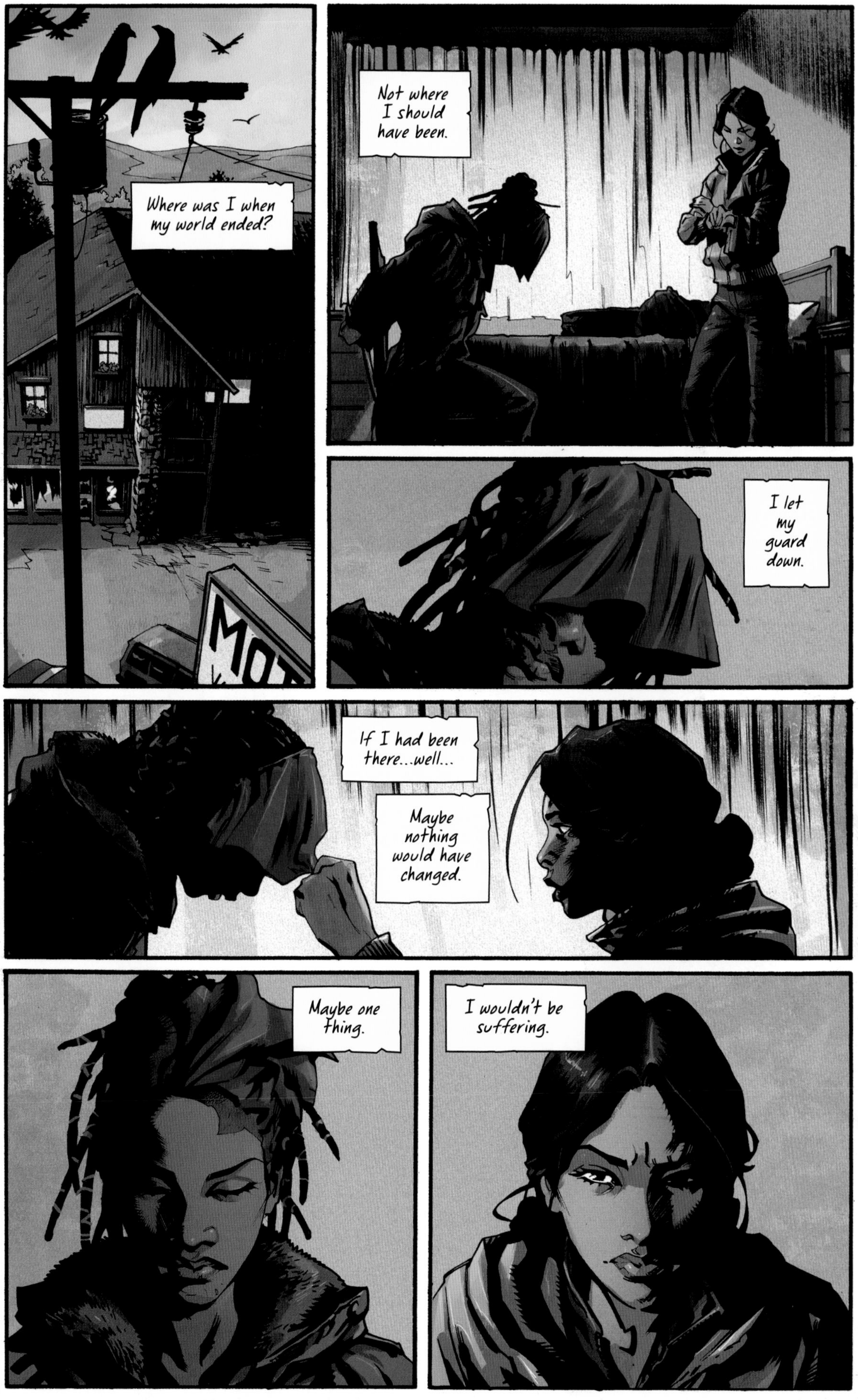

Where was I when my world ended?
Not where I should have been.
I let my guard down.
If I had been there...well...
Maybe nothing would have changed.
Maybe one thing.
I wouldn't be suffering.
MOT

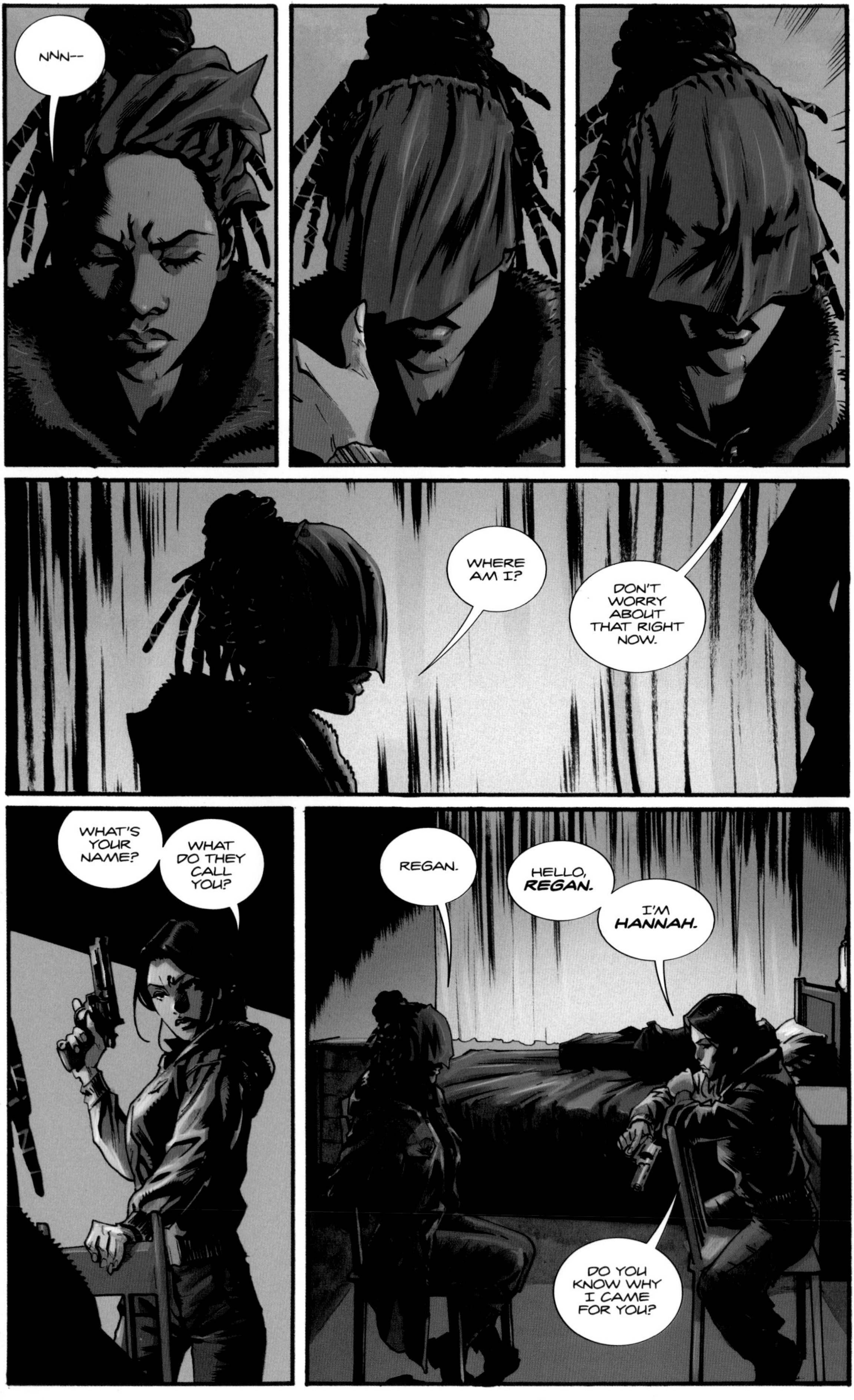
NNN--
WHERE AM I?
DON'T WORRY ABOUT THAT RIGHT NOW.
WHAT'S YOUR NAME?
WHAT DO THEY CALL YOU?
REGAN.
HELLO, **REGAN.**
I'M **HANNAH.**
DO YOU KNOW WHY I CAME FOR YOU?

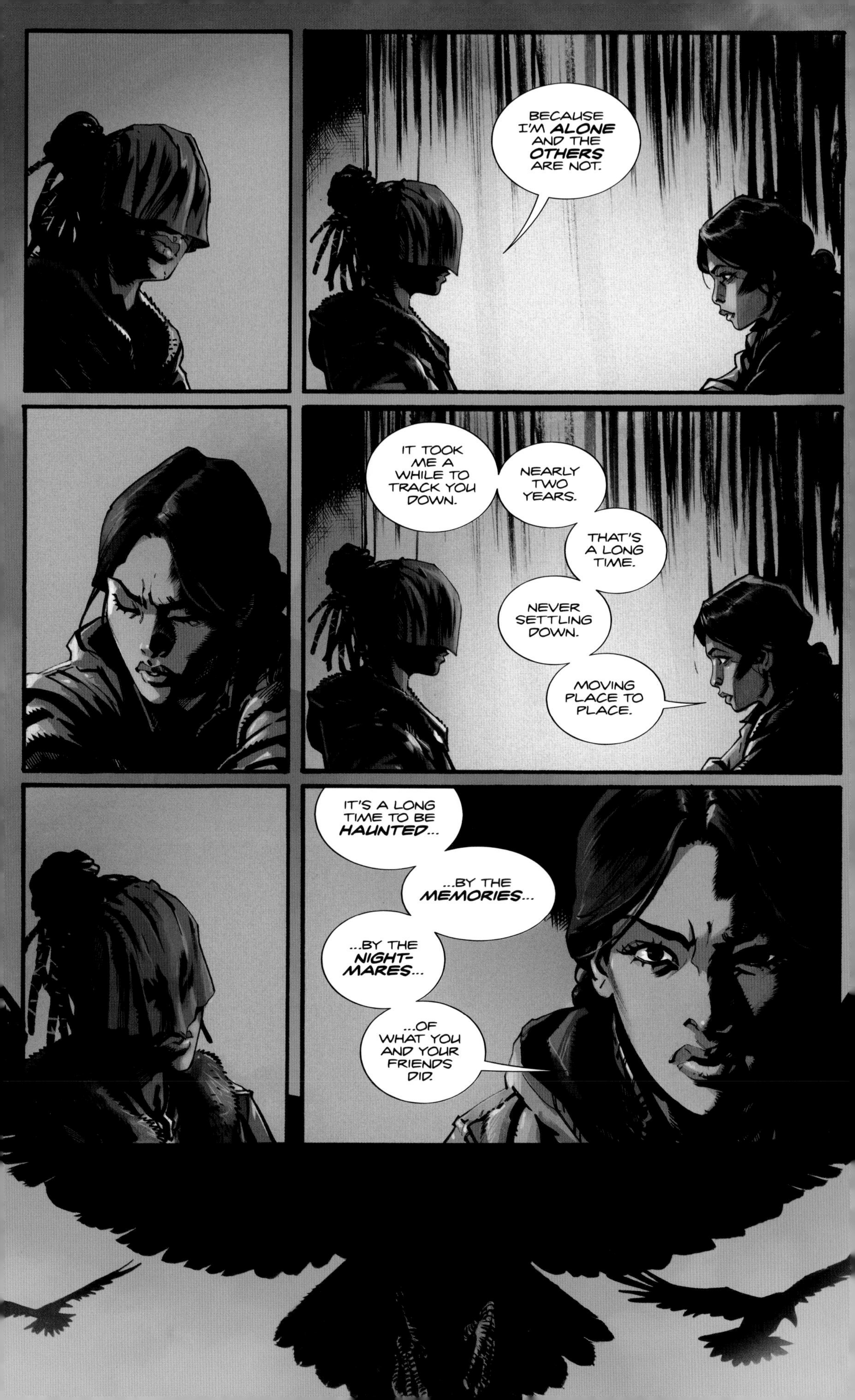
BECAUSE I'M ALONE AND THE OTHERS ARE NOT.
IT TOOK ME A WHILE TO TRACK YOU DOWN.
NEARLY TWO YEARS.
THAT'S A LONG TIME.
NEVER SETTLING DOWN.
MOVING PLACE TO PLACE.
IT'S A LONG TIME TO BE HAUNTED...
...BY THE MEMORIES...
...BY THE NIGHT-MARES...
...OF WHAT YOU AND YOUR FRIENDS DID.

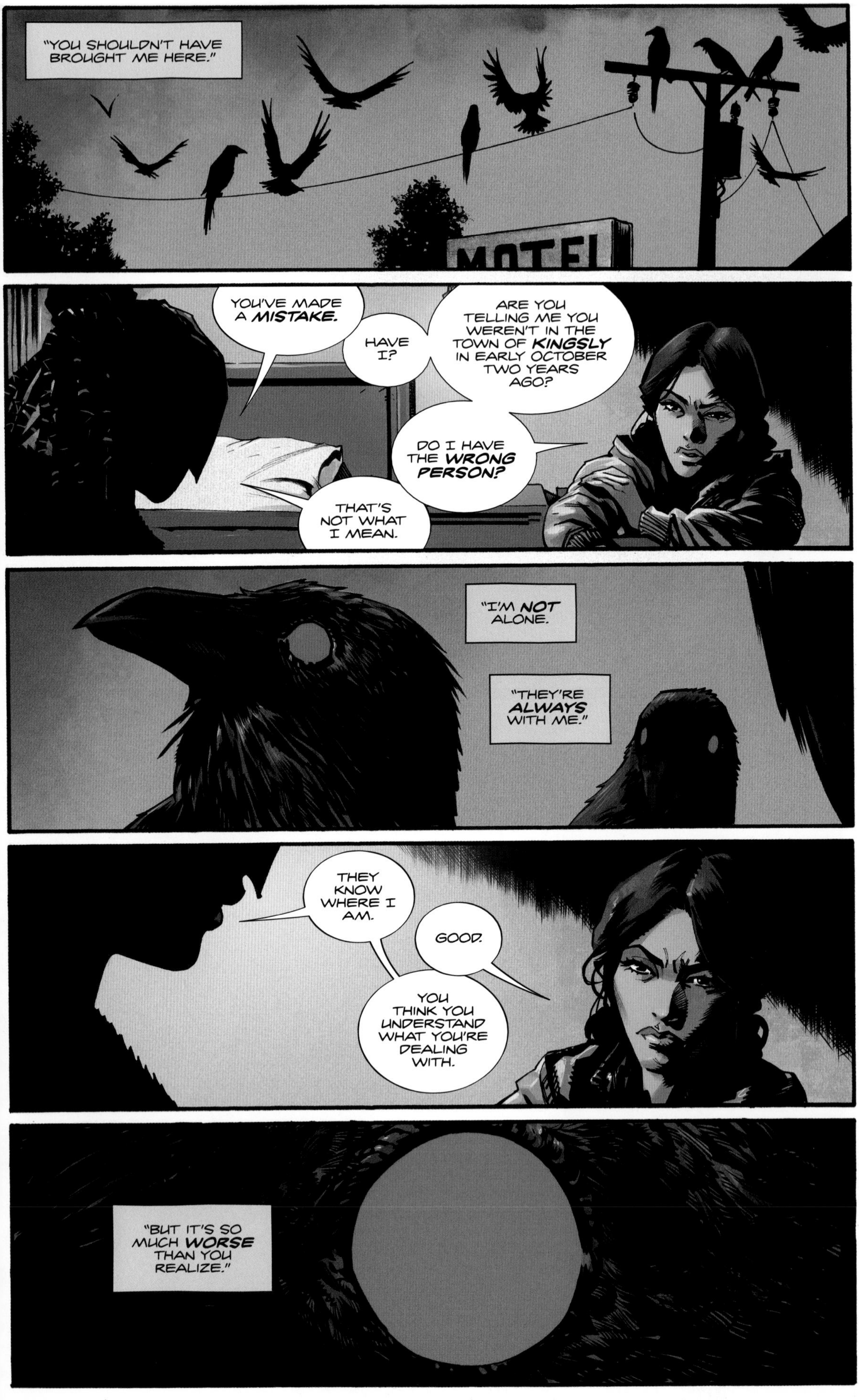
"YOU SHOULDN'T HAVE BROUGHT ME HERE."
MOTEL
YOU'VE MADE A MISTAKE.
HAVE I?
ARE YOU TELLING ME YOU WEREN'T IN THE TOWN OF KINGSLY IN EARLY OCTOBER TWO YEARS AGO?
DO I HAVE THE WRONG PERSON?
THAT'S NOT WHAT I MEAN.
"I'M NOT ALONE.
"THEY'RE ALWAYS WITH ME."
THEY KNOW WHERE I AM.
GOOD.
YOU THINK YOU UNDERSTAND WHAT YOU'RE DEALING WITH.
"BUT IT'S SO MUCH WORSE THAN YOU REALIZE."

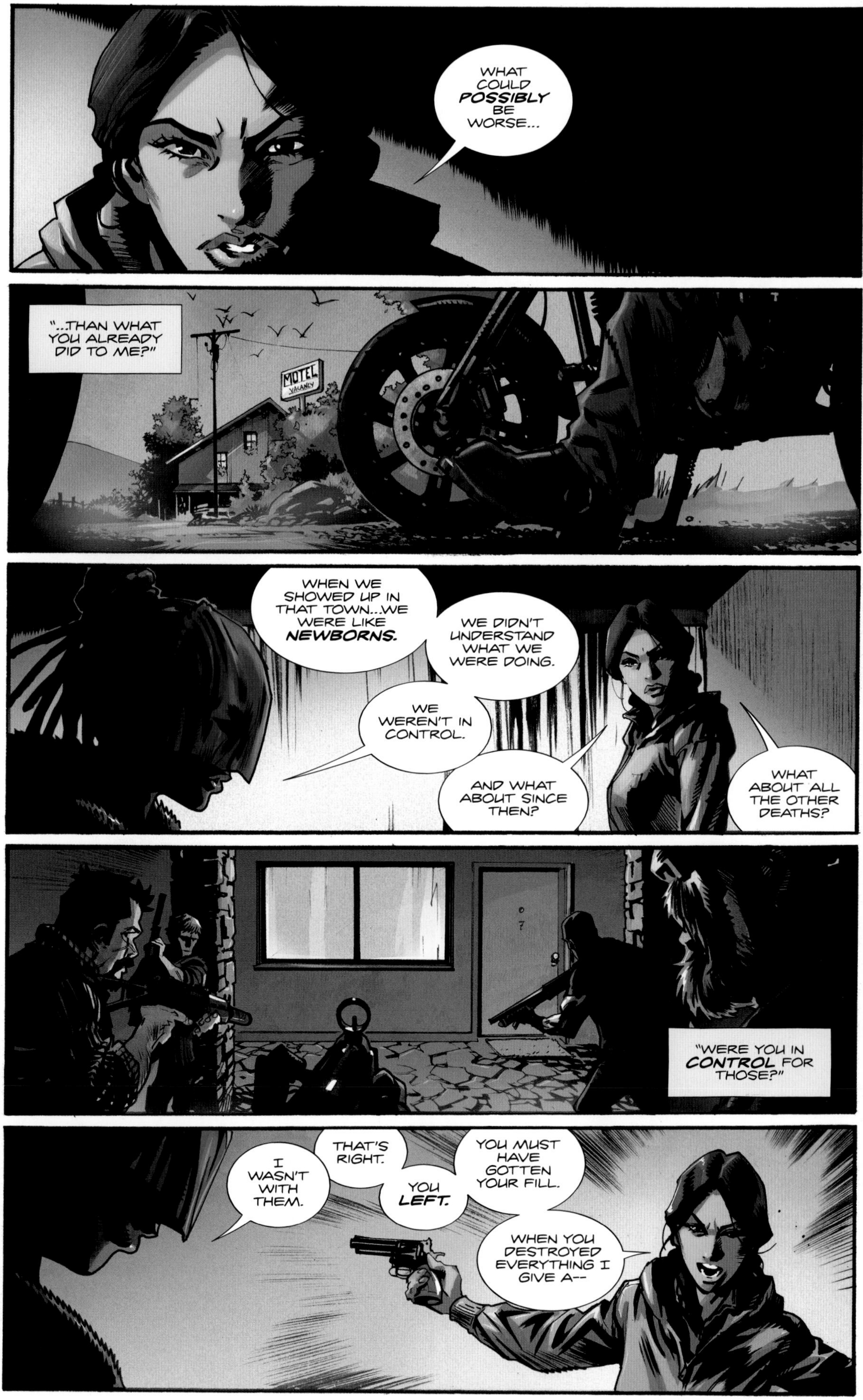
WHAT COULD **POSSIBLY** BE WORSE...
"...THAN WHAT YOU ALREADY DID TO ME?"
MOTEL VACANCY
WHEN WE SHOWED UP IN THAT TOWN...WE WERE LIKE **NEWBORNS.**
WE DIDN'T UNDERSTAND WHAT WE WERE DOING.
WE WEREN'T IN CONTROL.
AND WHAT ABOUT SINCE THEN?
WHAT ABOUT ALL THE OTHER DEATHS?
"WERE YOU IN **CONTROL** FOR THOSE?"
I WASN'T WITH THEM.
THAT'S RIGHT.
YOU **LEFT.**
YOU MUST HAVE GOTTEN YOUR FILL.
WHEN YOU DESTROYED EVERYTHING I GIVE A--

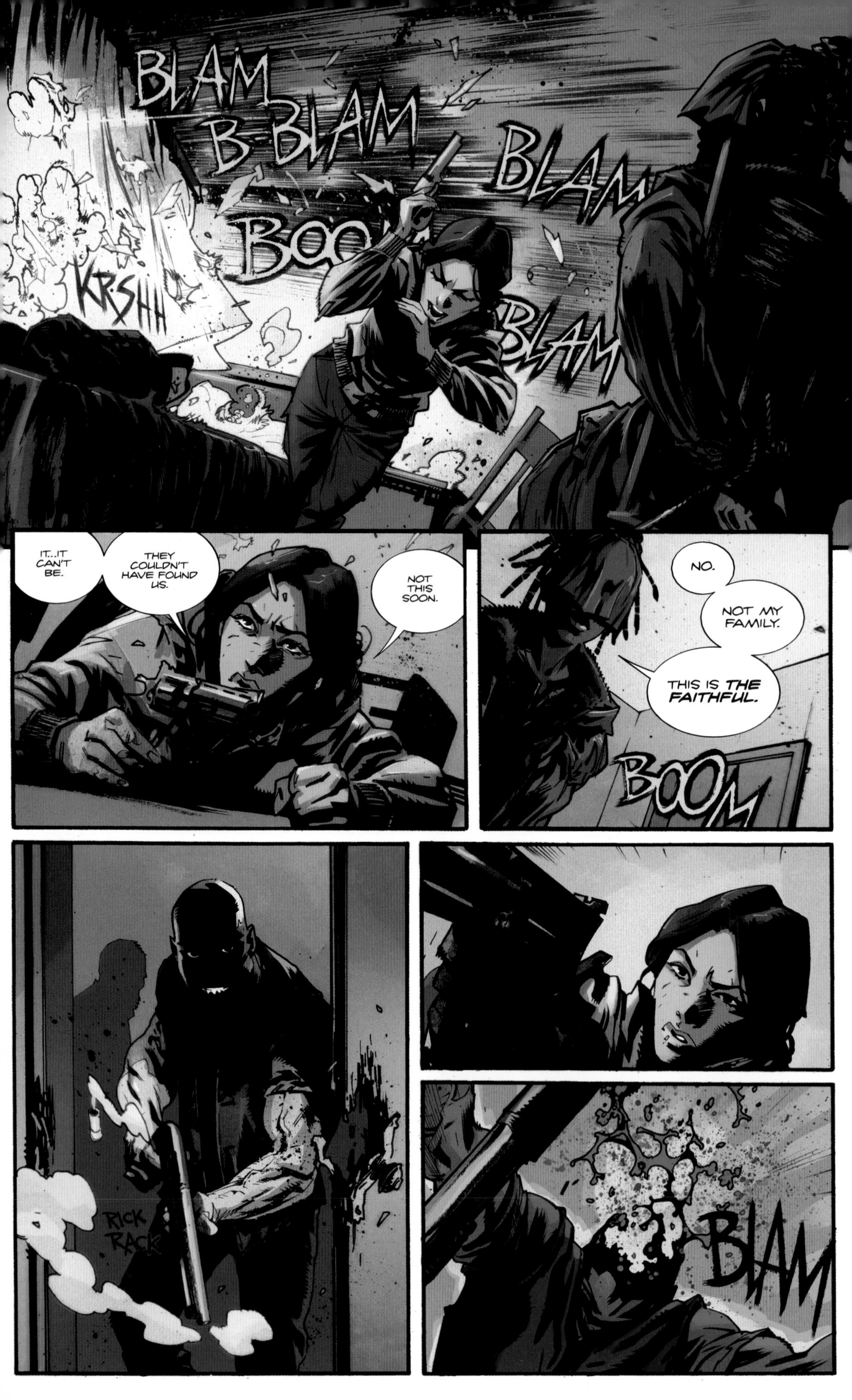
BLAM
B-BLAM
BLAM
BOOM
KRSHH
BLAM
IT... IT CAN'T BE.
THEY COULDN'T HAVE FOUND US.
NOT THIS SOON.
NO.
NOT MY FAMILY.
THIS IS **THE FAITHFUL.**
BOOM
RICK RACK
BLAM

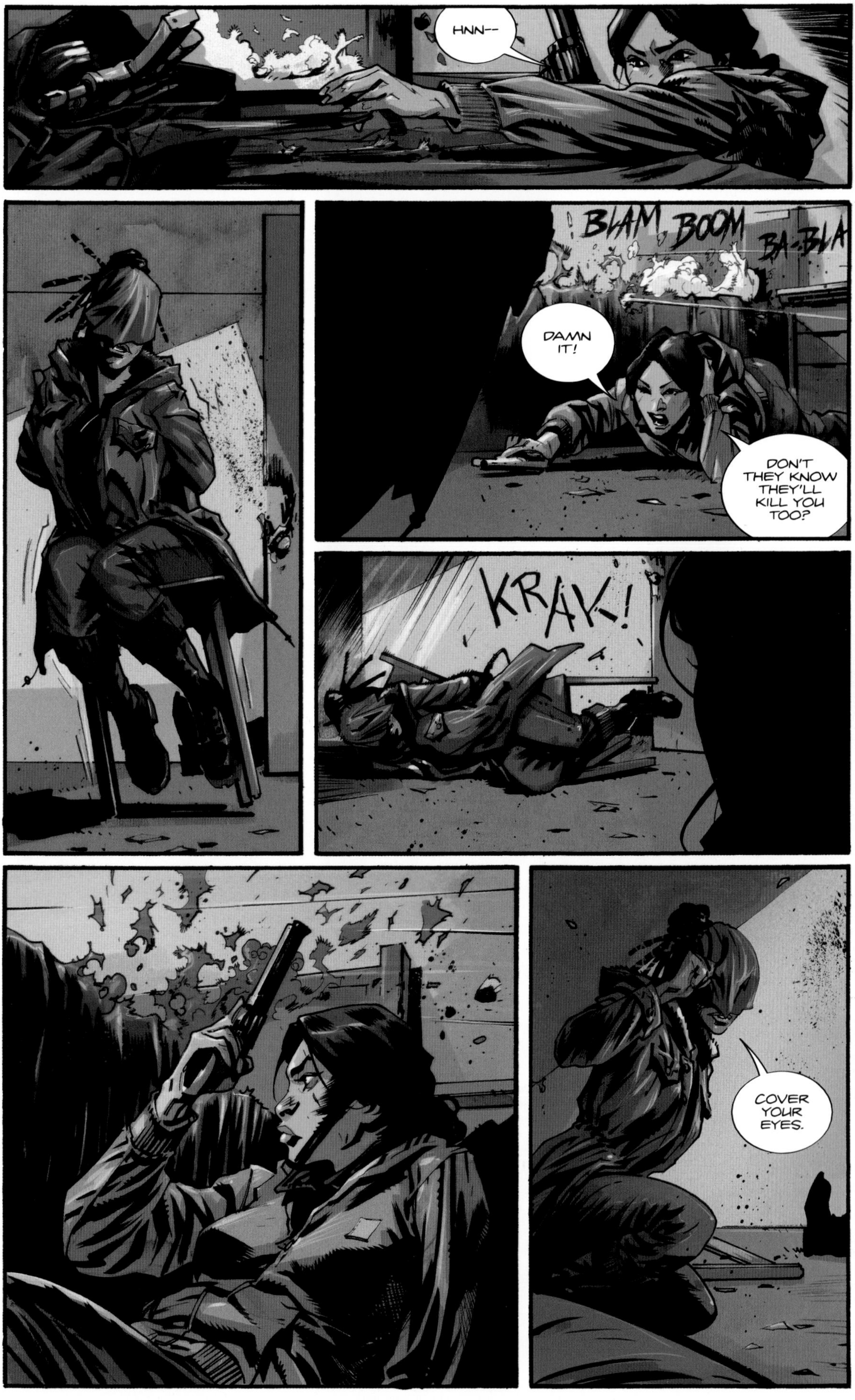
HNN--
BLAM BOOM BA-BLA
DAMN IT!
DON'T THEY KNOW THEY'LL KILL YOU TOO?
KRAK!
COVER YOUR EYES.

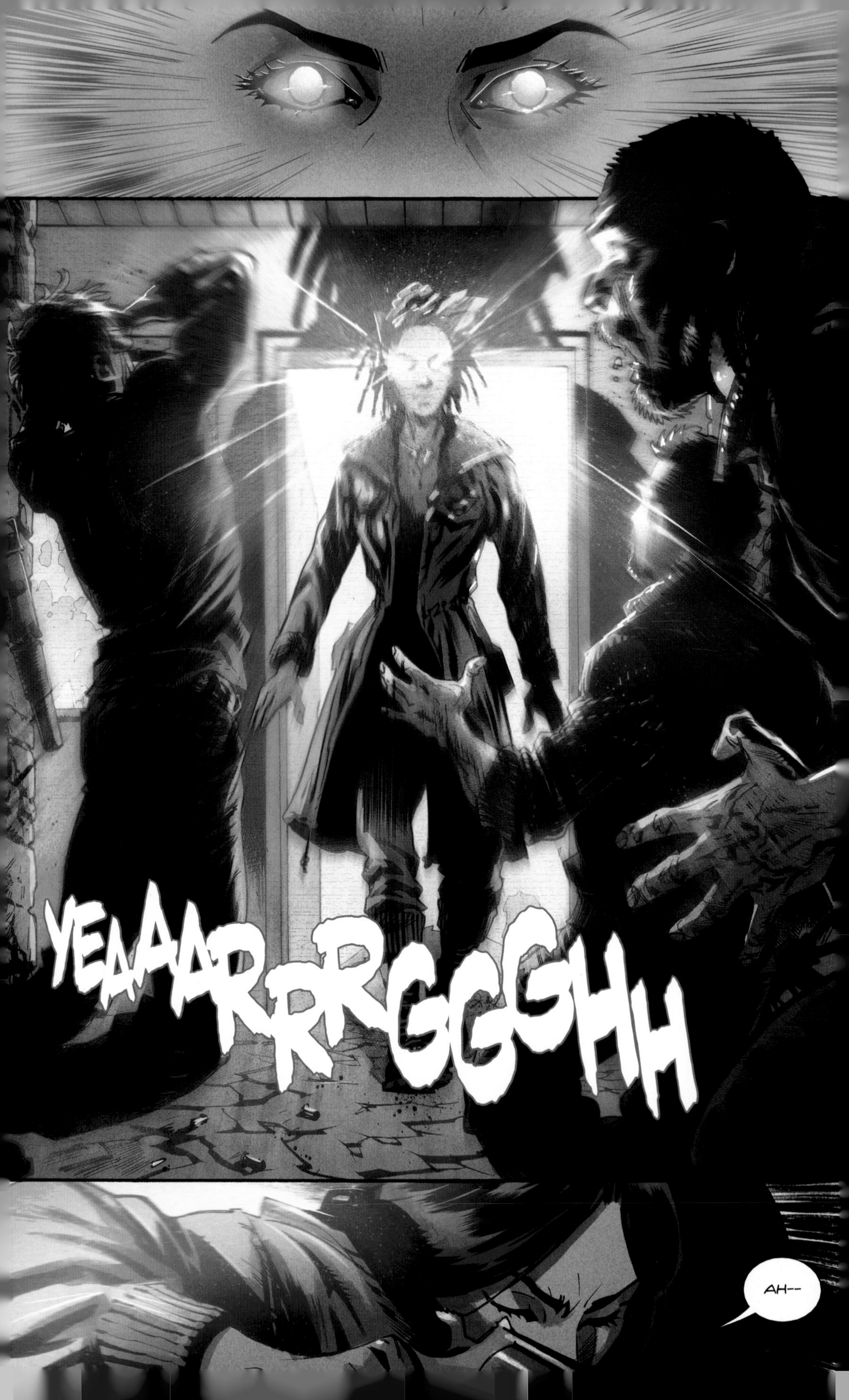
YEAAARRRGGGHH
AH--

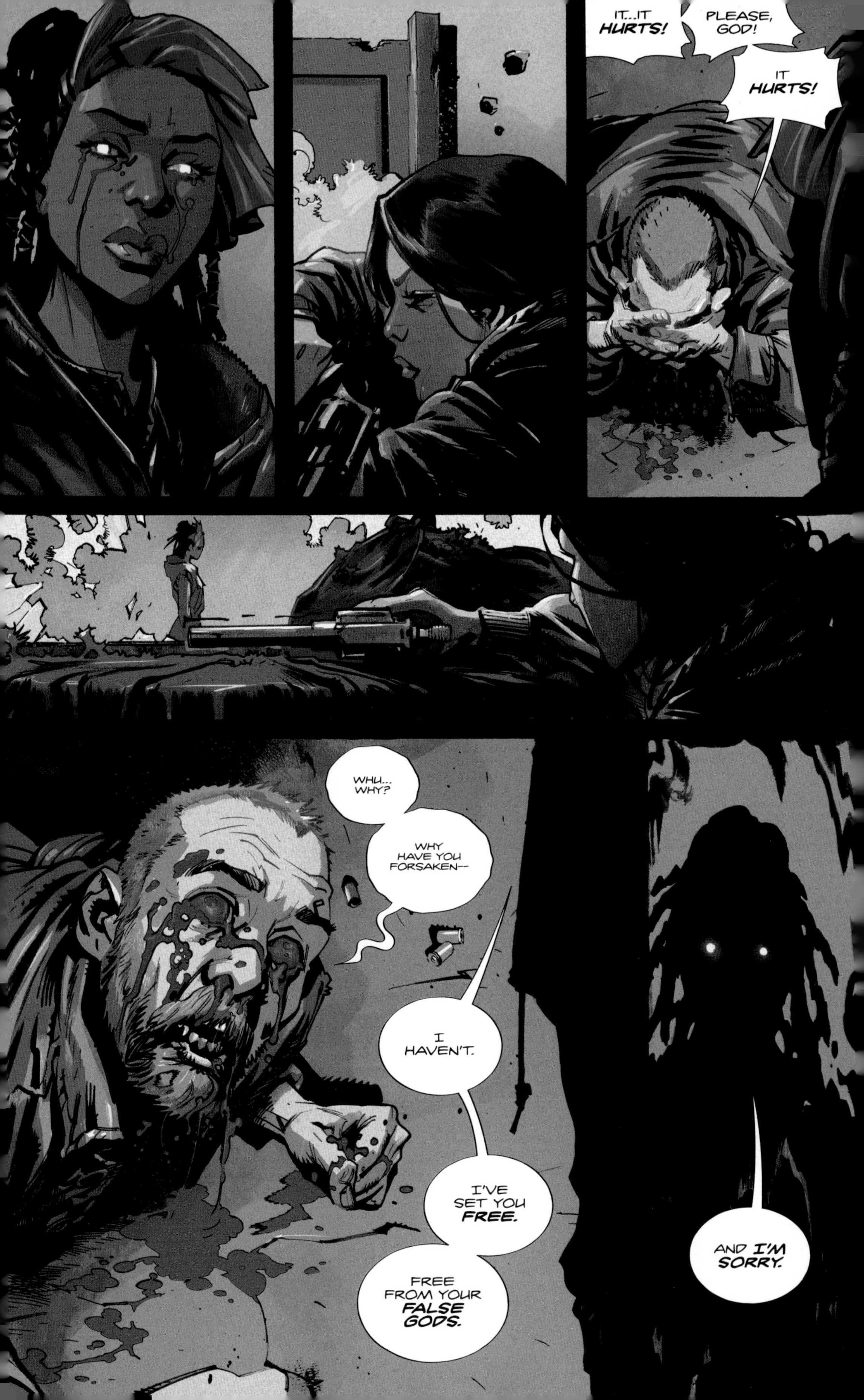
IT...IT HURTS!
PLEASE, GOD!
IT HURTS!
WHU... WHY?
WHY HAVE YOU FORSAKEN--
I HAVEN'T.
I'VE SET YOU FREE.
FREE FROM YOUR FALSE GODS.
AND I'M SORRY.

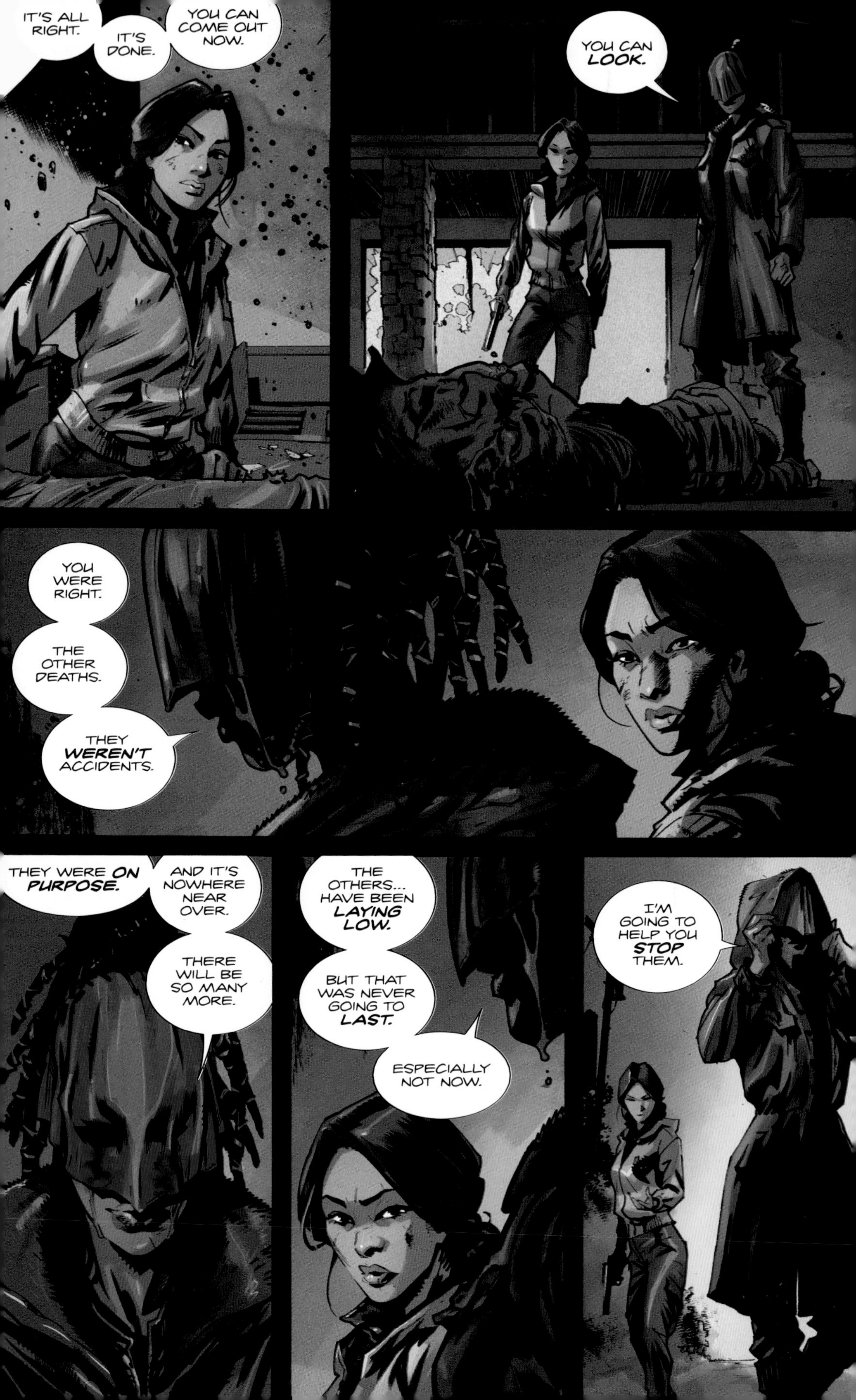
IT'S ALL RIGHT.
IT'S DONE.
YOU CAN COME OUT NOW.
YOU CAN LOOK.
YOU WERE RIGHT.
THE OTHER DEATHS.
THEY WEREN'T ACCIDENTS.
THEY WERE ON PURPOSE.
AND IT'S NOWHERE NEAR OVER.
THERE WILL BE SO MANY MORE.
THE OTHERS... HAVE BEEN LAYING LOW.
BUT THAT WAS NEVER GOING TO LAST.
ESPECIALLY NOT NOW.
I'M GOING TO HELP YOU STOP THEM.

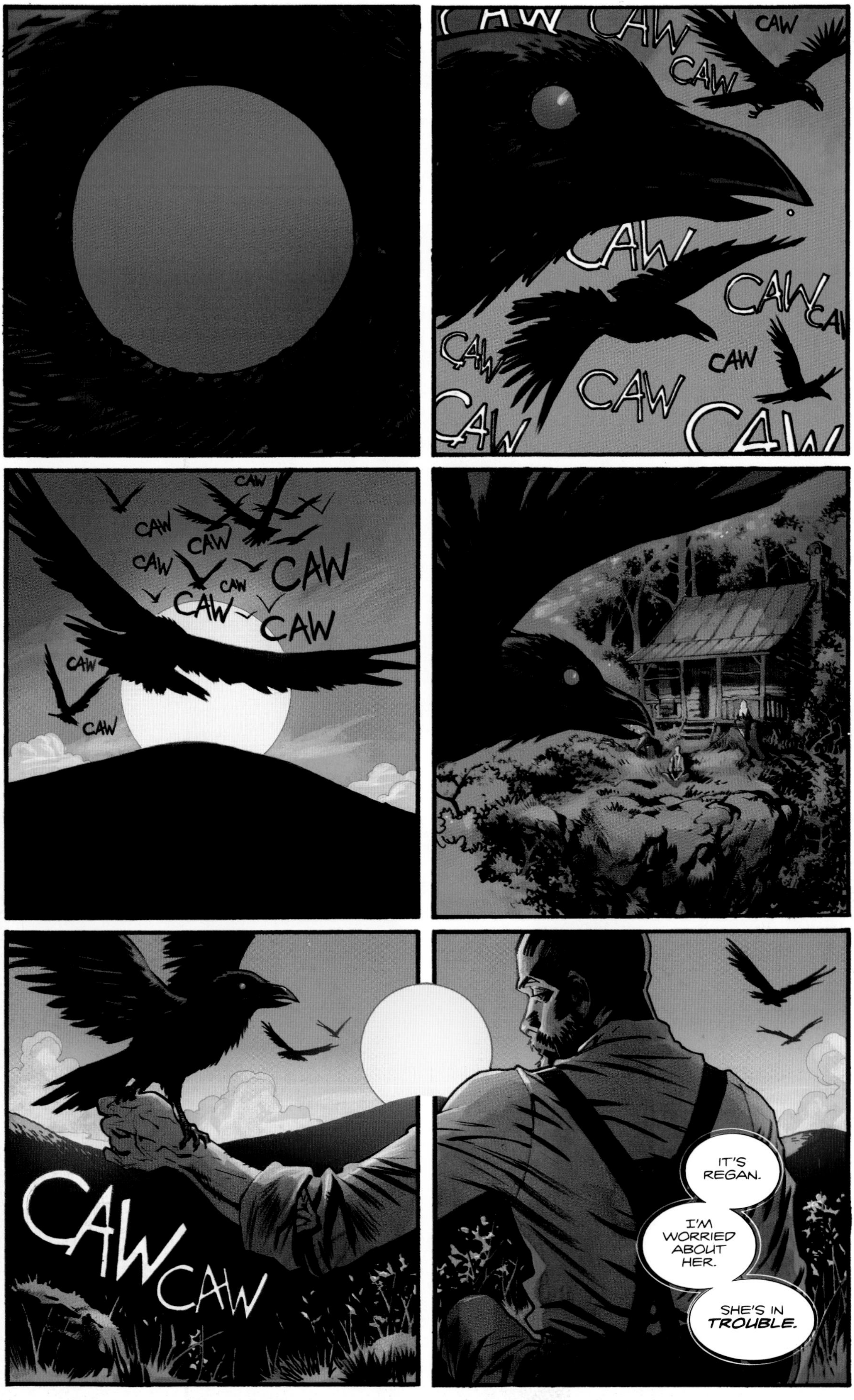
CAW CAW
CAW
CAW
CAW
CAW
CAW
CAW
CAW
CAW
CAW
CAW
CAW
CAW
CAW
CAW
CAW
CAW
CAW
CAW
CAW
CAW CAW
IT'S REGAN.
I'M WORRIED ABOUT HER.
SHE'S IN *TROUBLE.*

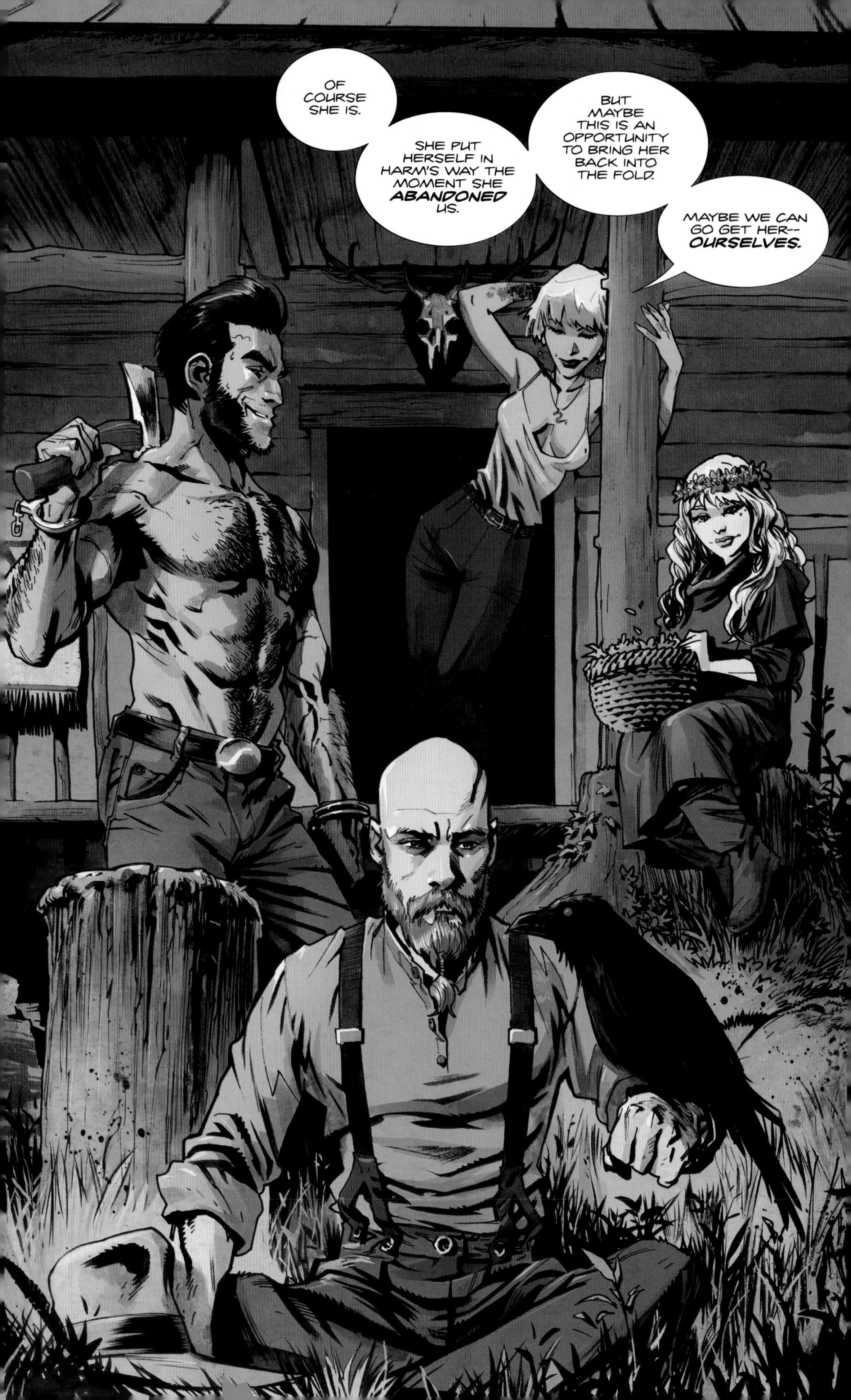
OF COURSE SHE IS.
SHE PUT HERSELF IN HARM'S WAY THE MOMENT SHE **ABANDONED** US.
BUT MAYBE THIS IS AN OPPORTUNITY TO BRING HER BACK INTO THE FOLD.
MAYBE WE CAN GO GET HER-- **OURSELVES.**

CHAPTER TWO

BLESSINGS OF
THE CHIMERA

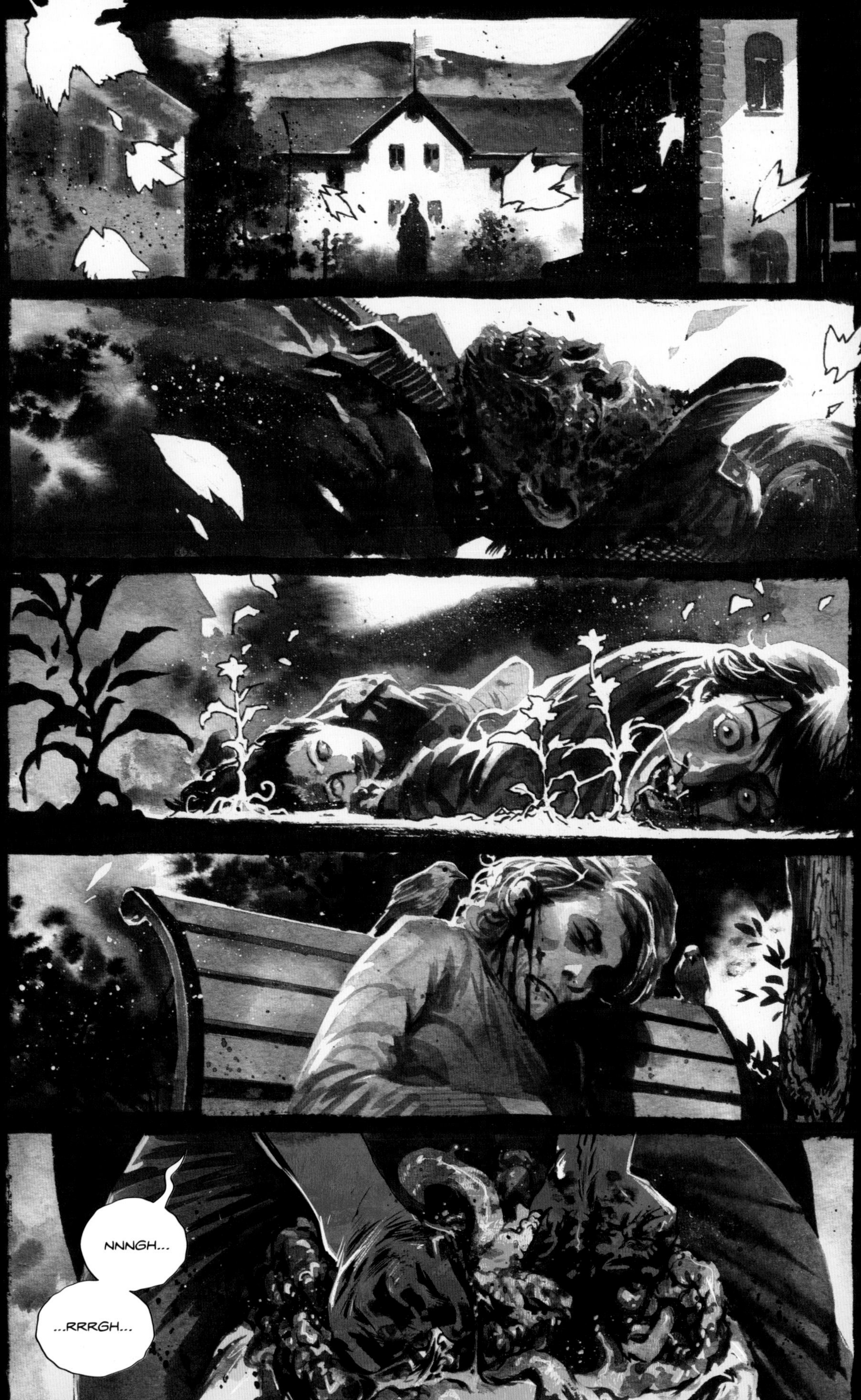
NNNGH...
...RRRGH...

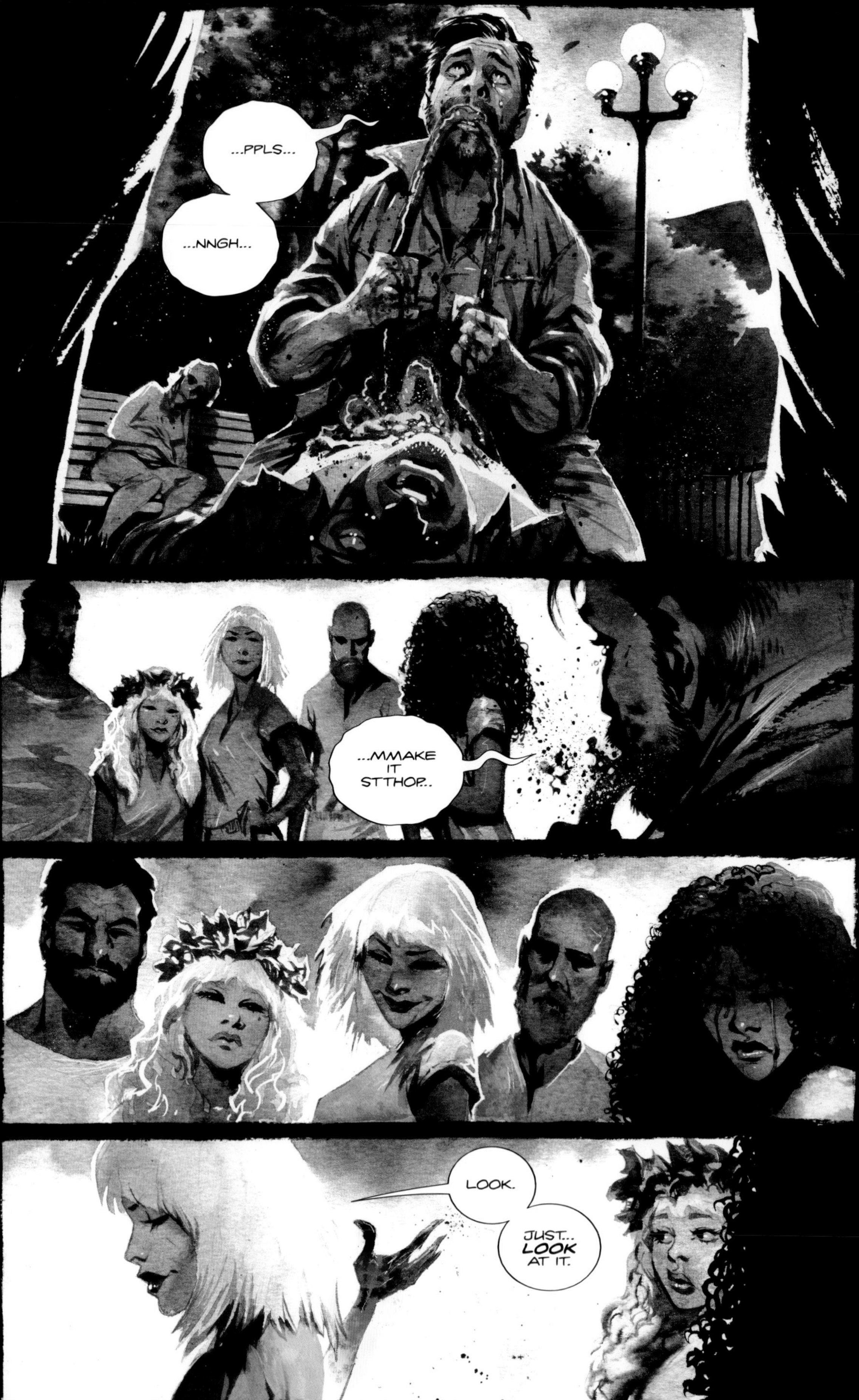
...PPLS...
...NNGH...
...MMAKE IT STTHOP...
LOOK.
JUST... **LOOK** AT IT.

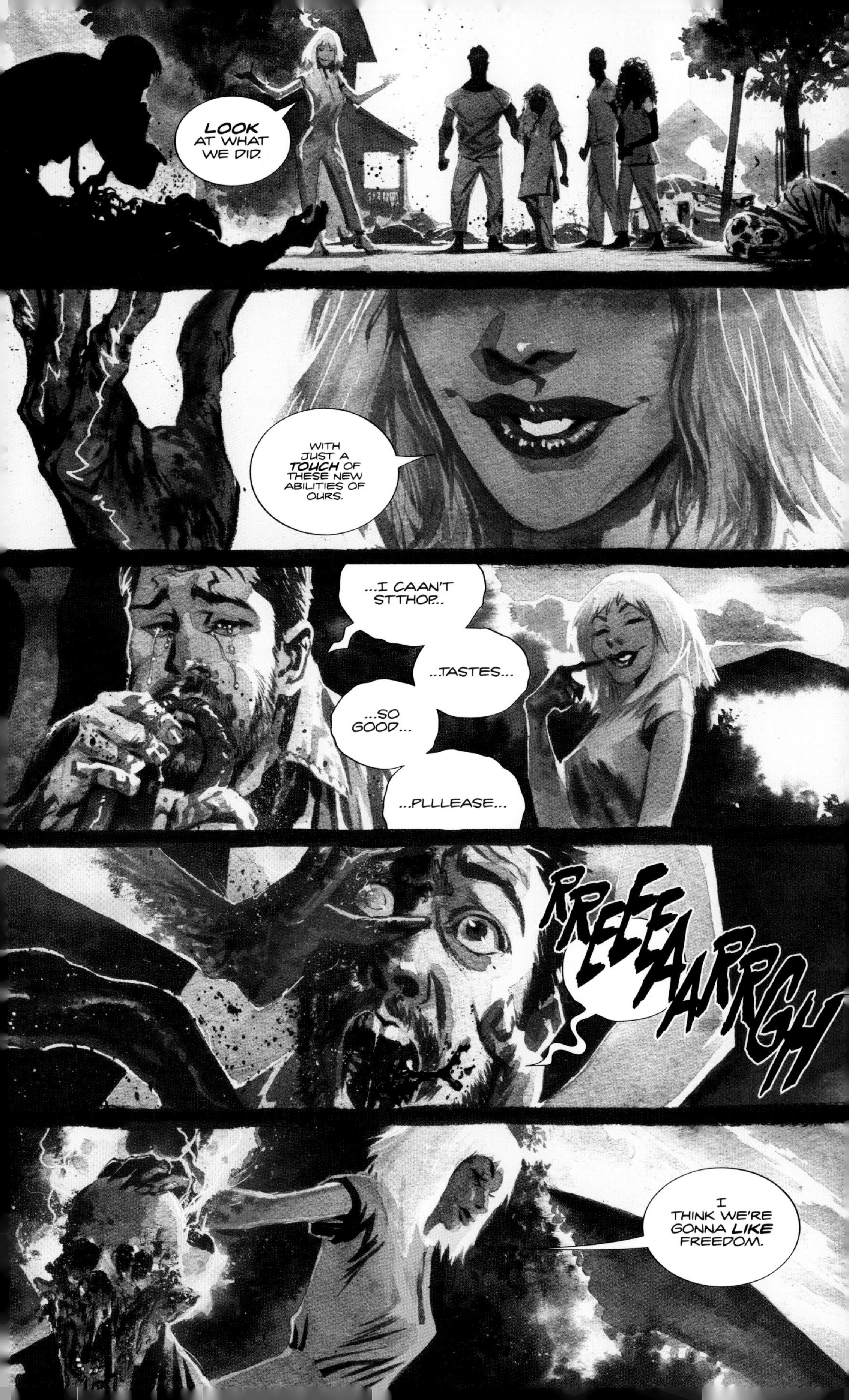
LOOK AT WHAT WE DID.
WITH JUST A TOUCH OF THESE NEW ABILITIES OF OURS.
...I CAAN'T STTHOP...
...TASTES...
...SO GOOD...
...PLLLEASE...
RREEEAARRGH
I THINK WE'RE GONNA LIKE FREEDOM.

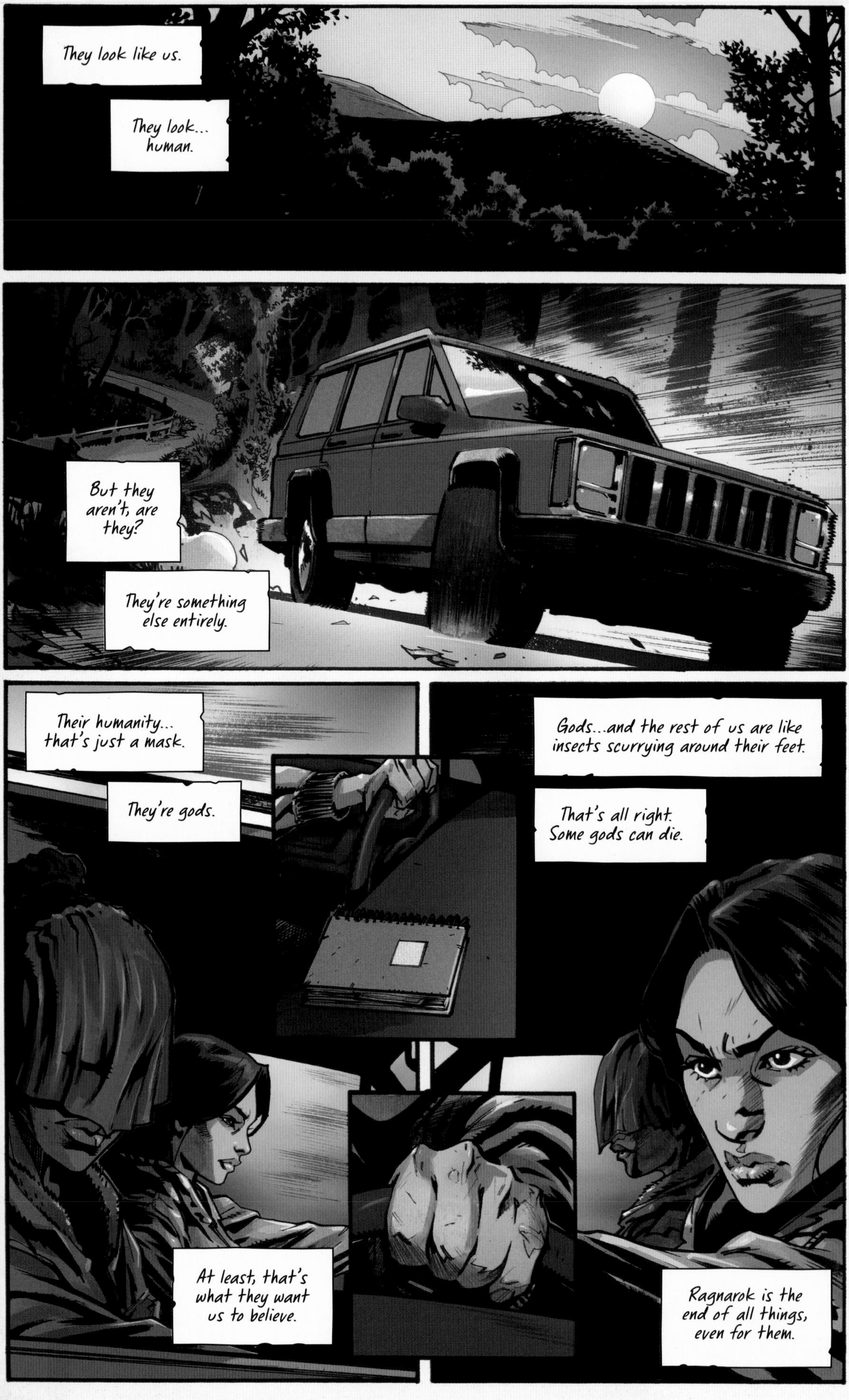
They look like us.
They look... human.
But they aren't, are they?
They're something else entirely.
Their humanity... that's just a mask.
They're gods.
Gods...and the rest of us are like insects scurrying around their feet.
That's all right. Some gods can die.
At least, that's what they want us to believe.
Ragnarok is the end of all things, even for them.

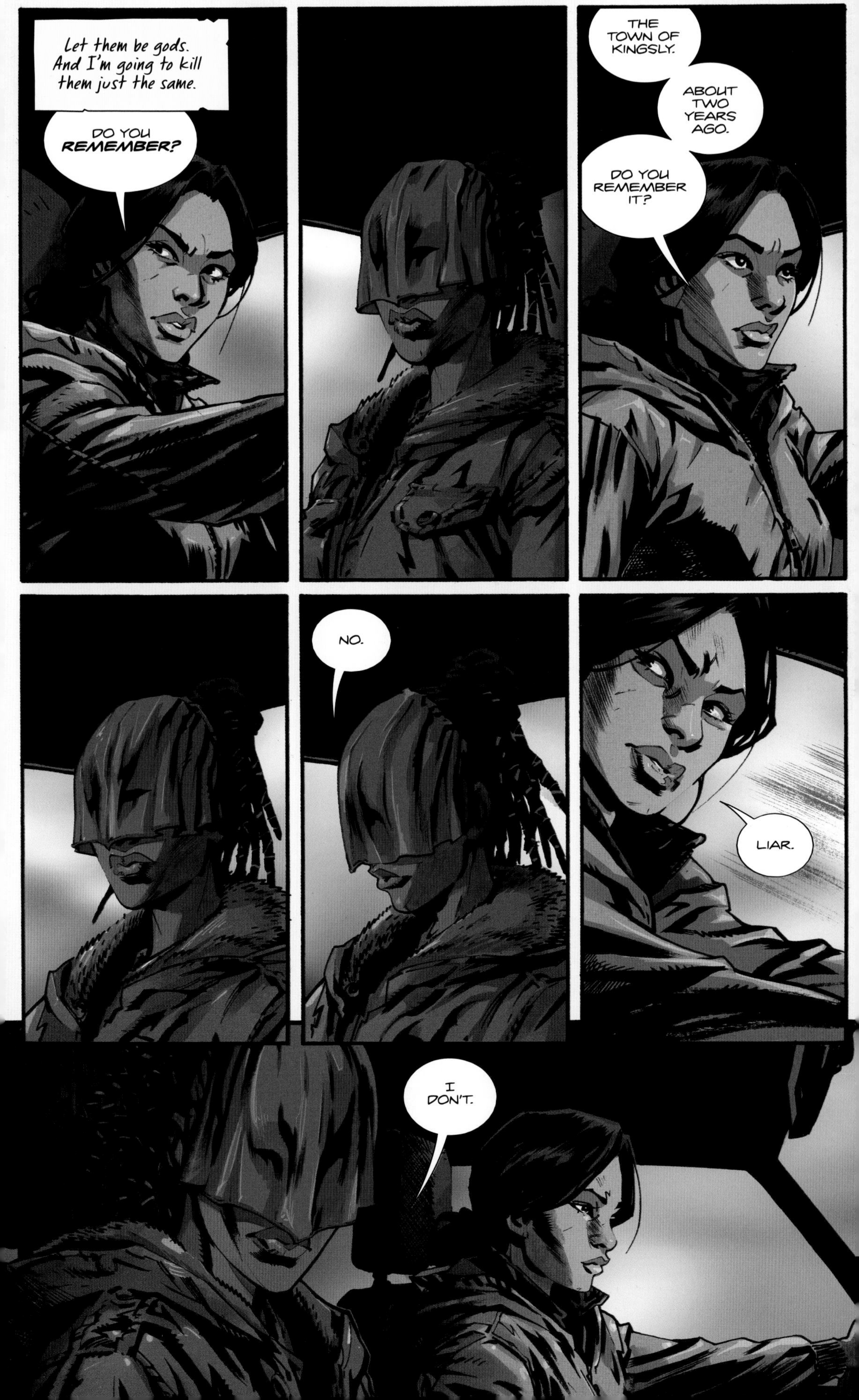
Let them be gods. And I'm going to kill them just the same.
DO YOU *REMEMBER?*
THE TOWN OF KINGSLY.
ABOUT TWO YEARS AGO.
DO YOU REMEMBER IT?
NO.
LIAR.
I DON'T.

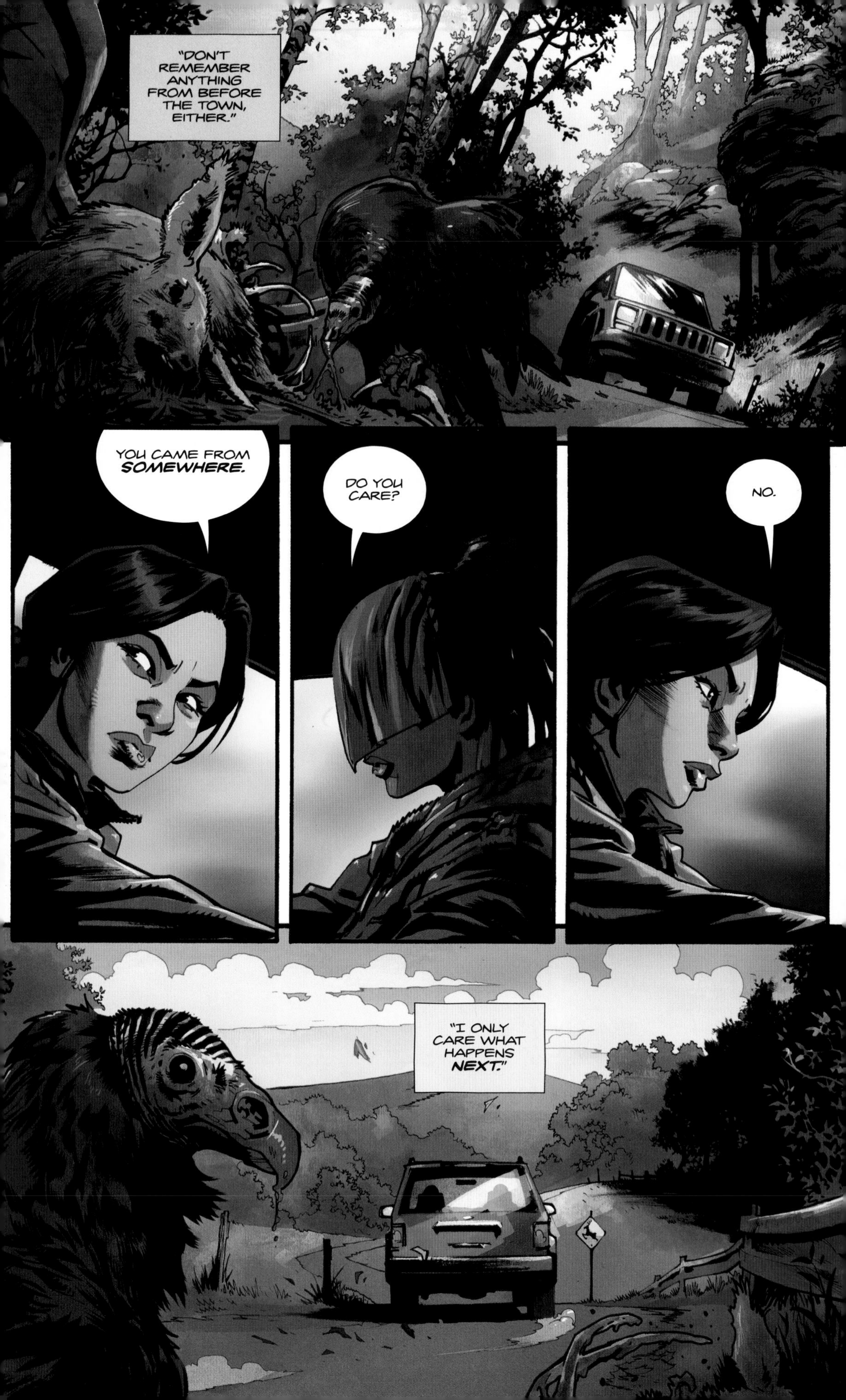
"DON'T REMEMBER ANYTHING FROM BEFORE THE TOWN, EITHER."
YOU CAME FROM SOMEWHERE.
DO YOU CARE?
NO.
"I ONLY CARE WHAT HAPPENS NEXT."

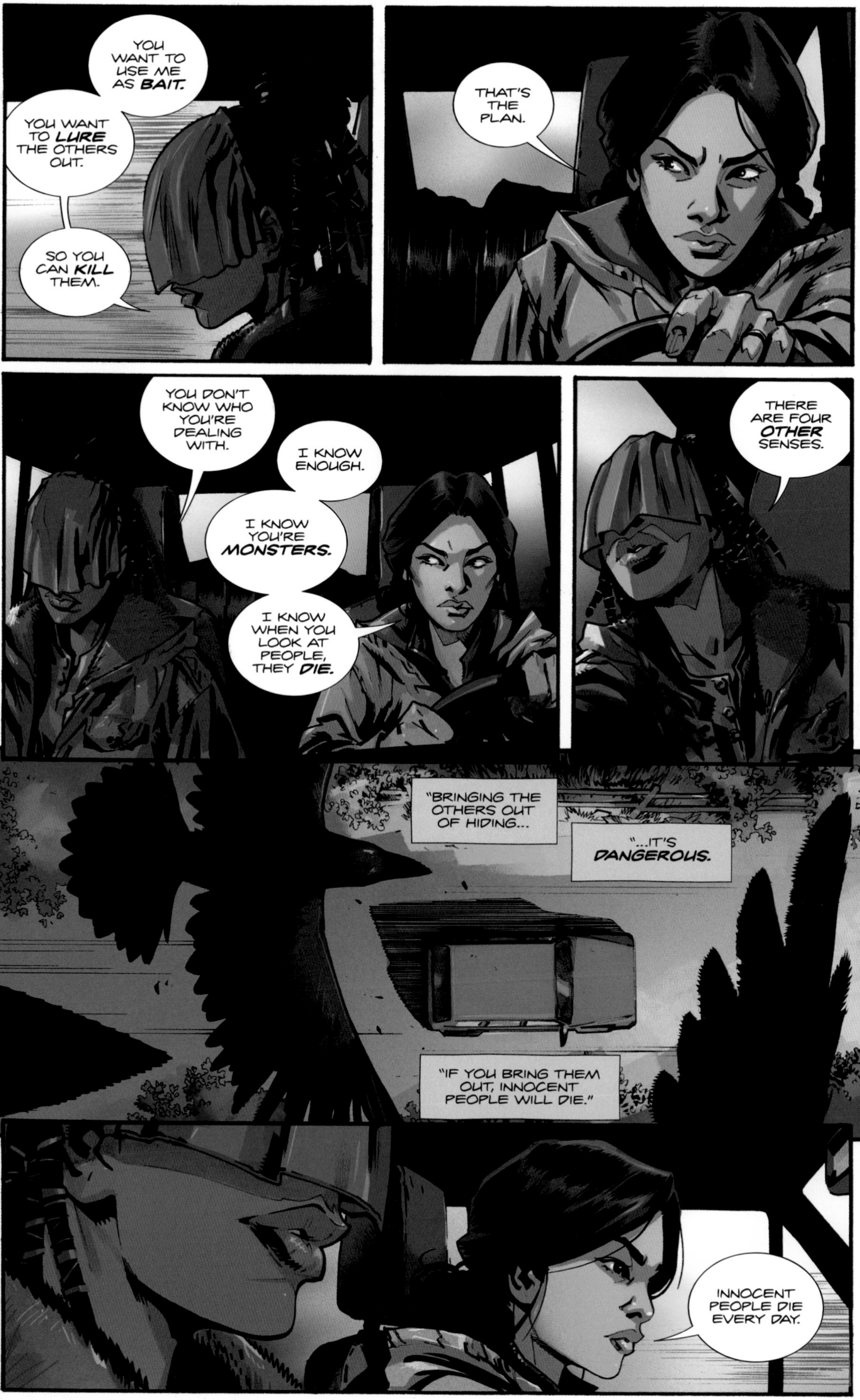
YOU WANT TO USE ME AS BAIT.
YOU WANT TO LURE THE OTHERS OUT.
SO YOU CAN KILL THEM.
THAT'S THE PLAN.
YOU DON'T KNOW WHO YOU'RE DEALING WITH.
I KNOW ENOUGH.
I KNOW YOU'RE MONSTERS.
I KNOW WHEN YOU LOOK AT PEOPLE, THEY DIE.
THERE ARE FOUR OTHER SENSES.
"BRINGING THE OTHERS OUT OF HIDING...
"...IT'S DANGEROUS.
"IF YOU BRING THEM OUT, INNOCENT PEOPLE WILL DIE."
INNOCENT PEOPLE DIE EVERY DAY.

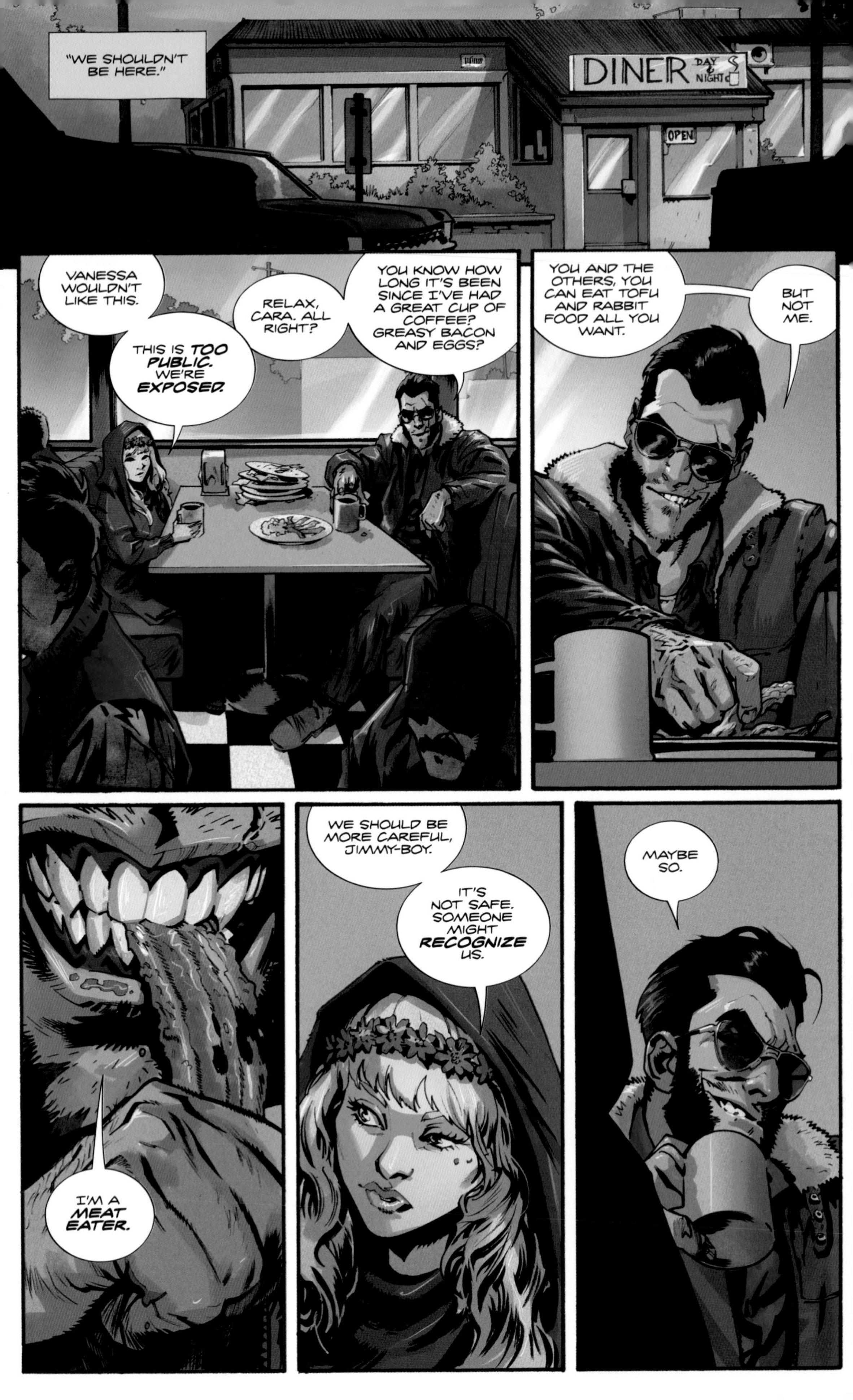
"WE SHOULDN'T BE HERE."
DINER DAY & NIGHT
OPEN
VANESSA WOULDN'T LIKE THIS.
THIS IS TOO PUBLIC. WE'RE EXPOSED.
RELAX, CARA. ALL RIGHT?
YOU KNOW HOW LONG IT'S BEEN SINCE I'VE HAD A GREAT CUP OF COFFEE? GREASY BACON AND EGGS?
YOU AND THE OTHERS, YOU CAN EAT TOFU AND RABBIT FOOD ALL YOU WANT.
BUT NOT ME.
I'M A MEAT EATER.
WE SHOULD BE MORE CAREFUL, JIMMY-BOY.
IT'S NOT SAFE. SOMEONE MIGHT RECOGNIZE US.
MAYBE SO.

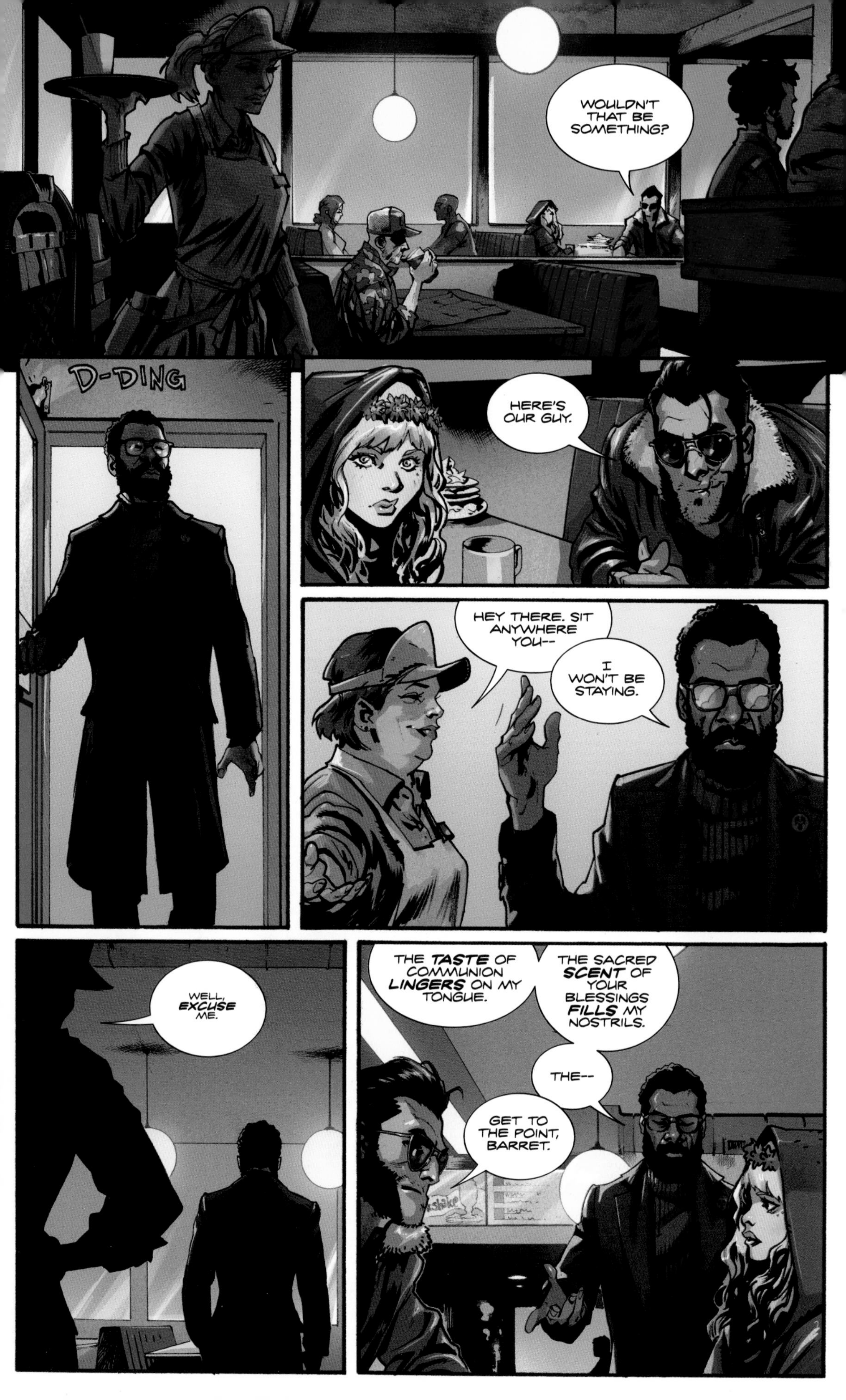
WOULDN'T THAT BE SOMETHING?
D-DING
HERE'S OUR GUY.
HEY THERE. SIT ANYWHERE YOU--
I WON'T BE STAYING.
WELL, *EXCUSE* ME.
THE *TASTE* OF COMMUNION *LINGERS* ON MY TONGUE.
THE SACRED *SCENT* OF YOUR BLESSINGS *FILLS* MY NOSTRILS.
THE--
GET TO THE POINT, BARRET.

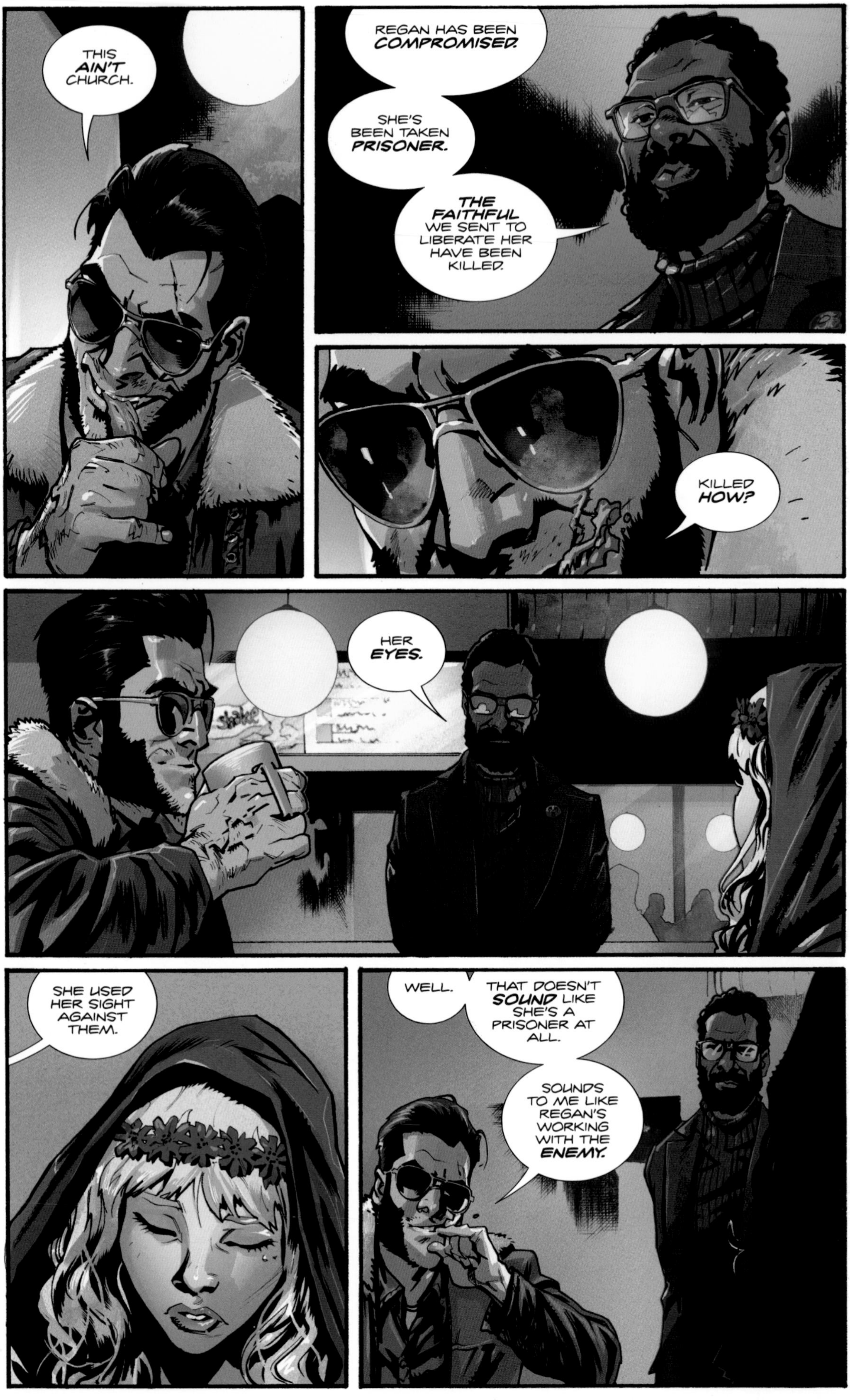
THIS AIN'T CHURCH.
REGAN HAS BEEN COMPROMISED.
SHE'S BEEN TAKEN PRISONER.
THE FAITHFUL WE SENT TO LIBERATE HER HAVE BEEN KILLED.
KILLED HOW?
HER EYES.
SHE USED HER SIGHT AGAINST THEM.
WELL.
THAT DOESN'T SOUND LIKE SHE'S A PRISONER AT ALL.
SOUNDS TO ME LIKE REGAN'S WORKING WITH THE ENEMY.

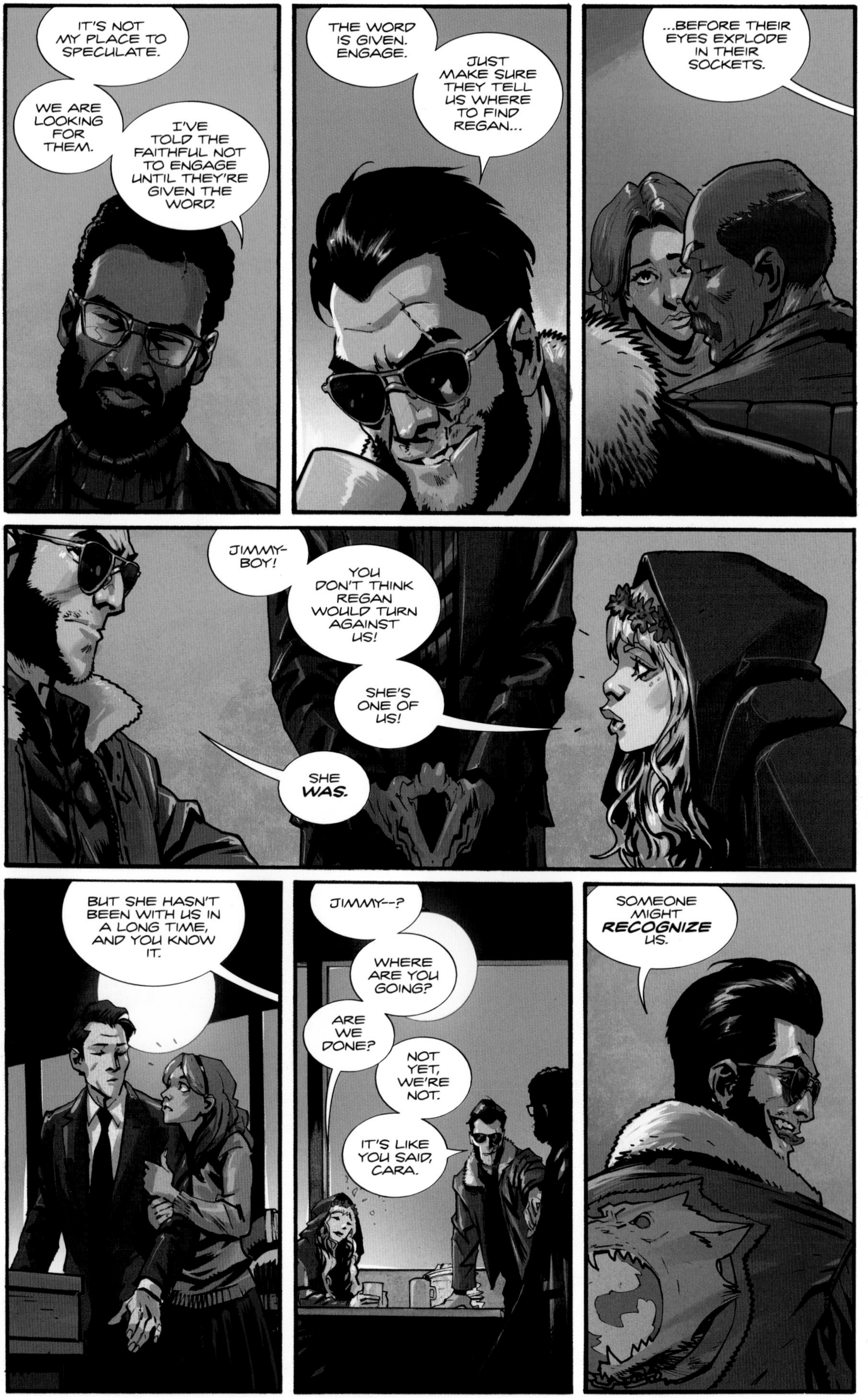
IT'S NOT MY PLACE TO SPECULATE.
WE ARE LOOKING FOR THEM.
I'VE TOLD THE FAITHFUL NOT TO ENGAGE UNTIL THEY'RE GIVEN THE WORD.
THE WORD IS GIVEN. ENGAGE.
JUST MAKE SURE THEY TELL US WHERE TO FIND REGAN...
...BEFORE THEIR EYES EXPLODE IN THEIR SOCKETS.
JIMMY-BOY!
YOU DON'T THINK REGAN WOULD TURN AGAINST US!
SHE'S ONE OF US!
SHE WAS.
BUT SHE HASN'T BEEN WITH US IN A LONG TIME, AND YOU KNOW IT.
JIMMY--?
WHERE ARE YOU GOING?
ARE WE DONE?
NOT YET, WE'RE NOT.
IT'S LIKE YOU SAID, CARA.
SOMEONE MIGHT RECOGNIZE US.

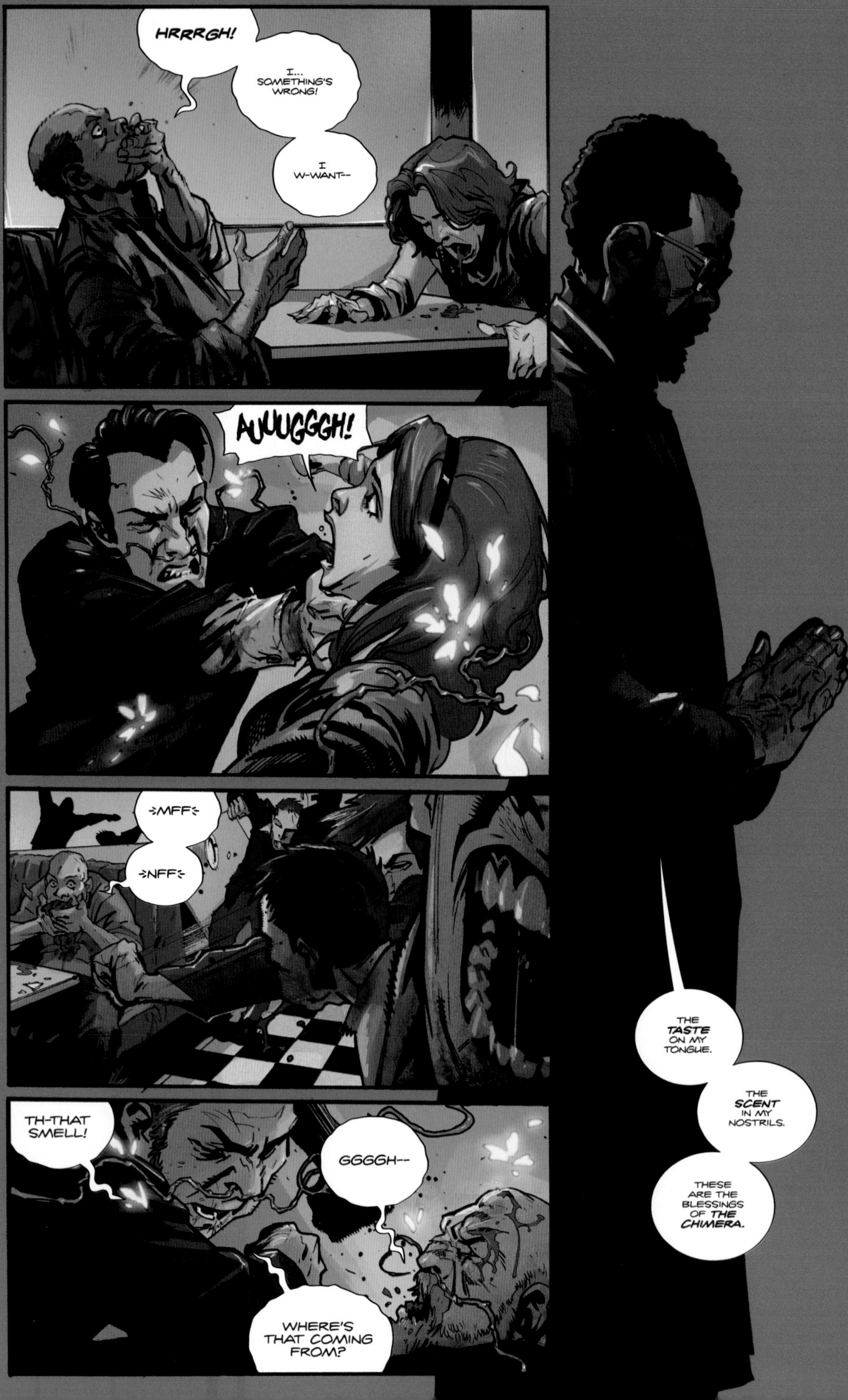
HRRRGH!
I... SOMETHING'S WRONG!
I W-WANT--
AUUUGGGH!
MFF
NFF
THE TASTE ON MY TONGUE.
TH-THAT SMELL!
GGGGH--
WHERE'S THAT COMING FROM?
THE SCENT IN MY NOSTRILS.
THESE ARE THE BLESSINGS OF THE CHIMERA.

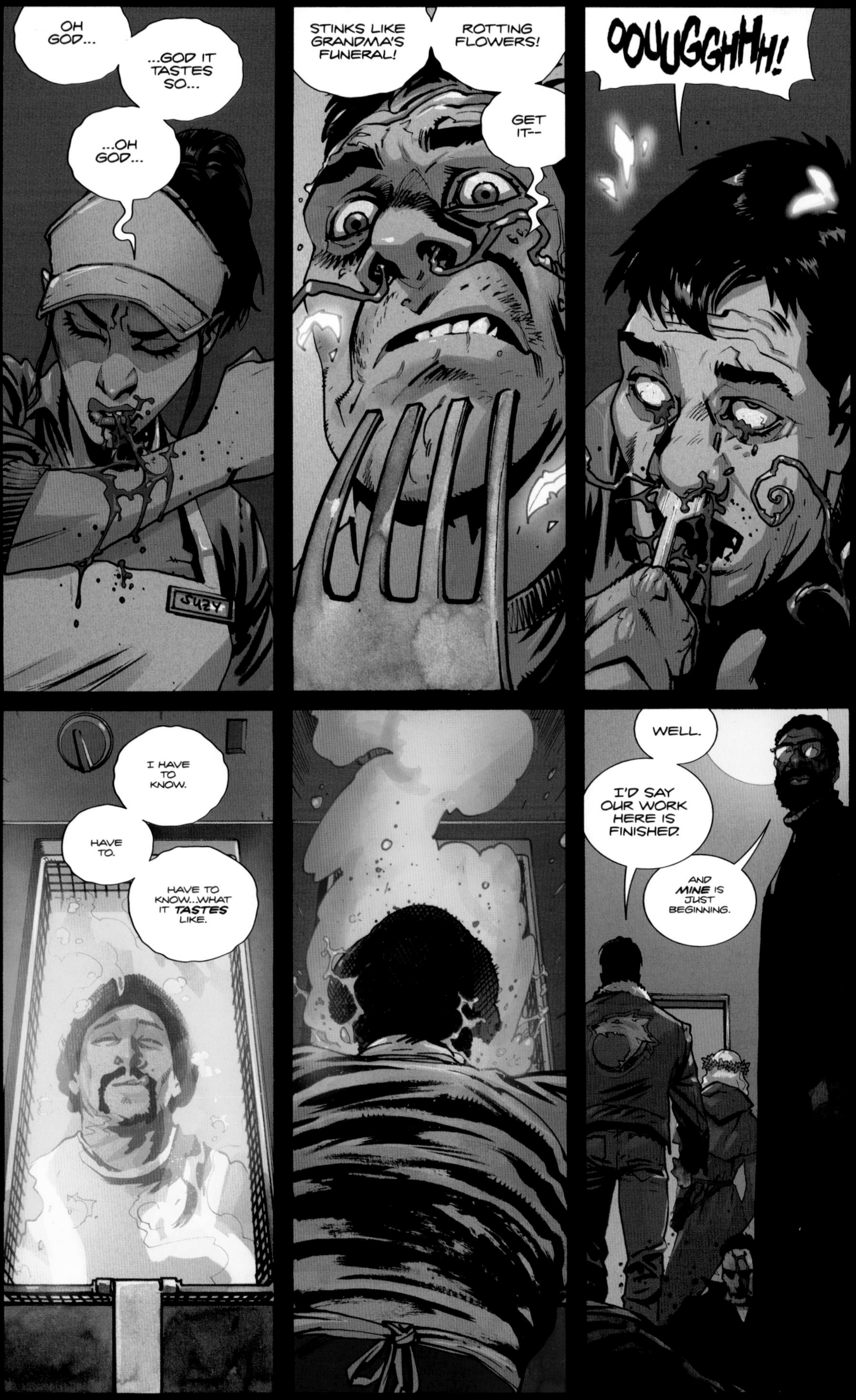
OH GOD...
...GOD IT TASTES SO...
...OH GOD...
STINKS LIKE GRANDMA'S FUNERAL!
ROTTING FLOWERS!
GET IT--
OOUUGGHHH!
I HAVE TO KNOW.
HAVE TO.
HAVE TO KNOW...WHAT IT TASTES LIKE.
WELL.
I'D SAY OUR WORK HERE IS FINISHED.
AND MINE IS JUST BEGINNING.

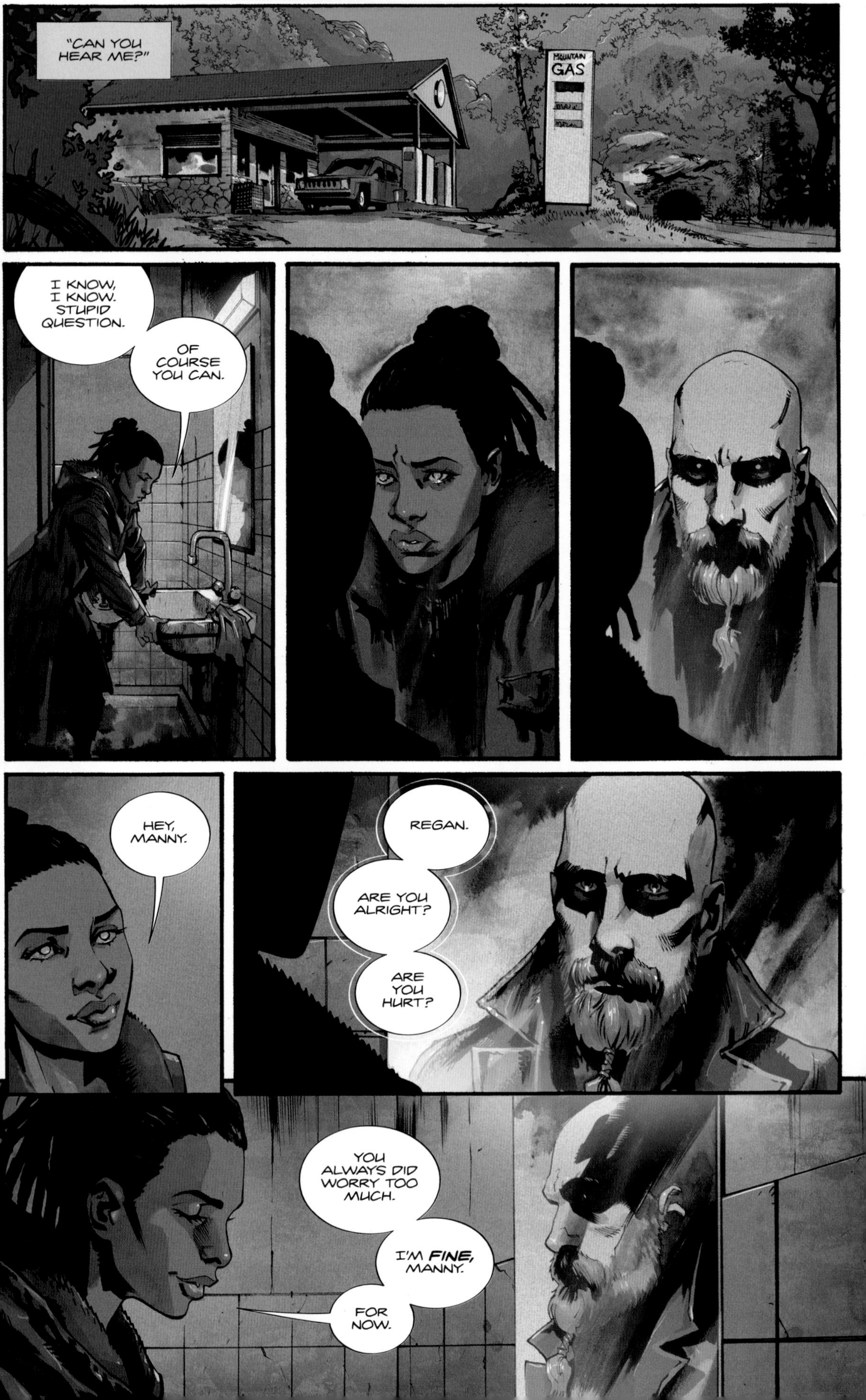
"CAN YOU HEAR ME?"
MOUNTAIN GAS
I KNOW, I KNOW. STUPID QUESTION.
OF COURSE YOU CAN.
HEY, MANNY.
REGAN.
ARE YOU ALRIGHT?
ARE YOU HURT?
YOU ALWAYS DID WORRY TOO MUCH.
I'M **FINE**, MANNY.
FOR NOW.

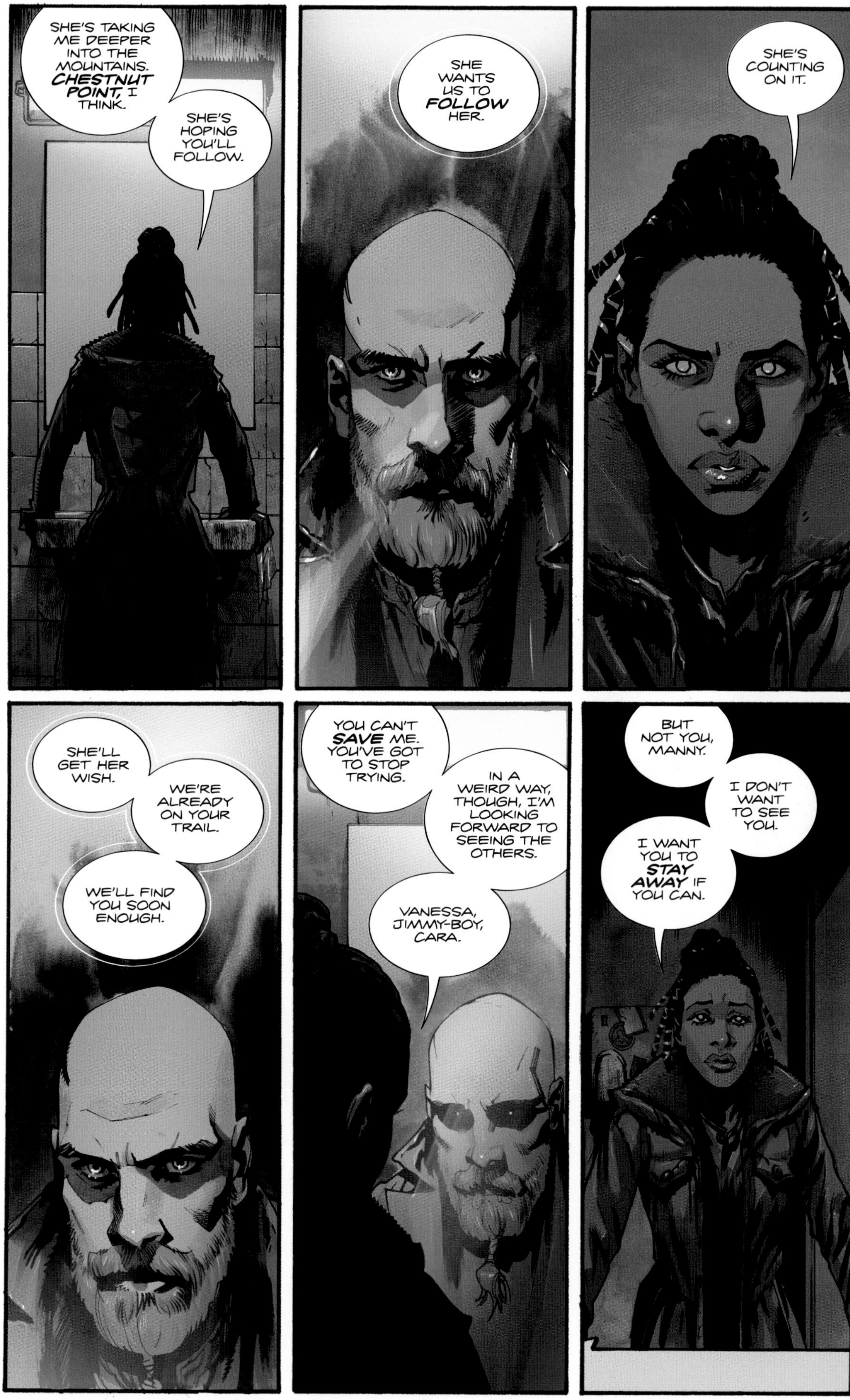
SHE'S TAKING ME DEEPER INTO THE MOUNTAINS. CHESTNUT POINT, I THINK.
SHE'S HOPING YOU'LL FOLLOW.
SHE WANTS US TO FOLLOW HER.
SHE'S COUNTING ON IT.
SHE'LL GET HER WISH.
WE'RE ALREADY ON YOUR TRAIL.
WE'LL FIND YOU SOON ENOUGH.
YOU CAN'T SAVE ME. YOU'VE GOT TO STOP TRYING.
IN A WEIRD WAY, THOUGH, I'M LOOKING FORWARD TO SEEING THE OTHERS.
VANESSA, JIMMY-BOY, CARA.
BUT NOT YOU, MANNY.
I DON'T WANT TO SEE YOU.
I WANT YOU TO STAY AWAY IF YOU CAN.

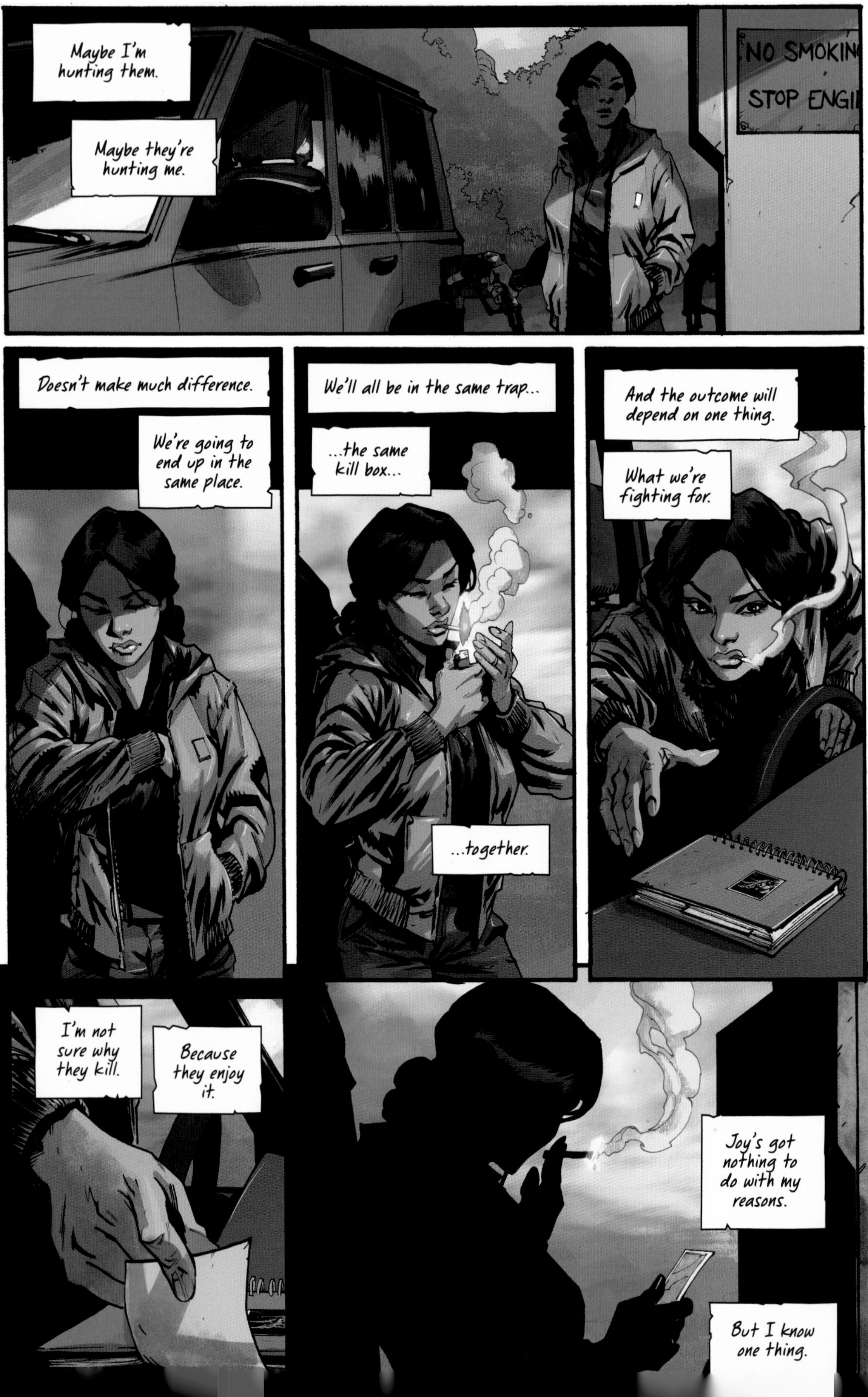
Maybe I'm hunting them.
Maybe they're hunting me.
NO SMOKING
STOP ENGI
Doesn't make much difference.
We're going to end up in the same place.
We'll all be in the same trap...
...the same kill box...
...together.
And the outcome will depend on one thing.
What we're fighting for.
I'm not sure why they kill.
Because they enjoy it.
Joy's got nothing to do with my reasons.
But I know one thing.

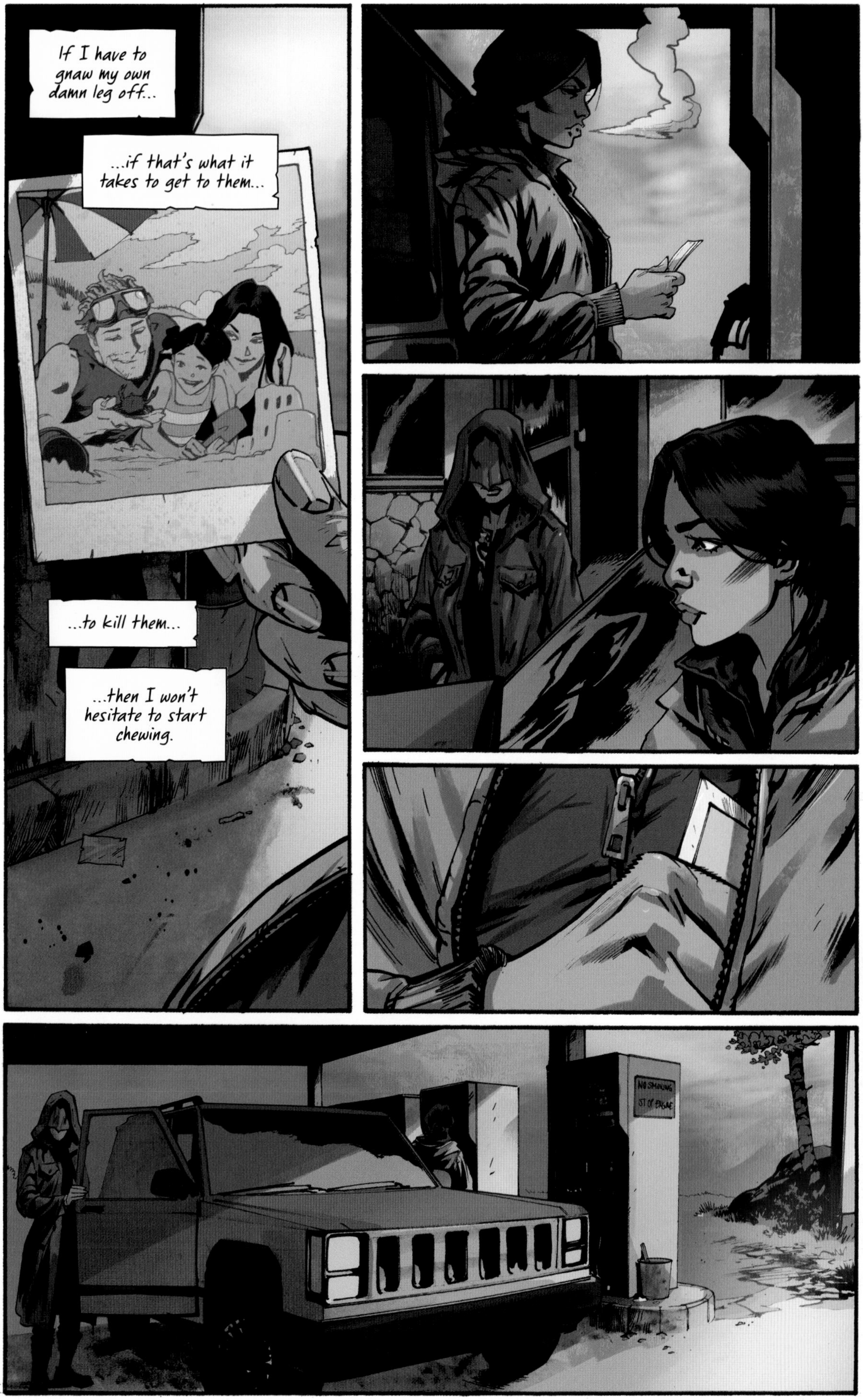
If I have to gnaw my own damn leg off...
...if that's what it takes to get to them...
...to kill them...
...then I won't hesitate to start chewing.

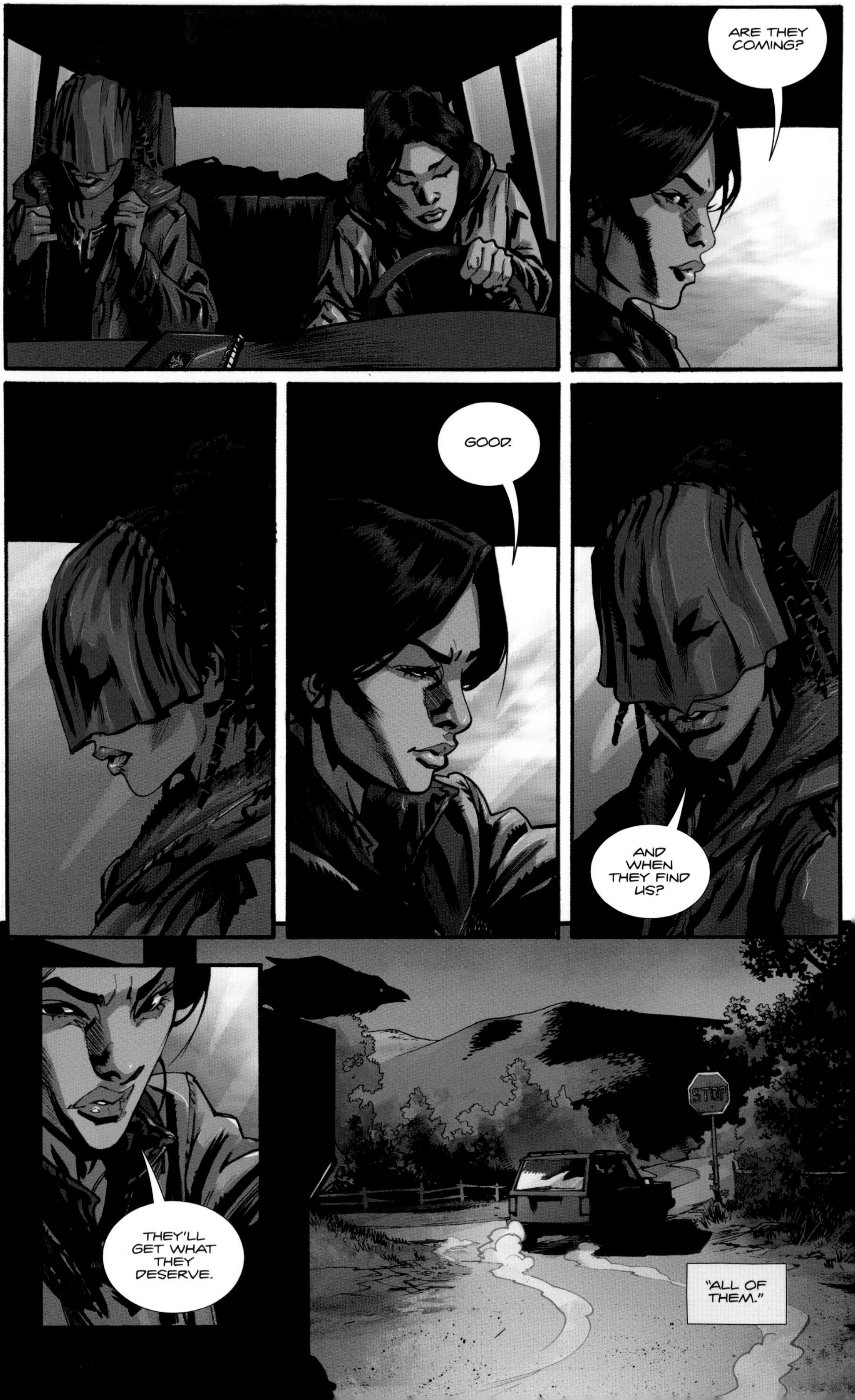
ARE THEY COMING?
GOOD.
AND WHEN THEY FIND US?
THEY'LL GET WHAT THEY DESERVE.
"ALL OF THEM."
STOP

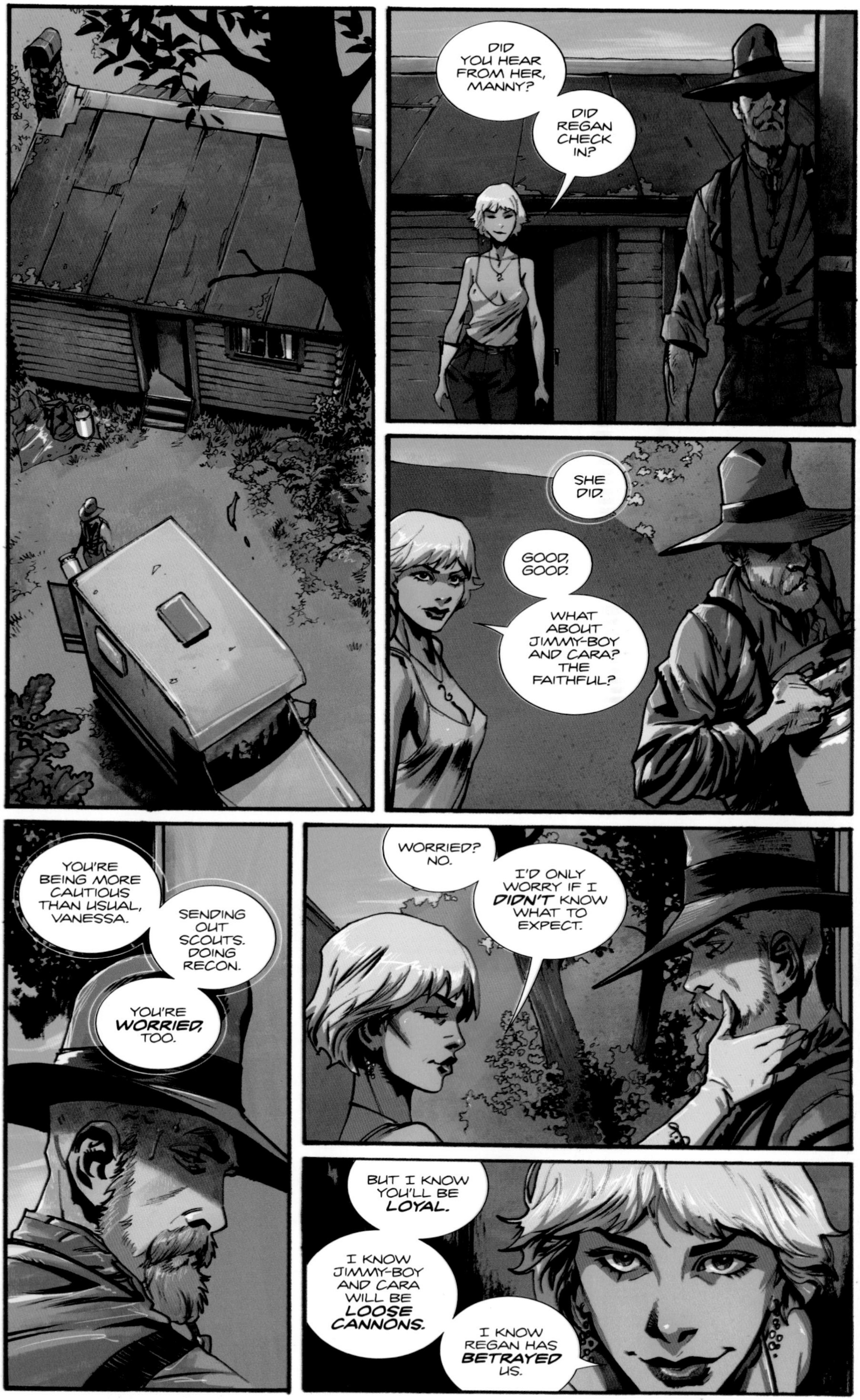
DID YOU HEAR FROM HER, MANNY?
DID REGAN CHECK IN?
SHE DID.
GOOD, GOOD.
WHAT ABOUT JIMMY-BOY AND CARA? THE FAITHFUL?
YOU'RE BEING MORE CAUTIOUS THAN USUAL, VANESSA.
SENDING OUT SCOUTS. DOING RECON.
YOU'RE **WORRIED,** TOO.
WORRIED? NO.
I'D ONLY WORRY IF I **DIDN'T** KNOW WHAT TO EXPECT.
BUT I KNOW YOU'LL BE **LOYAL.**
I KNOW JIMMY-BOY AND CARA WILL BE **LOOSE CANNONS.**
I KNOW REGAN HAS **BETRAYED** US.

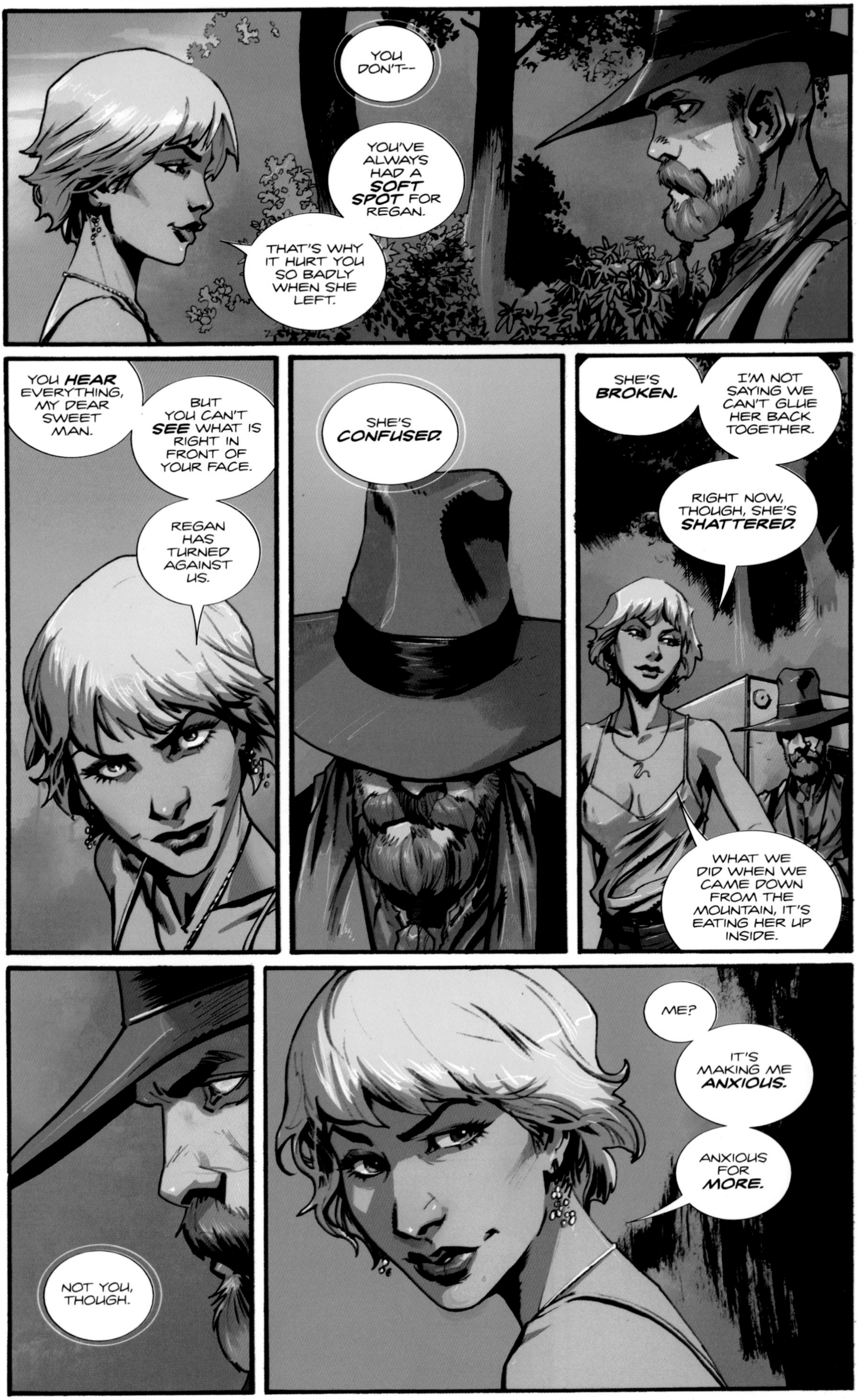
YOU DON'T--
YOU'VE ALWAYS HAD A SOFT SPOT FOR REGAN.
THAT'S WHY IT HURT YOU SO BADLY WHEN SHE LEFT.
YOU HEAR EVERYTHING, MY DEAR SWEET MAN.
BUT YOU CAN'T SEE WHAT IS RIGHT IN FRONT OF YOUR FACE.
REGAN HAS TURNED AGAINST US.
SHE'S CONFUSED.
SHE'S BROKEN.
I'M NOT SAYING WE CAN'T GLUE HER BACK TOGETHER.
RIGHT NOW, THOUGH, SHE'S SHATTERED.
WHAT WE DID WHEN WE CAME DOWN FROM THE MOUNTAIN, IT'S EATING HER UP INSIDE.
NOT YOU, THOUGH.
ME?
IT'S MAKING ME ANXIOUS.
ANXIOUS FOR MORE.

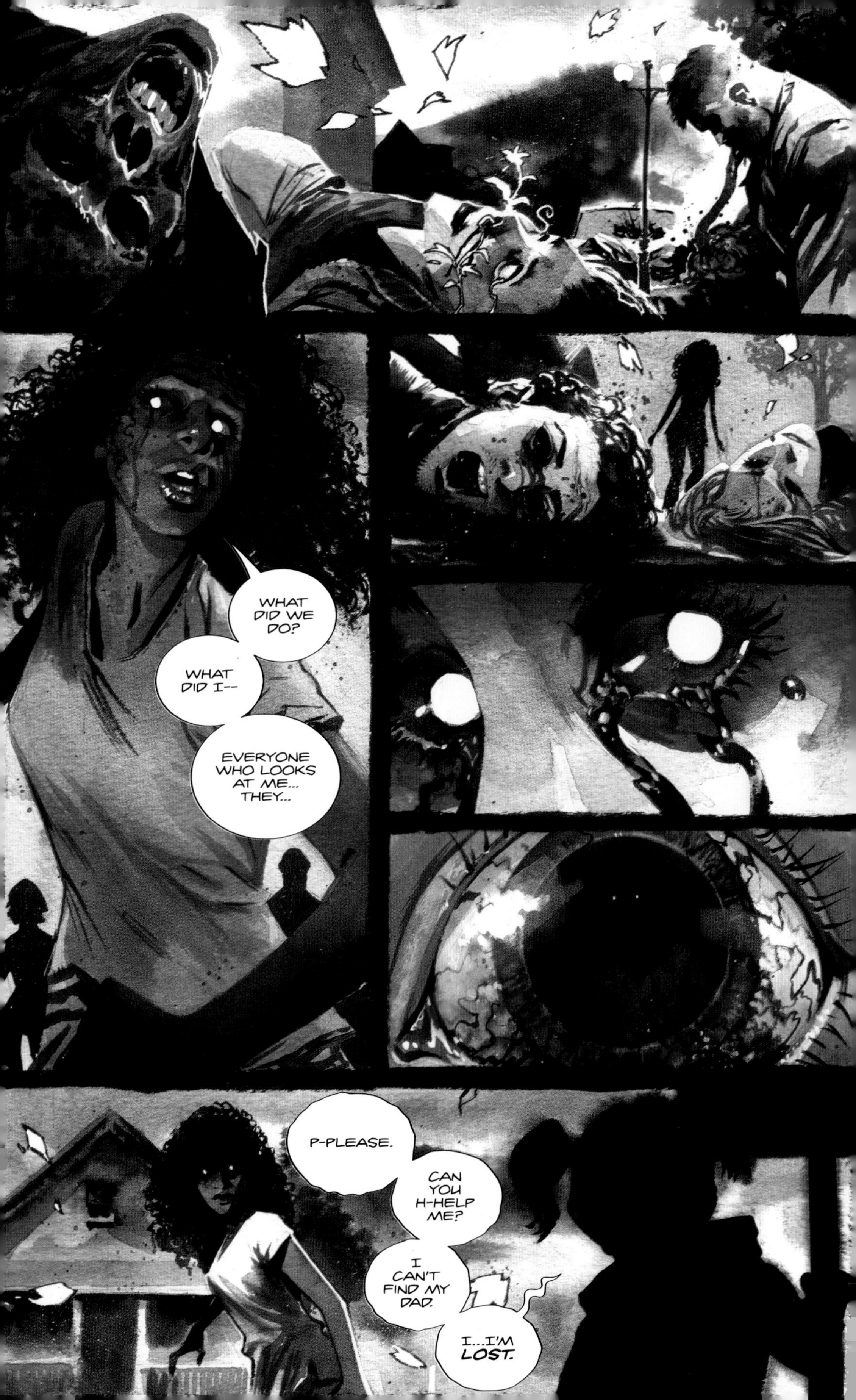
WHAT DID WE DO?
WHAT DID I--
EVERYONE WHO LOOKS AT ME... THEY...
P-PLEASE.
CAN YOU H-HELP ME?
I CAN'T FIND MY DAD.
I...I'M **LOST.**

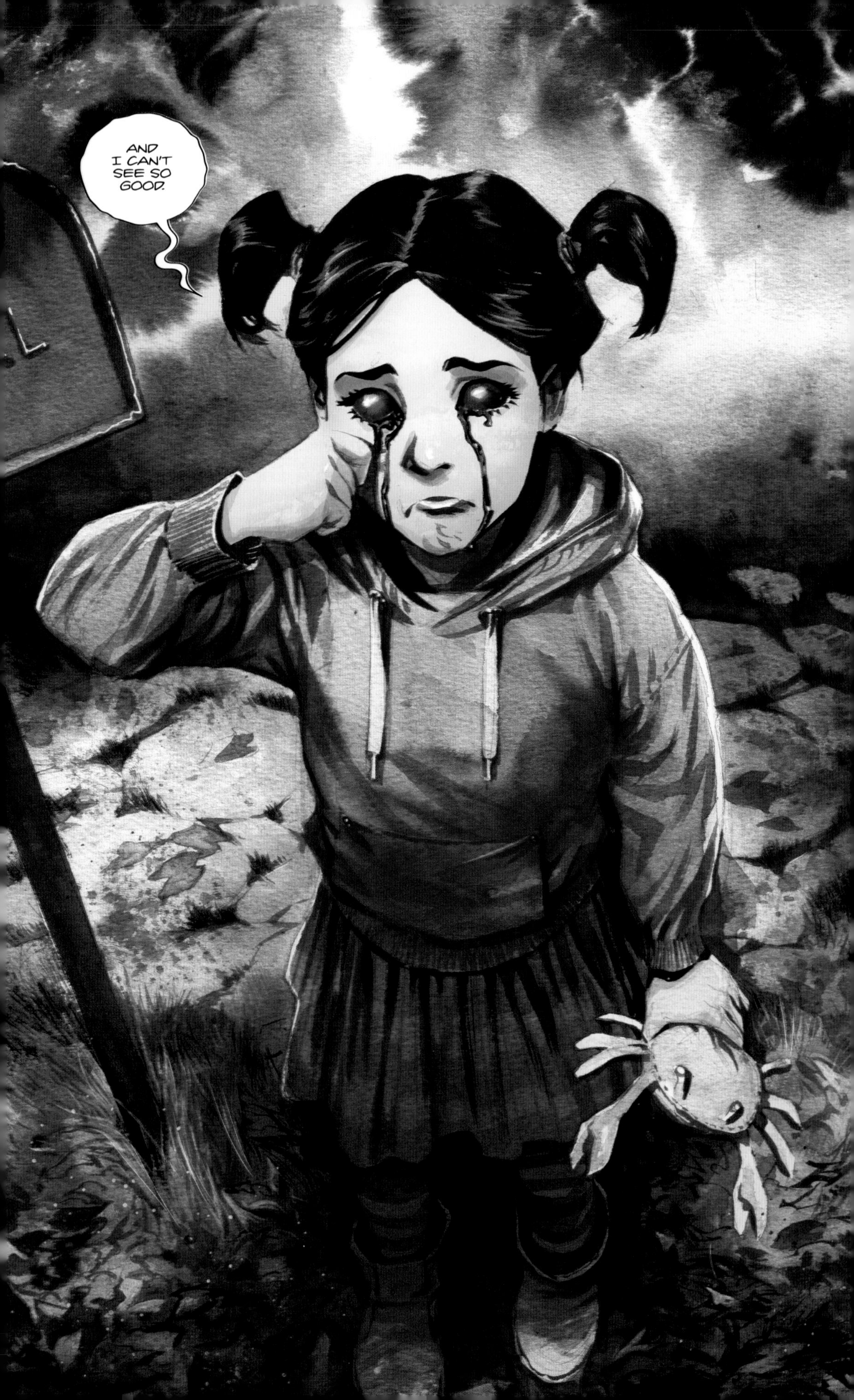
AND I CAN'T SEE SO GOOD.

CHAPTER THREE

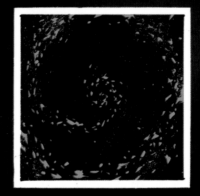

THAT TASTE
FOR BLOOD

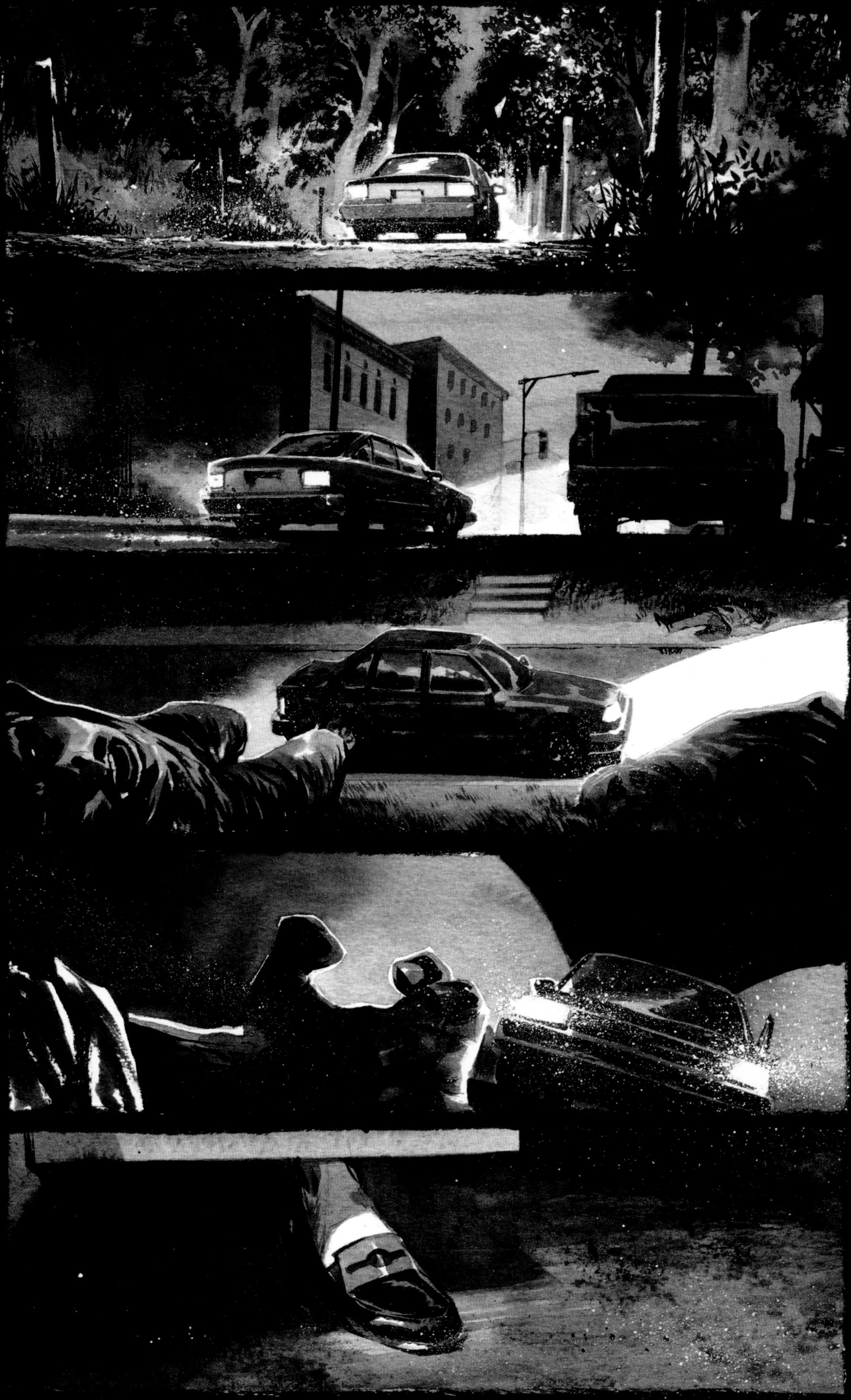

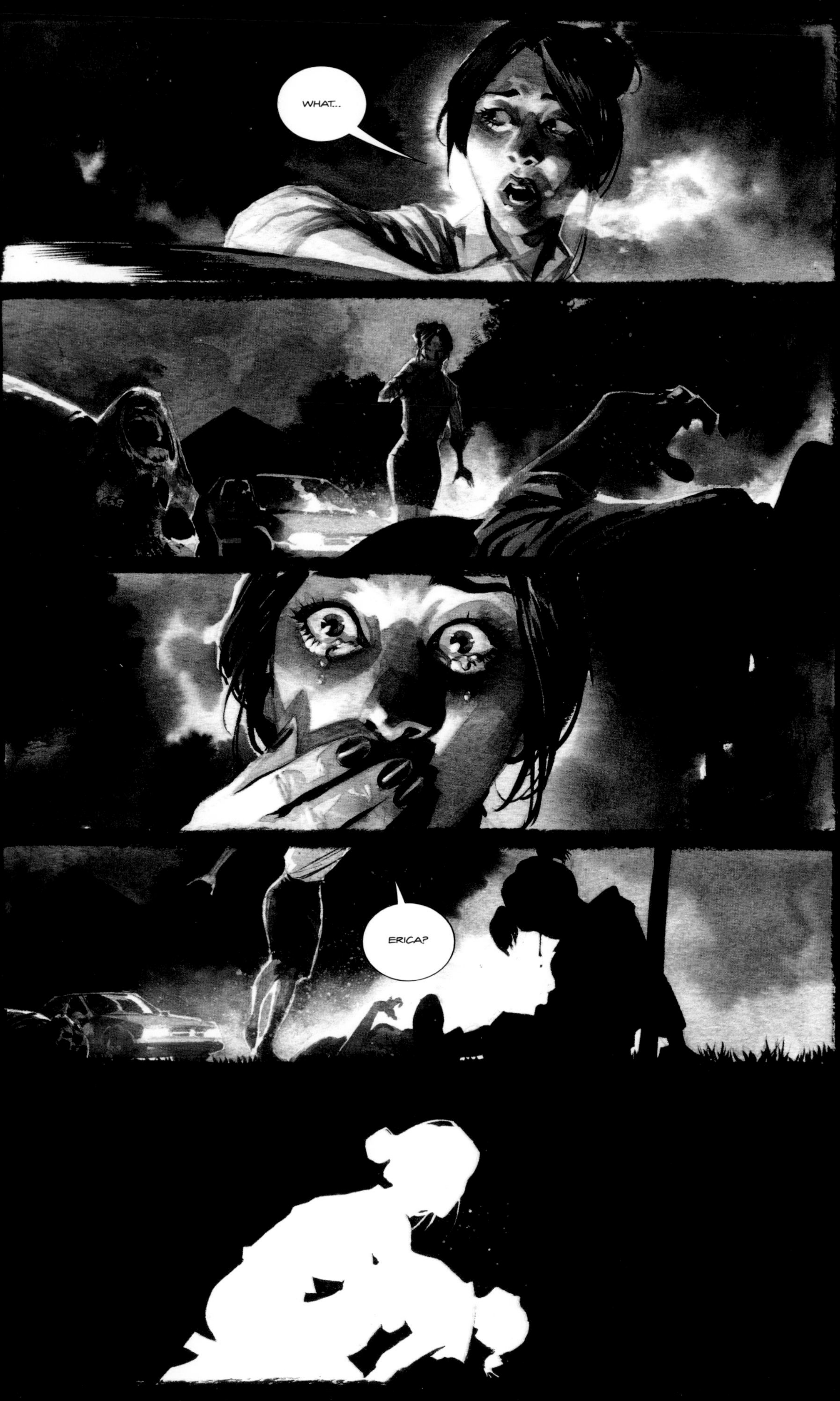
WHAT...
ERICA?

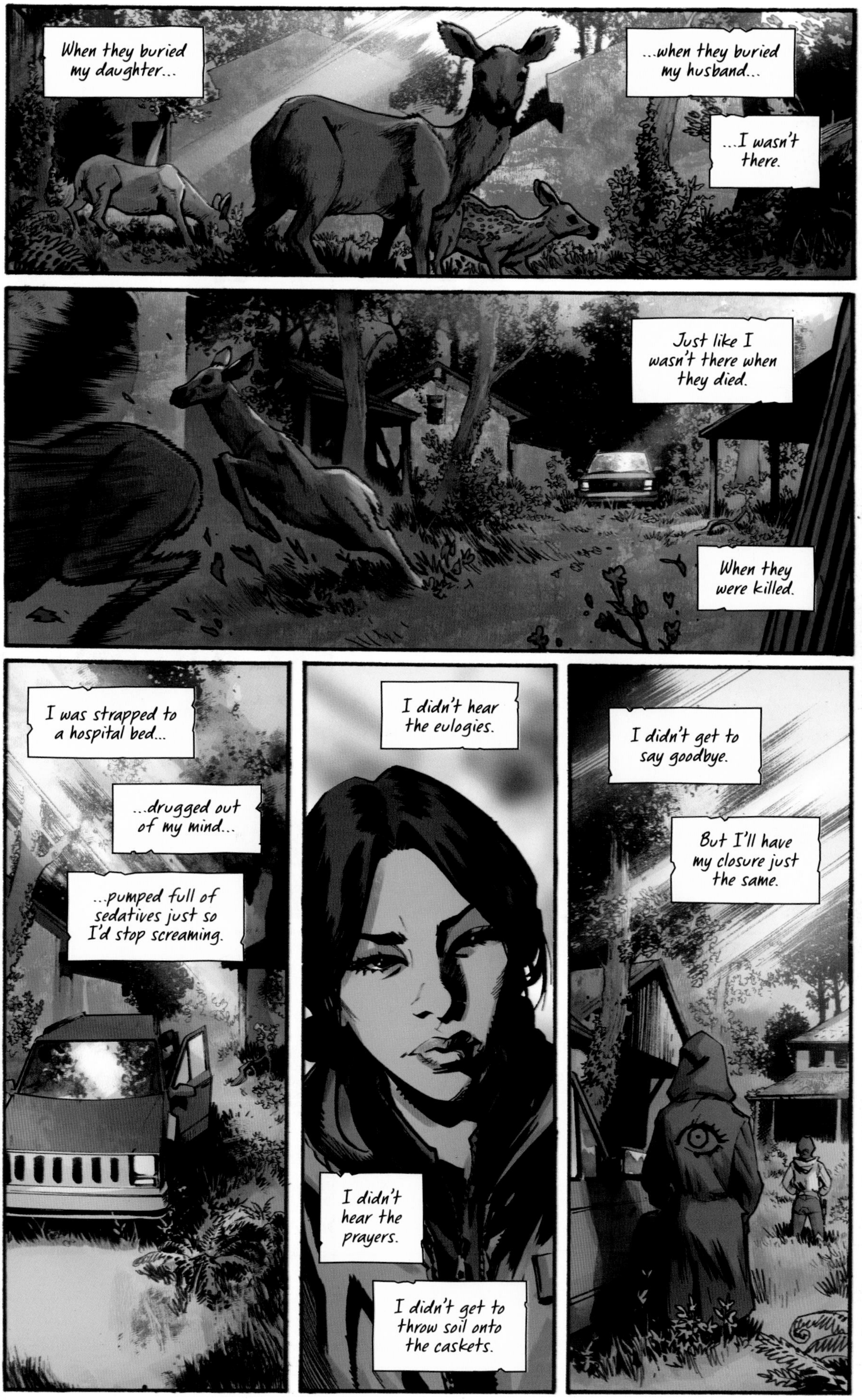
When they buried my daughter...
...when they buried my husband...
...I wasn't there.
Just like I wasn't there when they died.
When they were killed.
I was strapped to a hospital bed...
...drugged out of my mind...
...pumped full of sedatives just so I'd stop screaming.
I didn't hear the eulogies.
I didn't hear the prayers.
I didn't get to throw soil onto the caskets.
I didn't get to say goodbye.
But I'll have my closure just the same.

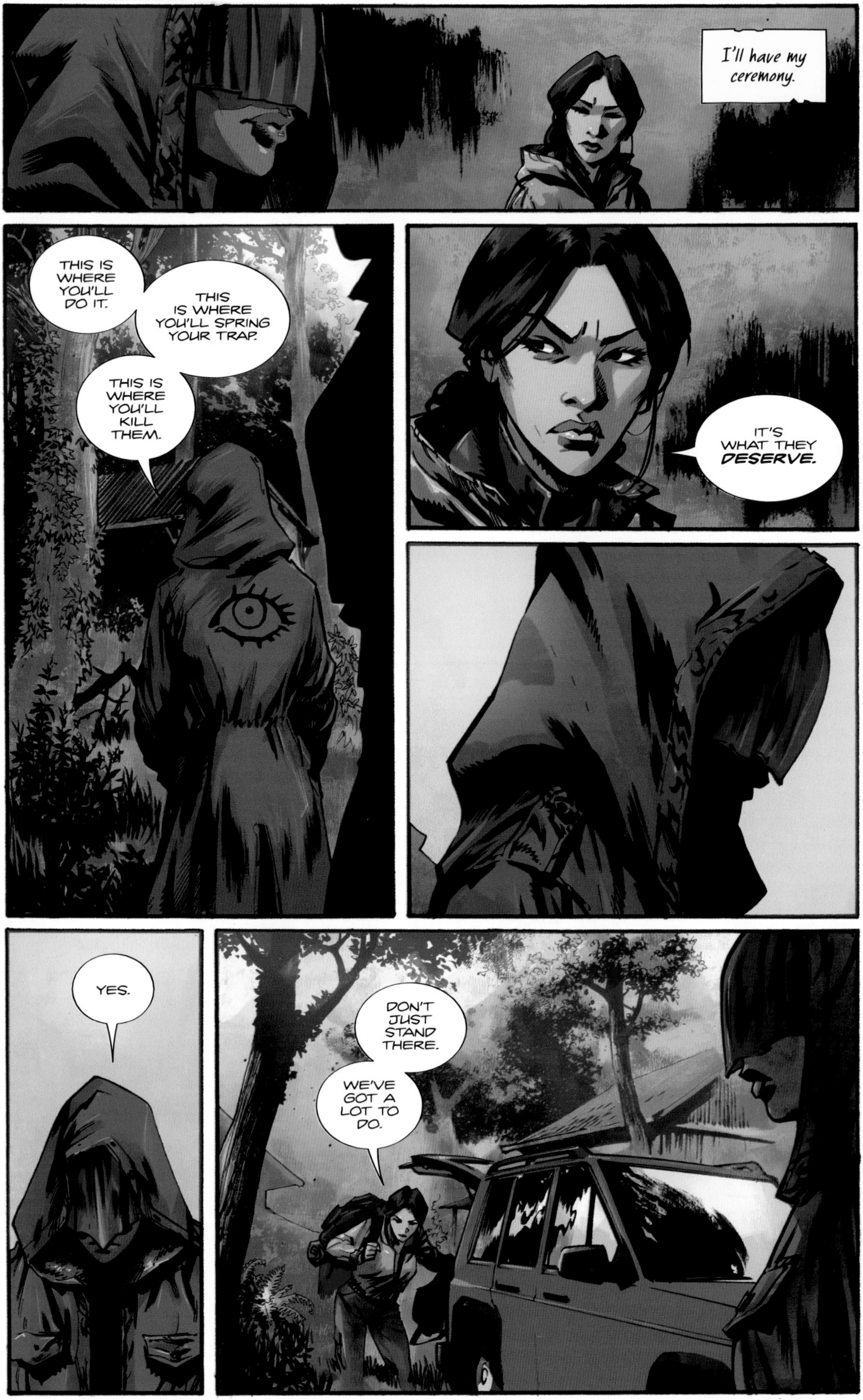
I'll have my ceremony.
THIS IS WHERE YOU'LL DO IT.
THIS IS WHERE YOU'LL SPRING YOUR TRAP.
THIS IS WHERE YOU'LL KILL THEM.
IT'S WHAT THEY DESERVE.
YES.
DON'T JUST STAND THERE.
WE'VE GOT A LOT TO DO.

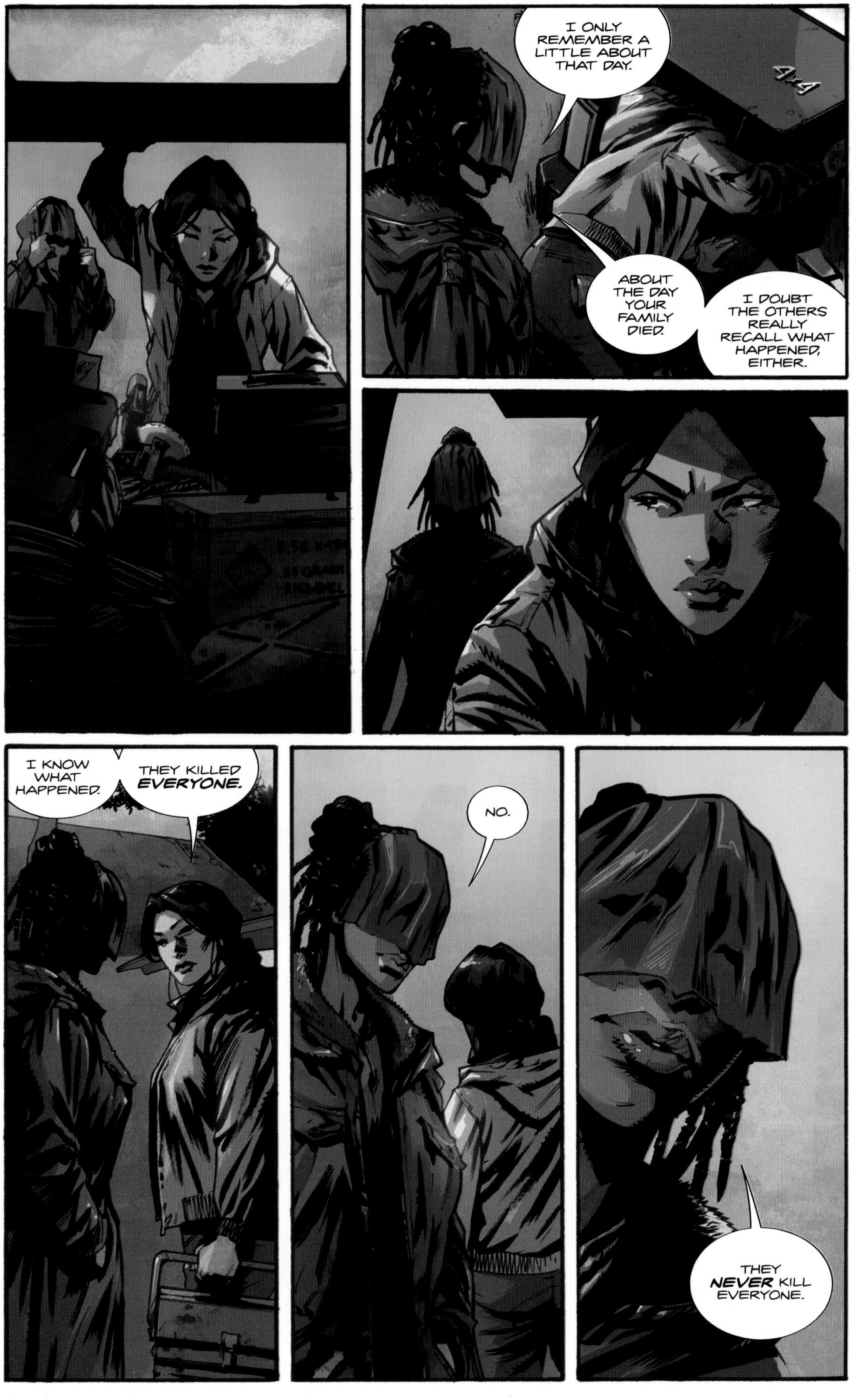
I ONLY REMEMBER A LITTLE ABOUT THAT DAY.
ABOUT THE DAY YOUR FAMILY DIED.
I DOUBT THE OTHERS REALLY RECALL WHAT HAPPENED, EITHER.
I KNOW WHAT HAPPENED.
THEY KILLED **EVERYONE.**
NO.
THEY **NEVER** KILL EVERYONE.

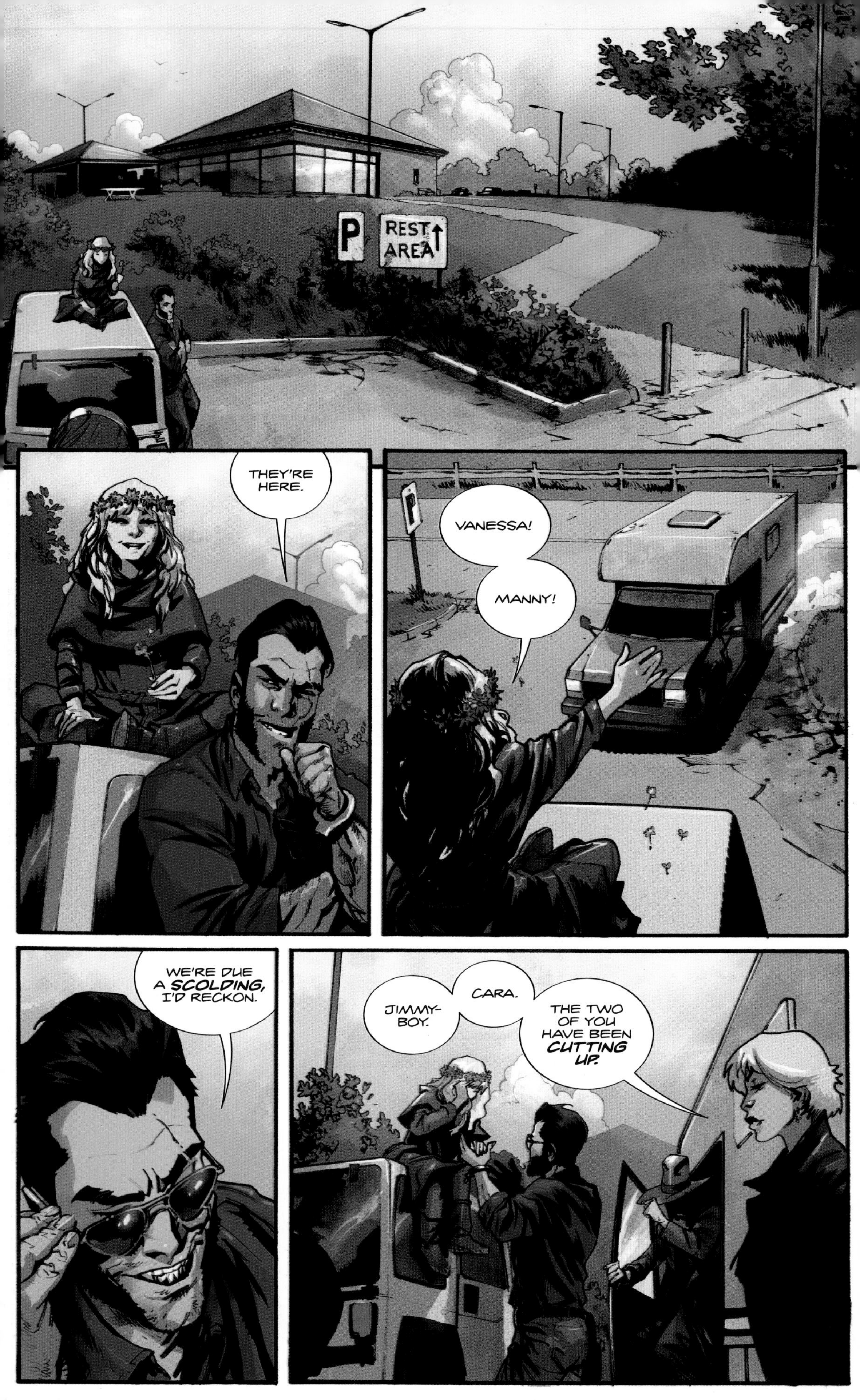
P
REST AREA
THEY'RE HERE.
VANESSA!
MANNY!
WE'RE DUE A SCOLDING, I'D RECKON.
JIMMY-BOY.
CARA.
THE TWO OF YOU HAVE BEEN CUTTING UP.

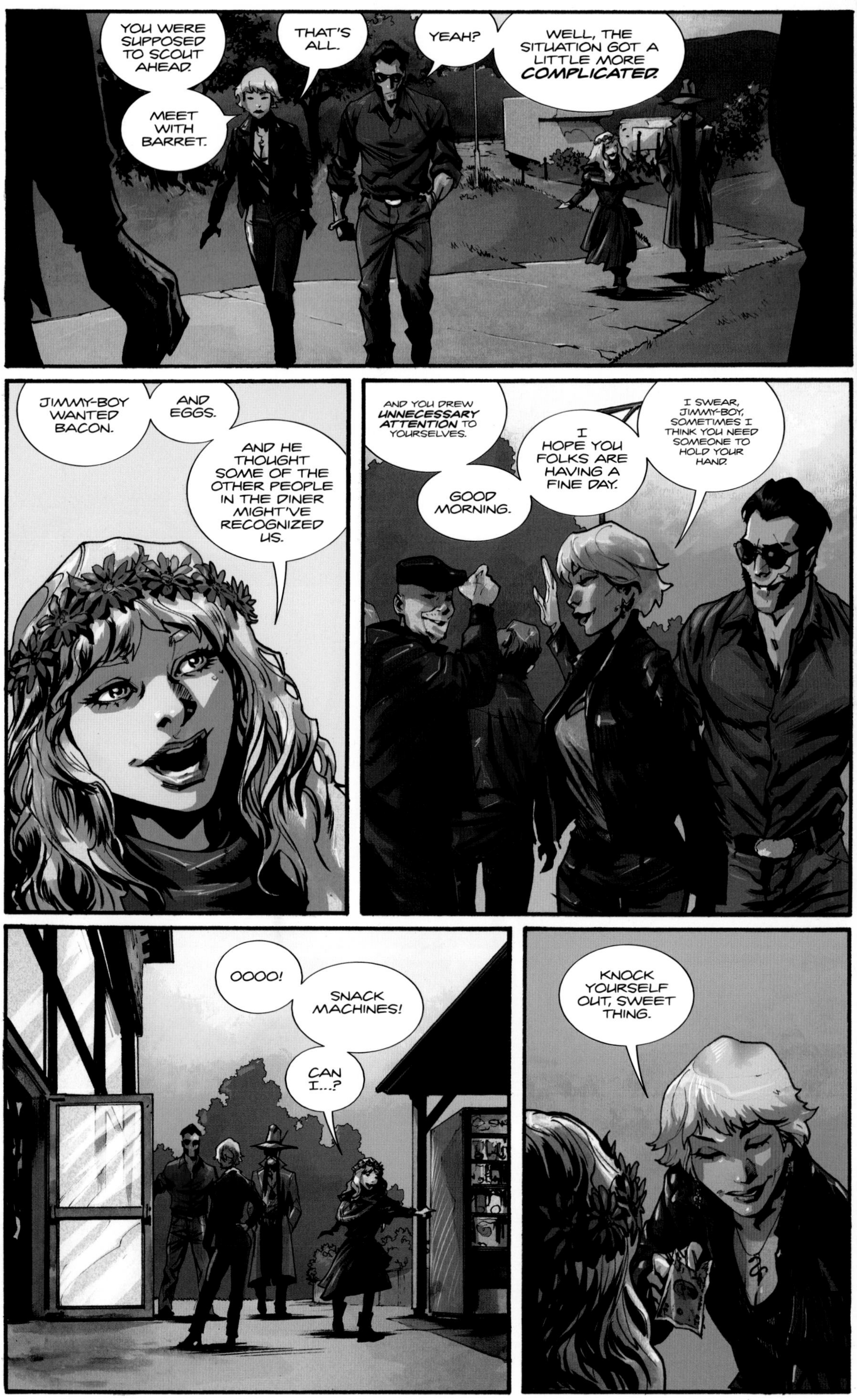
YOU WERE SUPPOSED TO SCOUT AHEAD.
MEET WITH BARRET.
THAT'S ALL.
YEAH?
WELL, THE SITUATION GOT A LITTLE MORE COMPLICATED.
JIMMY-BOY WANTED BACON.
AND EGGS.
AND HE THOUGHT SOME OF THE OTHER PEOPLE IN THE DINER MIGHT'VE RECOGNIZED US.
AND YOU DREW UNNECESSARY ATTENTION TO YOURSELVES.
GOOD MORNING.
I HOPE YOU FOLKS ARE HAVING A FINE DAY.
I SWEAR, JIMMY-BOY, SOMETIMES I THINK YOU NEED SOMEONE TO HOLD YOUR HAND.
OOOO!
SNACK MACHINES!
CAN I...?
KNOCK YOURSELF OUT, SWEET THING.

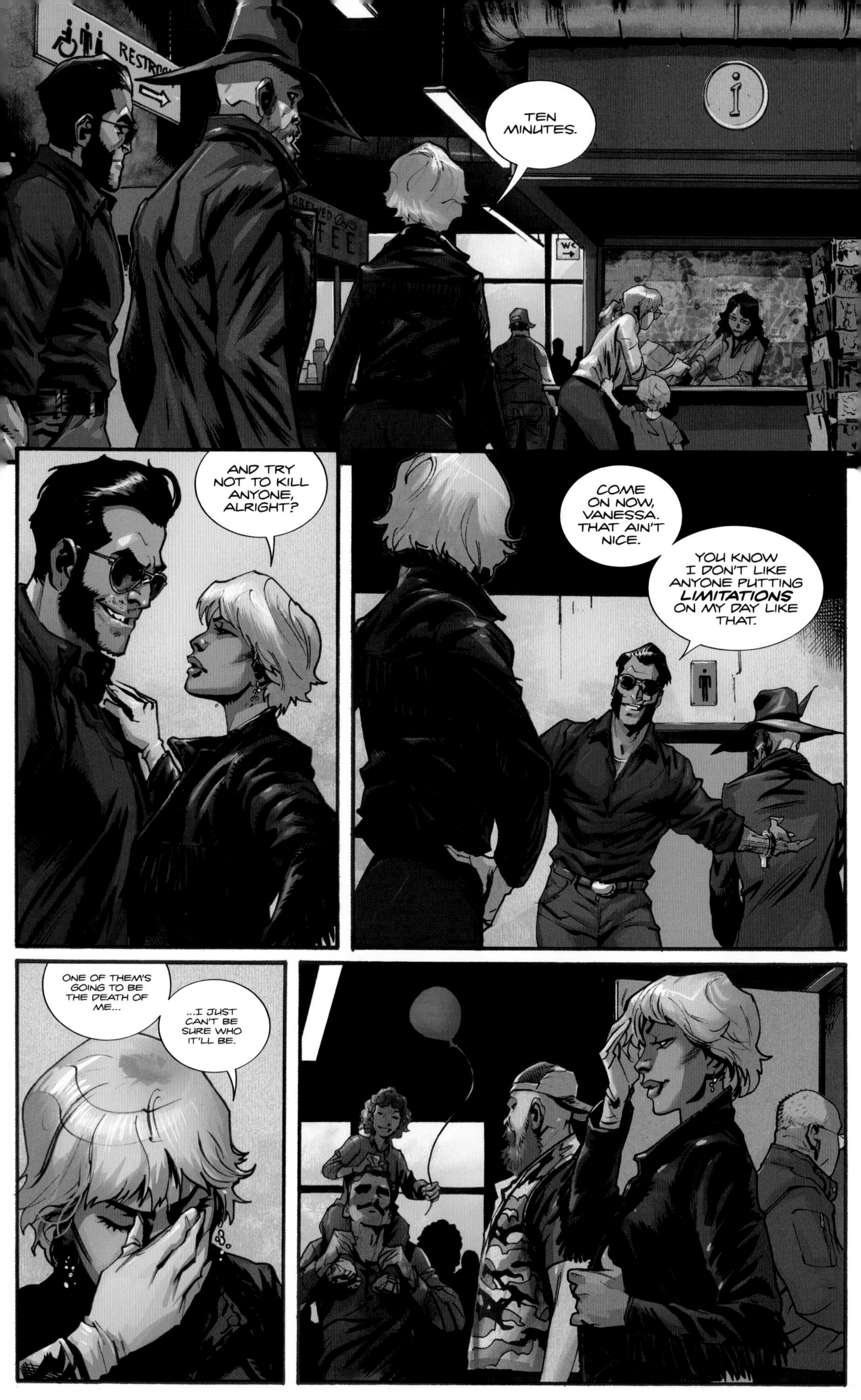
RESTROOMS
BREWED COFFEE
TEN MINUTES.
AND TRY NOT TO KILL ANYONE, ALRIGHT?
COME ON NOW, VANESSA. THAT AIN'T NICE.
YOU KNOW I DON'T LIKE ANYONE PUTTING **LIMITATIONS** ON MY DAY LIKE THAT.
ONE OF THEM'S GOING TO BE THE DEATH OF ME...
...I JUST CAN'T BE SURE WHO IT'LL BE.

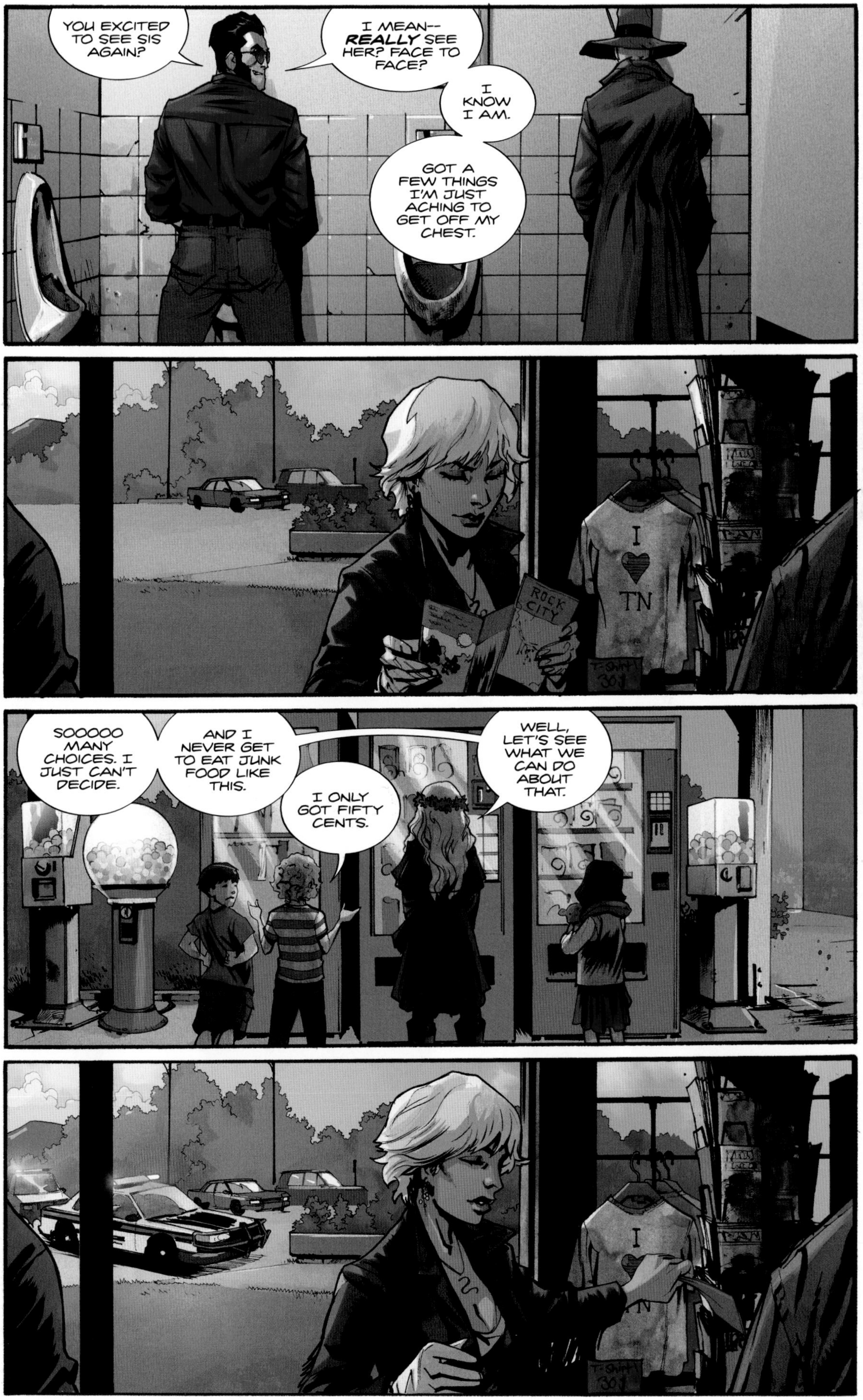
YOU EXCITED TO SEE SIS AGAIN?
I MEAN-- **REALLY** SEE HER? FACE TO FACE?
I KNOW I AM.
GOT A FEW THINGS I'M JUST ACHING TO GET OFF MY CHEST.
ROCK CITY
I ♥ TN
SOOOOO MANY CHOICES. I JUST CAN'T DECIDE.
AND I NEVER GET TO EAT JUNK FOOD LIKE THIS.
I ONLY GOT FIFTY CENTS.
WELL, LET'S SEE WHAT WE CAN DO ABOUT THAT.

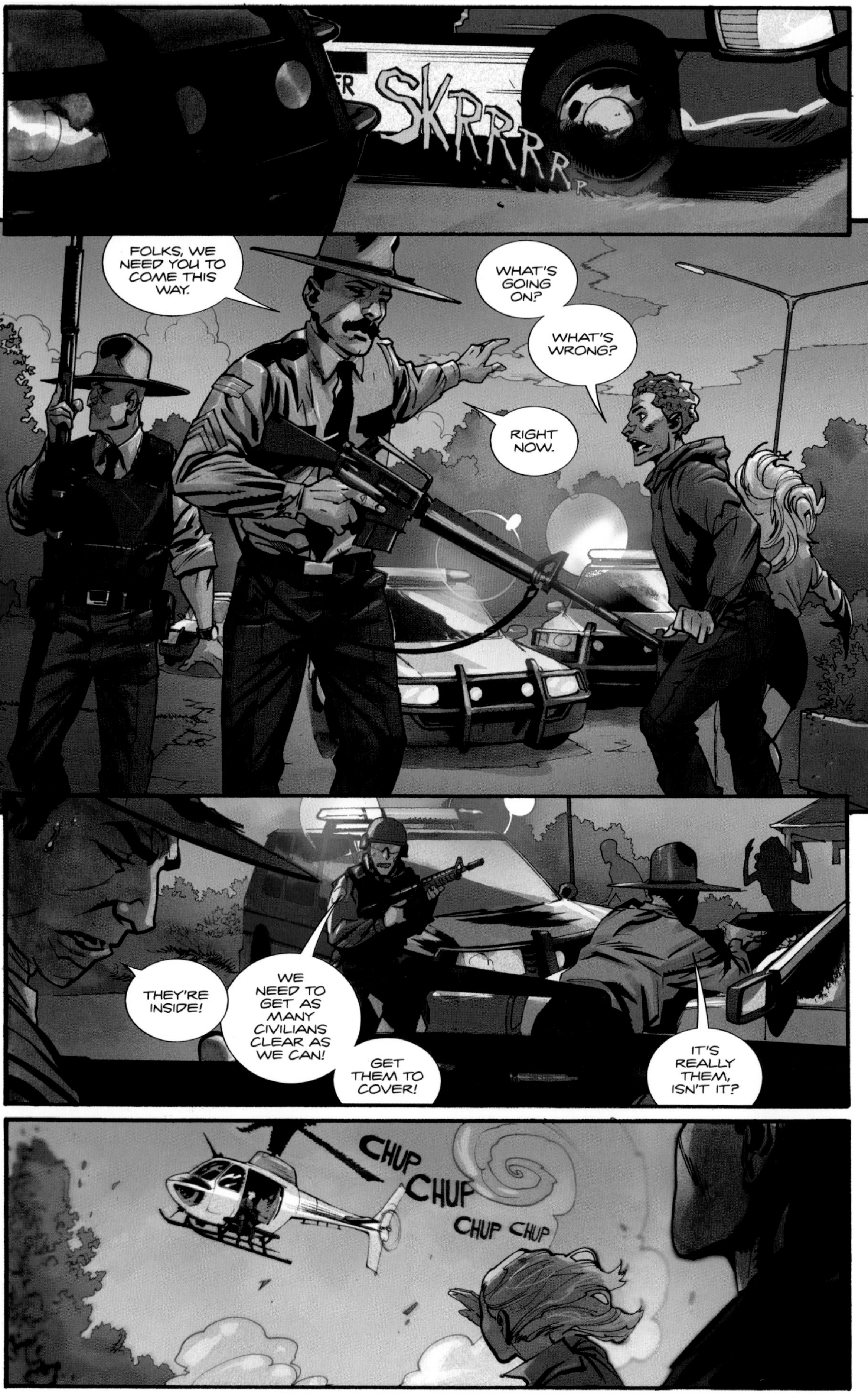
SKRRRRRp
FOLKS, WE NEED YOU TO COME THIS WAY.
WHAT'S GOING ON?
WHAT'S WRONG?
RIGHT NOW.
THEY'RE INSIDE!
WE NEED TO GET AS MANY CIVILIANS CLEAR AS WE CAN!
GET THEM TO COVER!
IT'S REALLY THEM, ISN'T IT?
CHUP CHUP CHUP CHUP

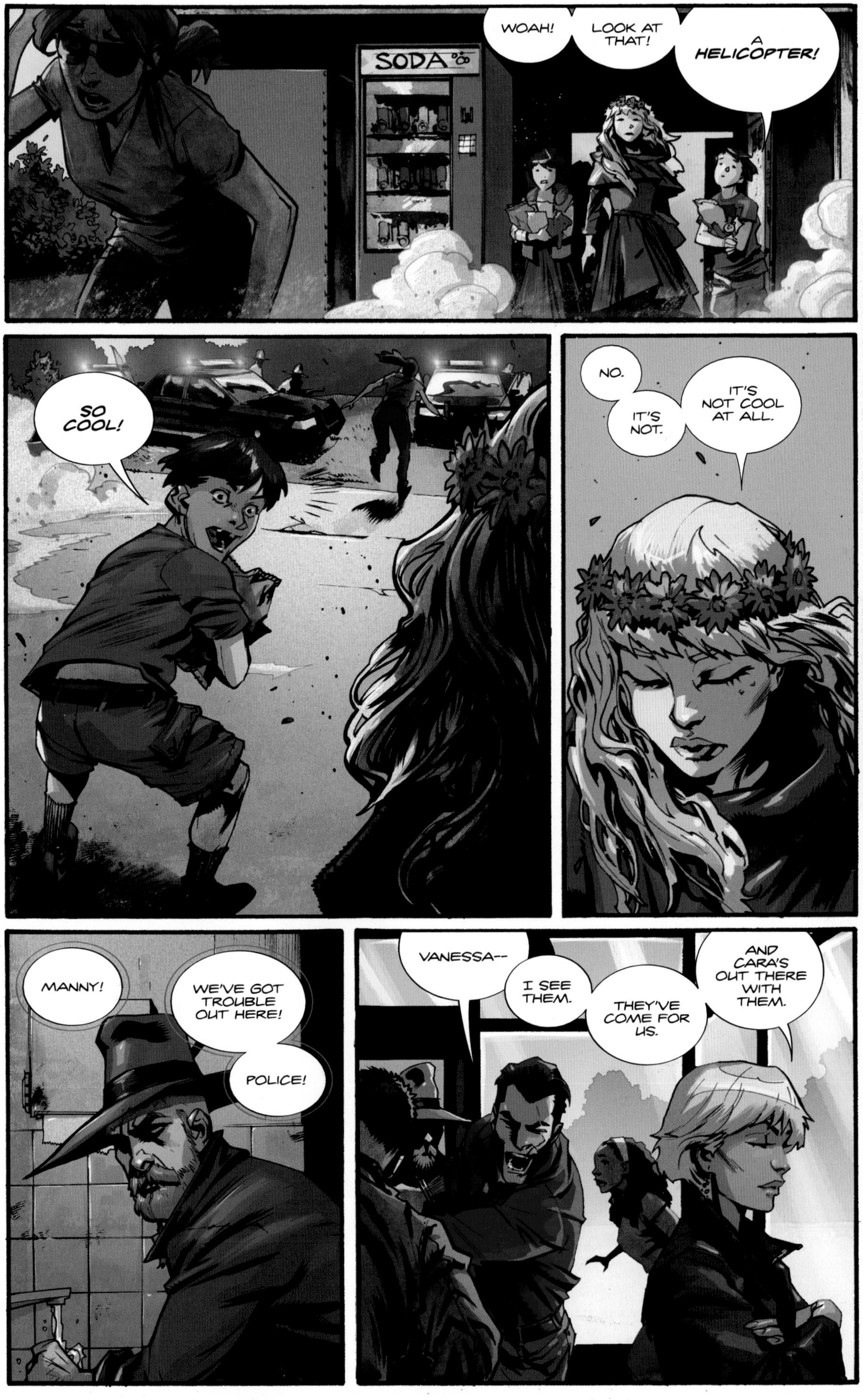
SODA
WOAH!
LOOK AT THAT!
A HELICOPTER!
SO COOL!
NO.
IT'S NOT.
IT'S NOT COOL AT ALL.
MANNY!
WE'VE GOT TROUBLE OUT HERE!
POLICE!
VANESSA--
I SEE THEM.
THEY'VE COME FOR US.
AND CARA'S OUT THERE WITH THEM.

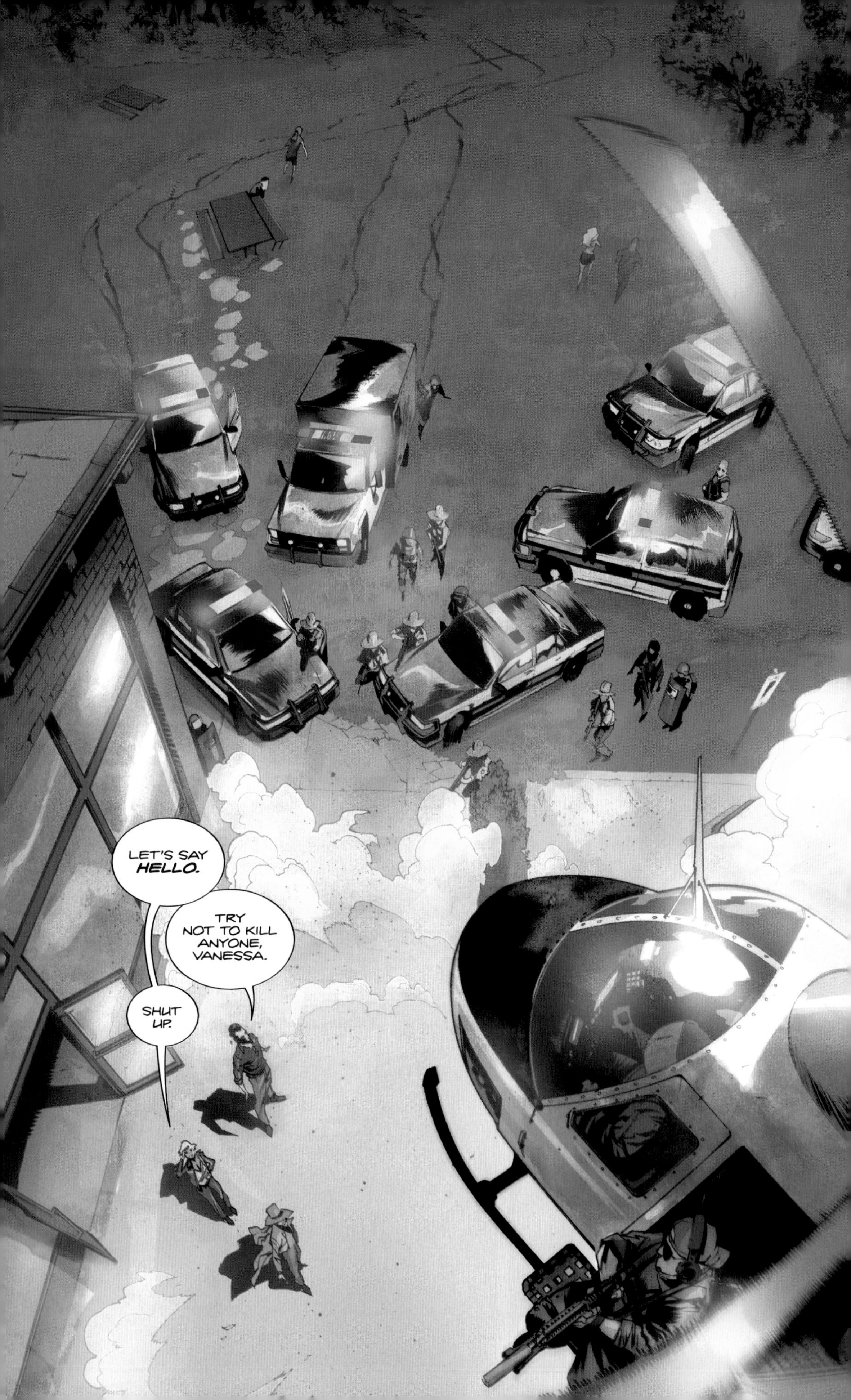
LET'S SAY HELLO.
TRY NOT TO KILL ANYONE, VANESSA.
SHUT UP.

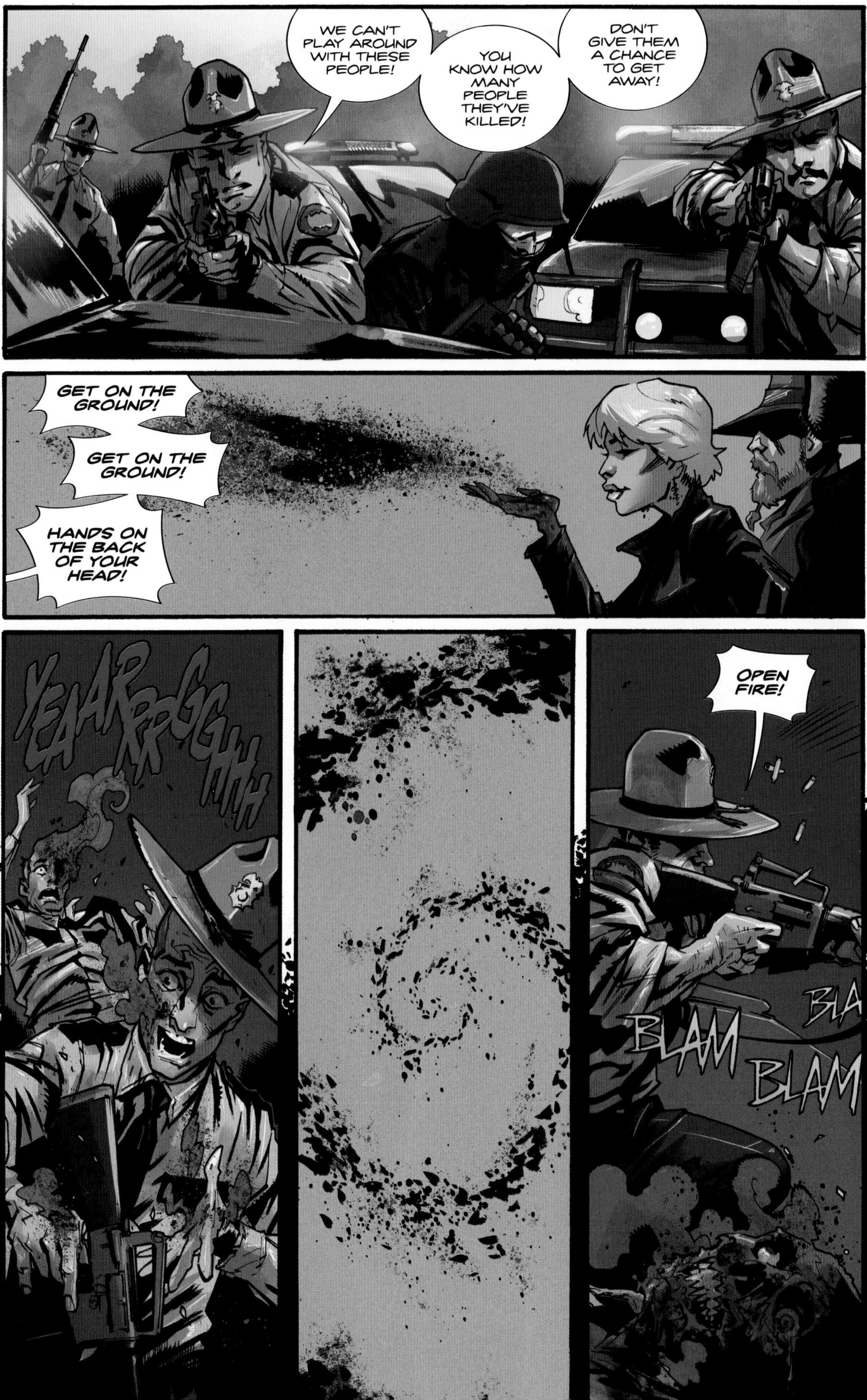
WE CAN'T PLAY AROUND WITH THESE PEOPLE!
YOU KNOW HOW MANY PEOPLE THEY'VE KILLED!
DON'T GIVE THEM A CHANCE TO GET AWAY!
GET ON THE GROUND!
GET ON THE GROUND!
HANDS ON THE BACK OF YOUR HEAD!
YEAARRRGGHHH
OPEN FIRE!
BLA
BLAM
BLAM

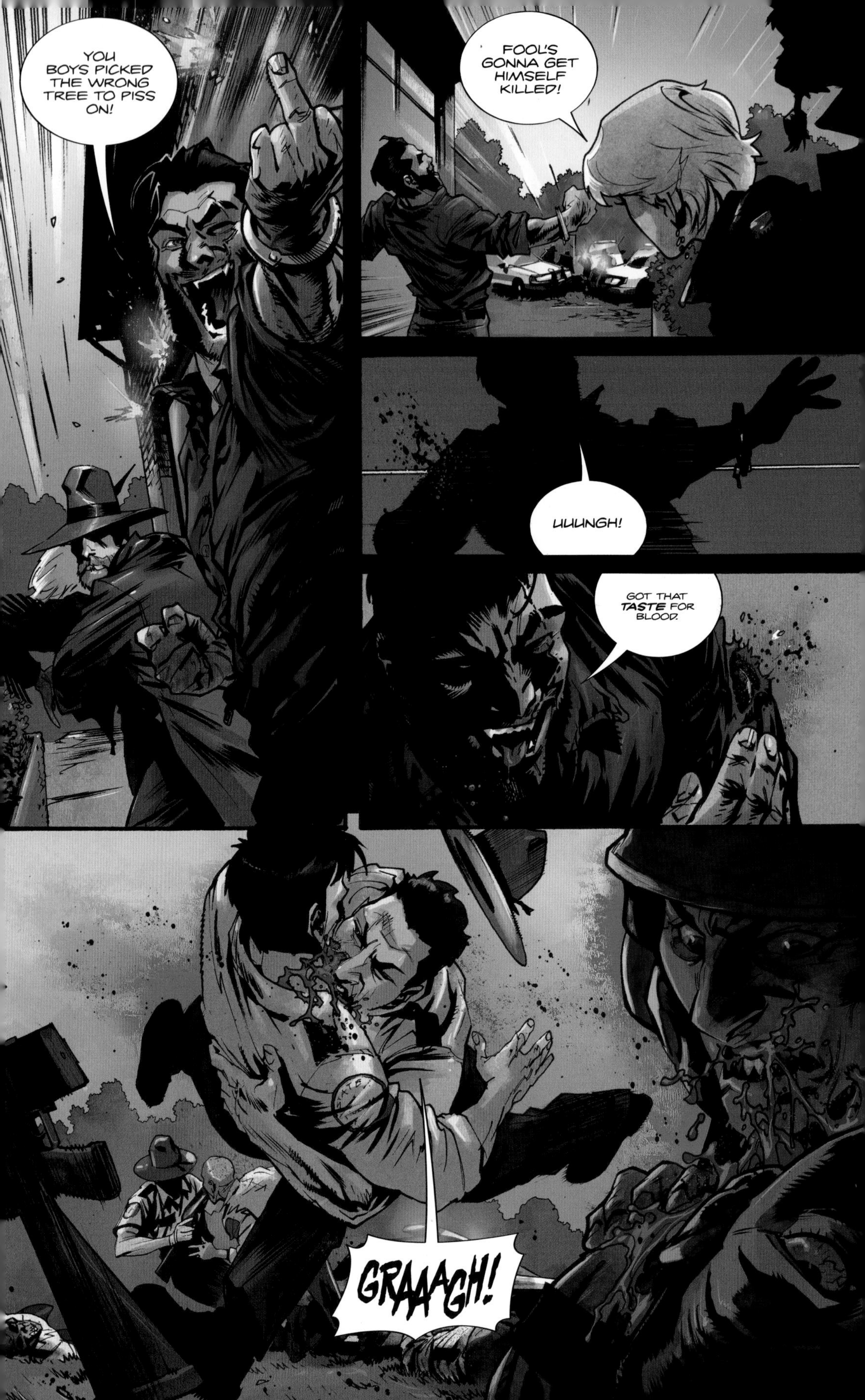
YOU BOYS PICKED THE WRONG TREE TO PISS ON!
FOOL'S GONNA GET HIMSELF KILLED!
UUUNGH!
GOT THAT *TASTE* FOR BLOOD.
GRAAAGH!

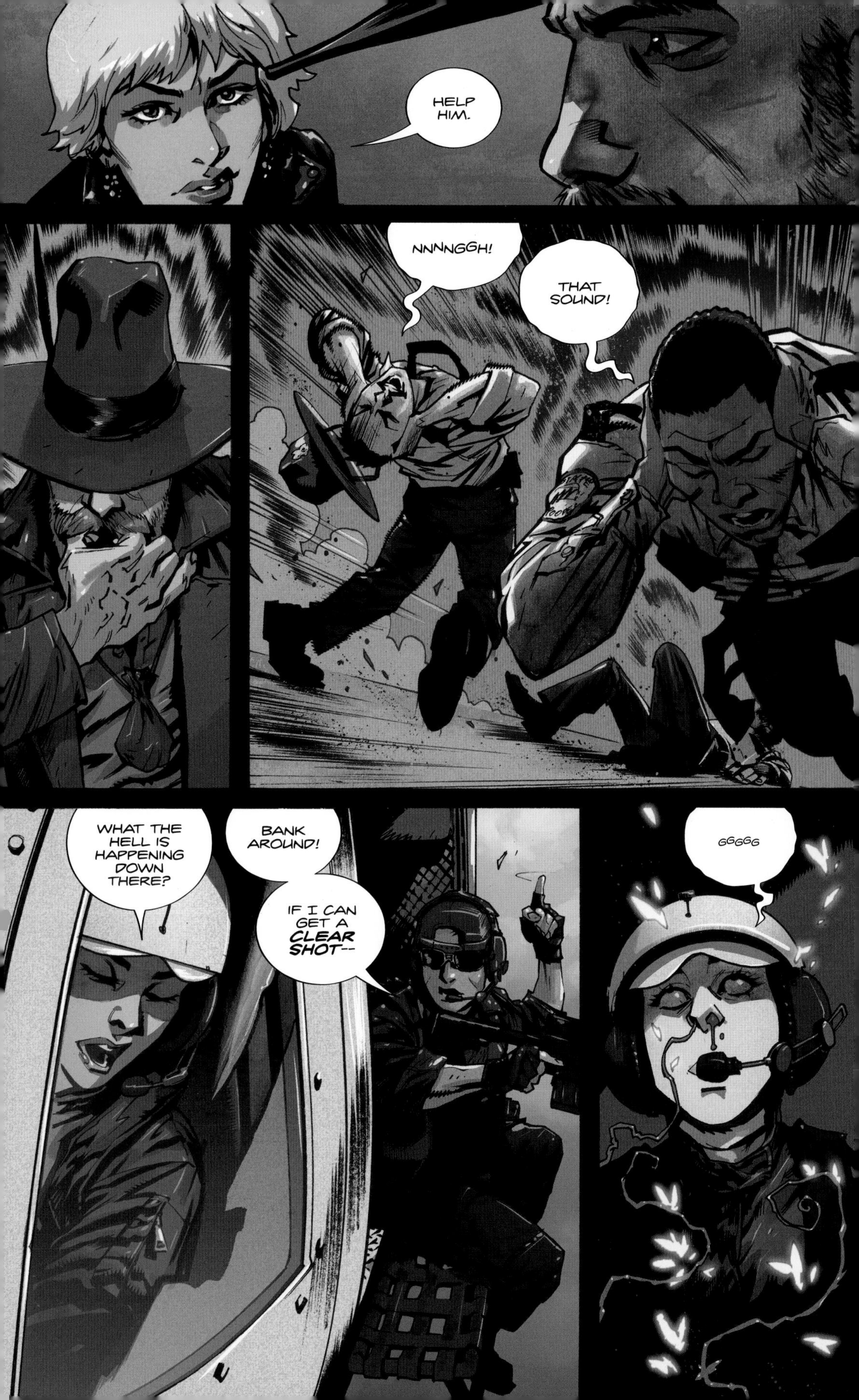
HELP HIM.
NNNNGGH!
THAT SOUND!
WHAT THE HELL IS HAPPENING DOWN THERE?
BANK AROUND!
IF I CAN GET A CLEAR SHOT--
GGGGG

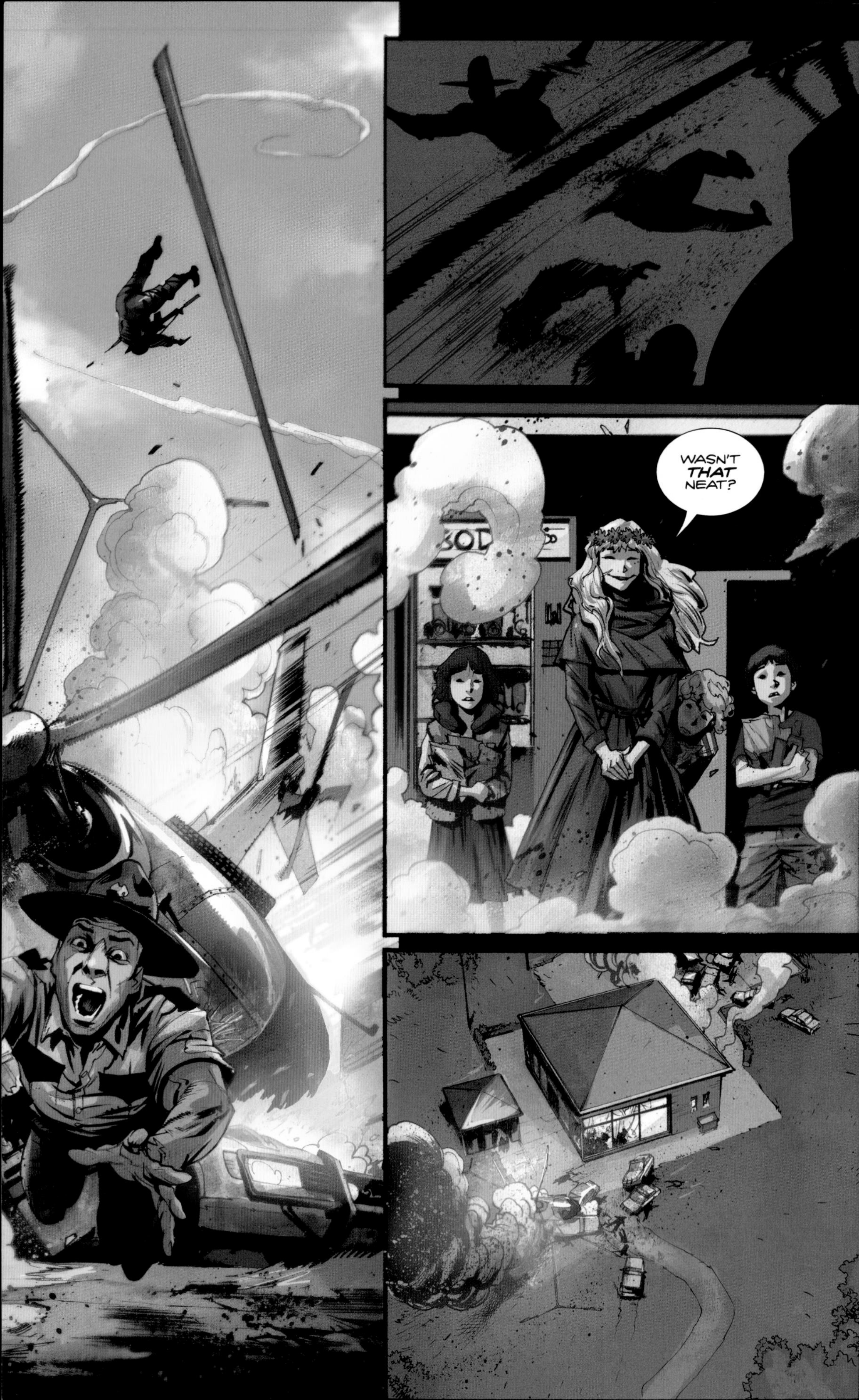
WASN'T THAT NEAT?

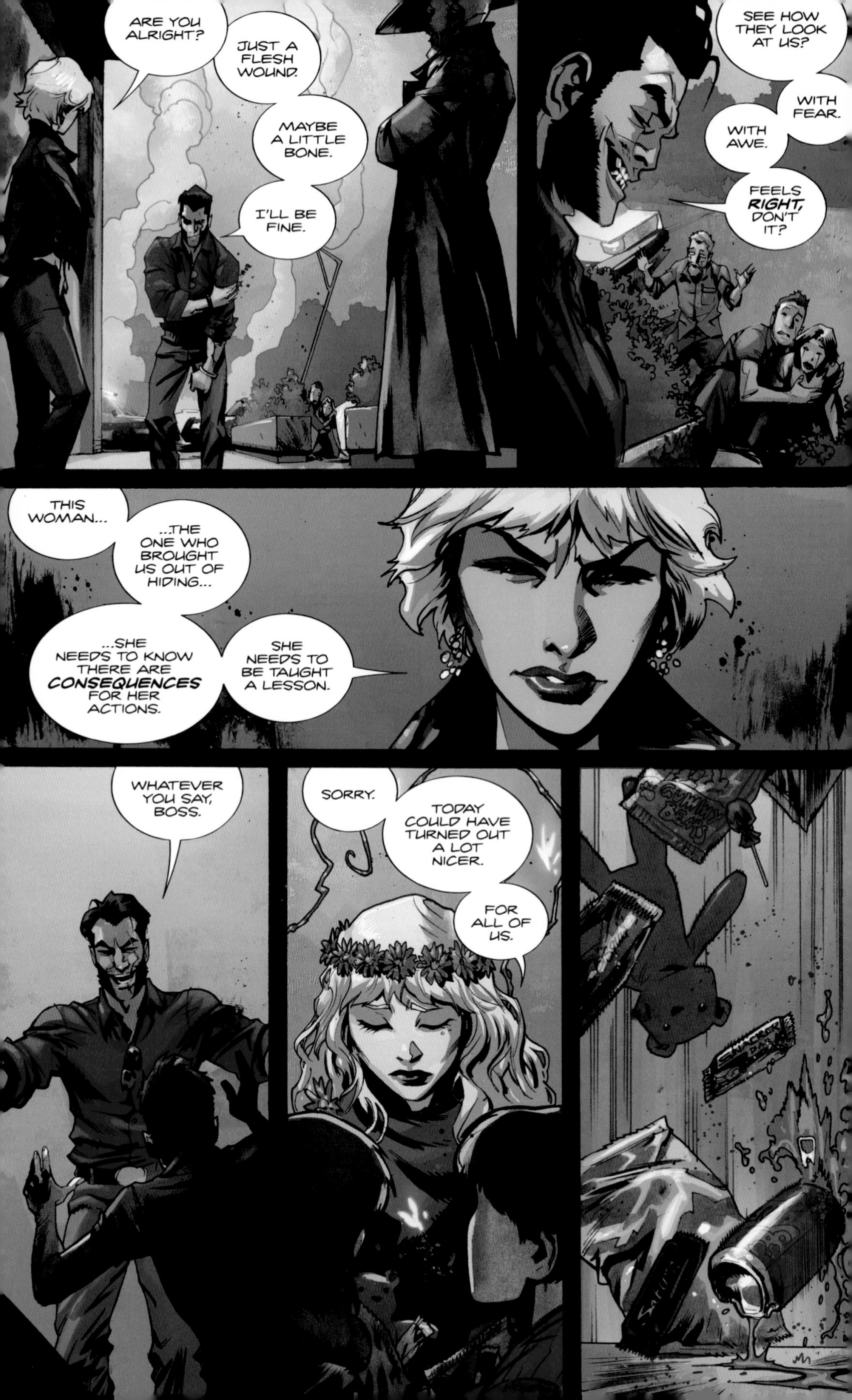
ARE YOU ALRIGHT?
JUST A FLESH WOUND.
MAYBE A LITTLE BONE.
I'LL BE FINE.
SEE HOW THEY LOOK AT US?
WITH AWE.
WITH FEAR.
FEELS **RIGHT,** DON'T IT?
THIS WOMAN...
...THE ONE WHO BROUGHT US OUT OF HIDING...
...SHE NEEDS TO KNOW THERE ARE **CONSEQUENCES** FOR HER ACTIONS.
SHE NEEDS TO BE TAUGHT A LESSON.
WHATEVER YOU SAY, BOSS.
SORRY.
TODAY COULD HAVE TURNED OUT A LOT NICER.
FOR ALL OF US.
GUMMY BEARS

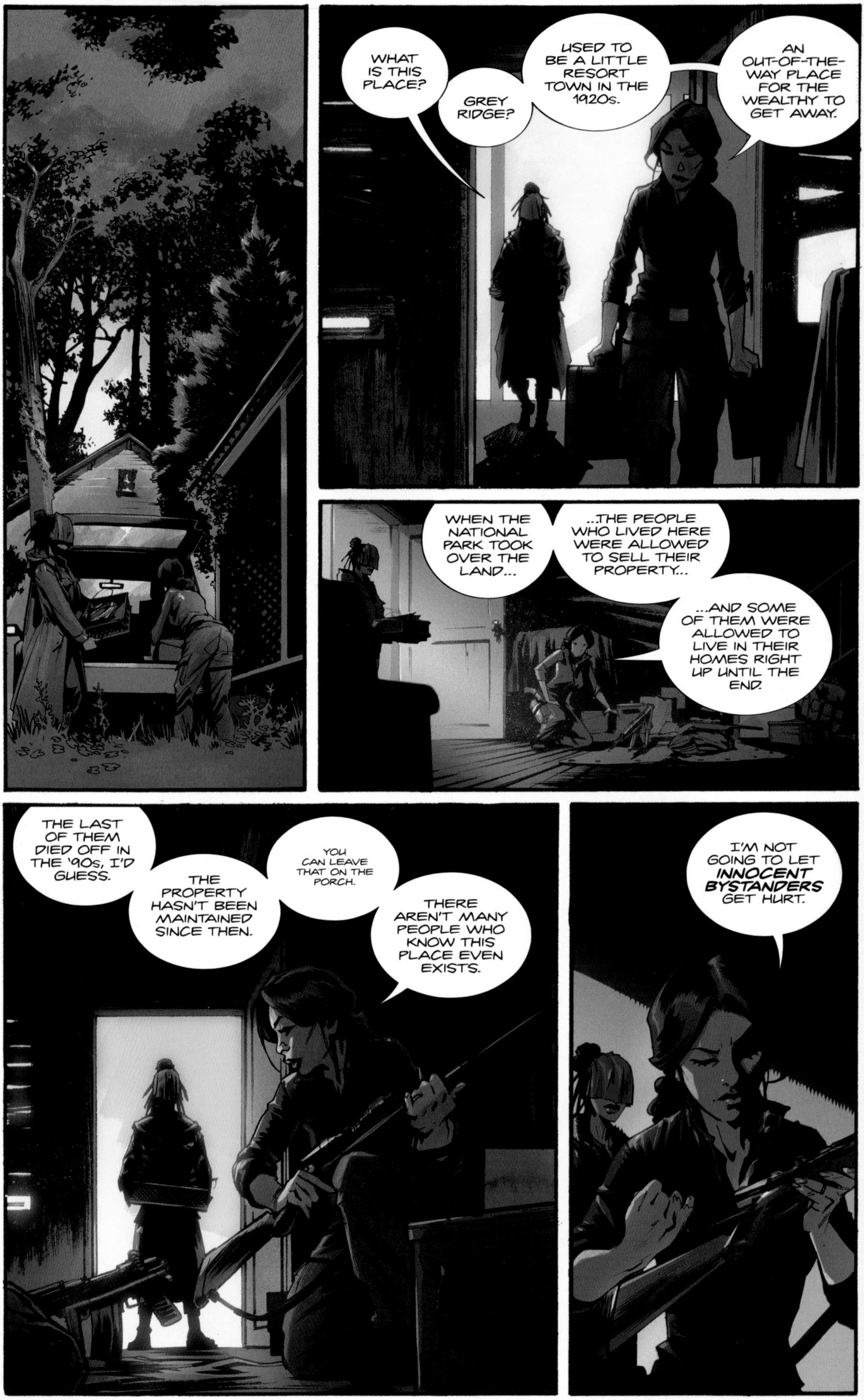
WHAT IS THIS PLACE?
GREY RIDGE?
USED TO BE A LITTLE RESORT TOWN IN THE 1920s.
AN OUT-OF-THE-WAY PLACE FOR THE WEALTHY TO GET AWAY.
WHEN THE NATIONAL PARK TOOK OVER THE LAND...
...THE PEOPLE WHO LIVED HERE WERE ALLOWED TO SELL THEIR PROPERTY...
...AND SOME OF THEM WERE ALLOWED TO LIVE IN THEIR HOMES RIGHT UP UNTIL THE END.
THE LAST OF THEM DIED OFF IN THE '90s, I'D GUESS.
THE PROPERTY HASN'T BEEN MAINTAINED SINCE THEN.
YOU CAN LEAVE THAT ON THE PORCH.
THERE AREN'T MANY PEOPLE WHO KNOW THIS PLACE EVEN EXISTS.
I'M NOT GOING TO LET ***INNOCENT BYSTANDERS*** GET HURT.

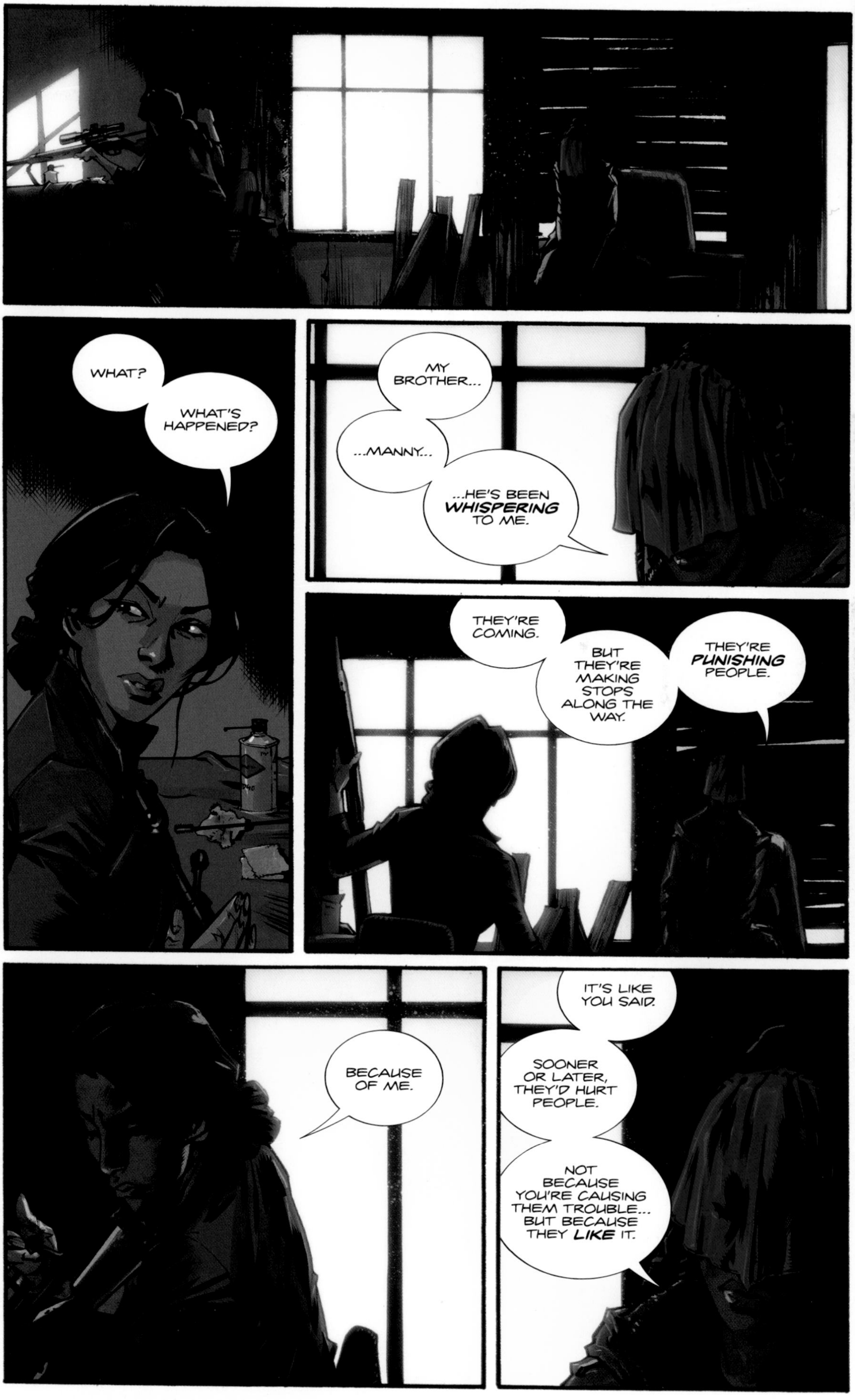
WHAT?
WHAT'S HAPPENED?
MY BROTHER...
...MANNY...
...HE'S BEEN **WHISPERING** TO ME.
THEY'RE COMING.
BUT THEY'RE MAKING STOPS ALONG THE WAY.
THEY'RE **PUNISHING** PEOPLE.
BECAUSE OF ME.
IT'S LIKE YOU SAID.
SOONER OR LATER, THEY'D HURT PEOPLE.
NOT BECAUSE YOU'RE CAUSING THEM TROUBLE... BUT BECAUSE THEY **LIKE** IT.

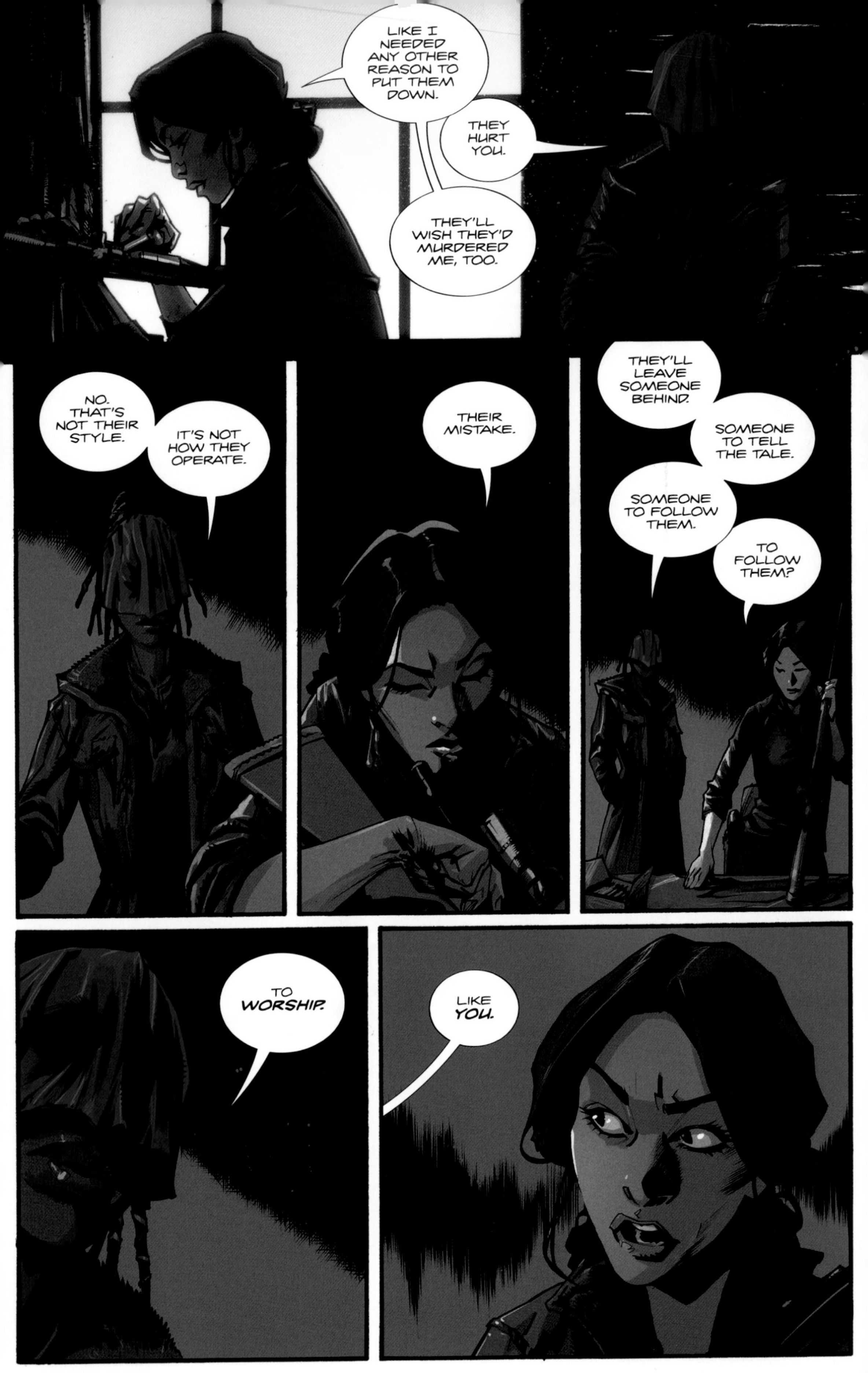
LIKE I NEEDED ANY OTHER REASON TO PUT THEM DOWN.
THEY HURT YOU.
THEY'LL WISH THEY'D MURDERED ME, TOO.
NO. THAT'S NOT THEIR STYLE.
IT'S NOT HOW THEY OPERATE.
THEIR MISTAKE.
THEY'LL LEAVE SOMEONE BEHIND.
SOMEONE TO TELL THE TALE.
SOMEONE TO FOLLOW THEM.
TO FOLLOW THEM?
TO WORSHIP.
LIKE YOU.

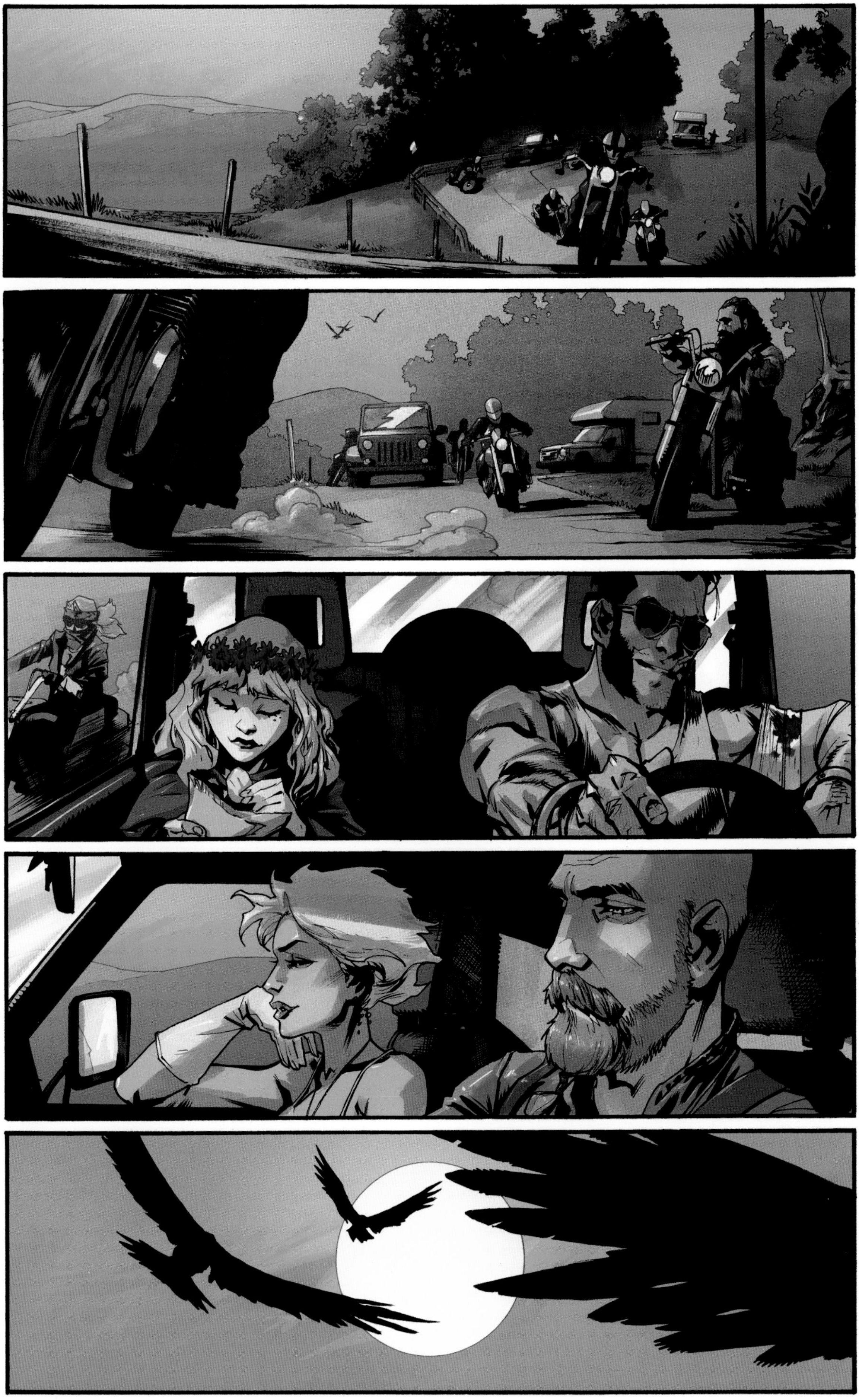

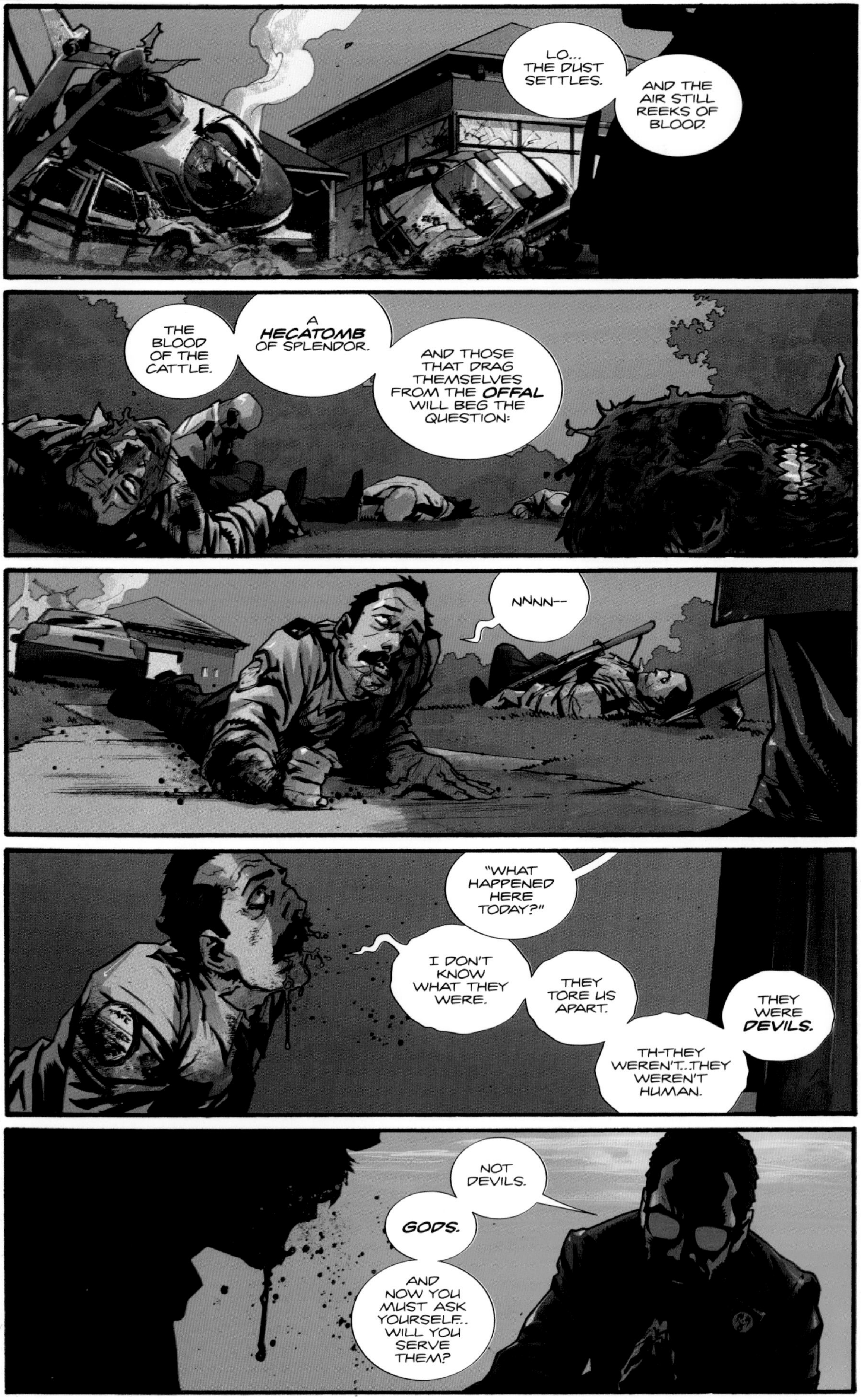
LO... THE DUST SETTLES.
AND THE AIR STILL REEKS OF BLOOD.
THE BLOOD OF THE CATTLE.
A HECATOMB OF SPLENDOR.
AND THOSE THAT DRAG THEMSELVES FROM THE OFFAL WILL BEG THE QUESTION:
NNNN--
"WHAT HAPPENED HERE TODAY?"
I DON'T KNOW WHAT THEY WERE.
THEY TORE US APART.
THEY WERE DEVILS.
TH-THEY WEREN'T...THEY WEREN'T HUMAN.
NOT DEVILS.
GODS.
AND NOW YOU MUST ASK YOURSELF... WILL YOU SERVE THEM?

CHAPTER FOUR

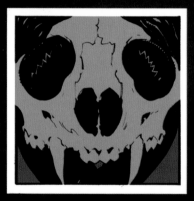

CONSEQUENCES

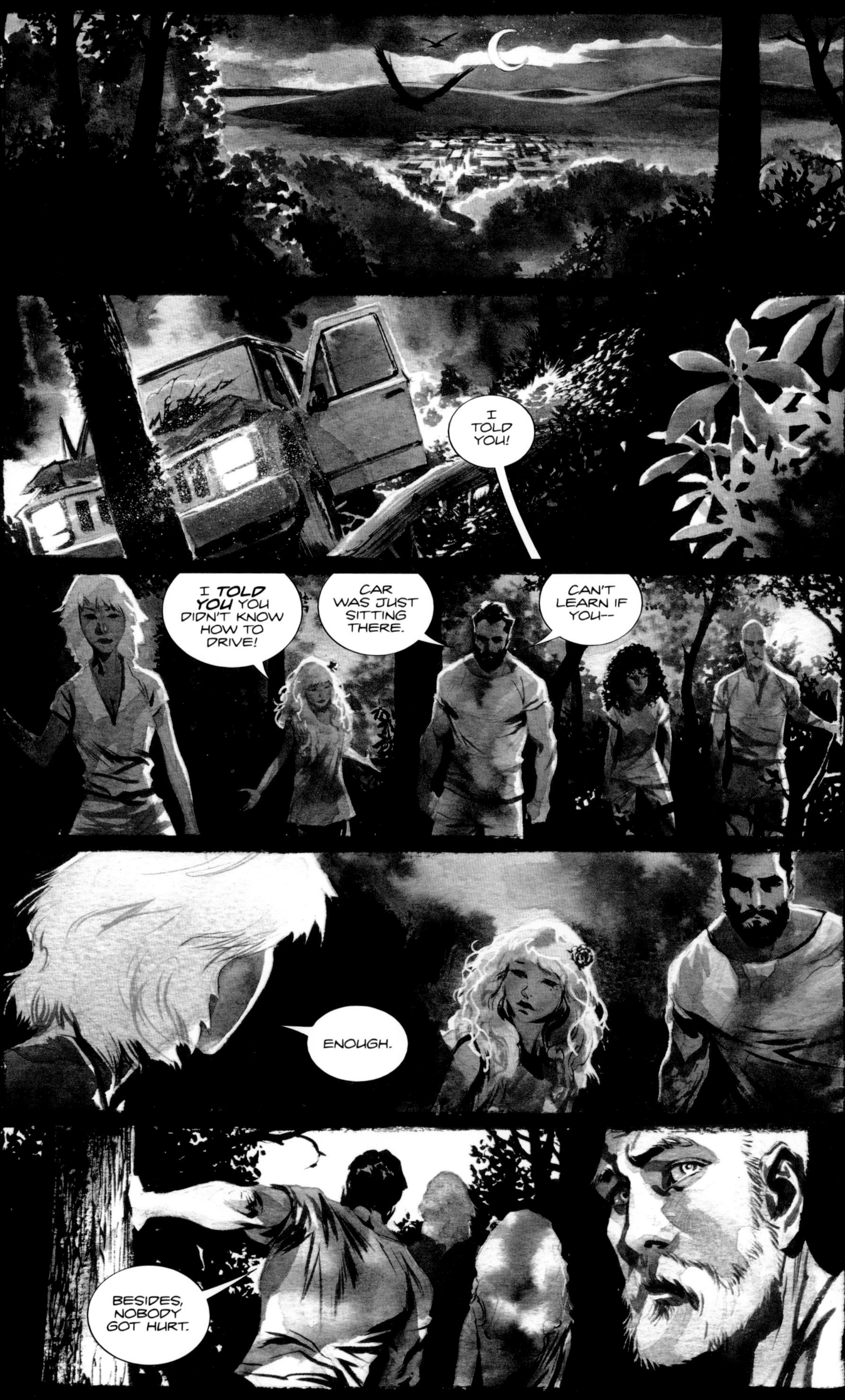
I TOLD YOU!
I TOLD YOU YOU DIDN'T KNOW HOW TO DRIVE!
CAR WAS JUST SITTING THERE.
CAN'T LEARN IF YOU--
ENOUGH.
BESIDES, NOBODY GOT HURT.

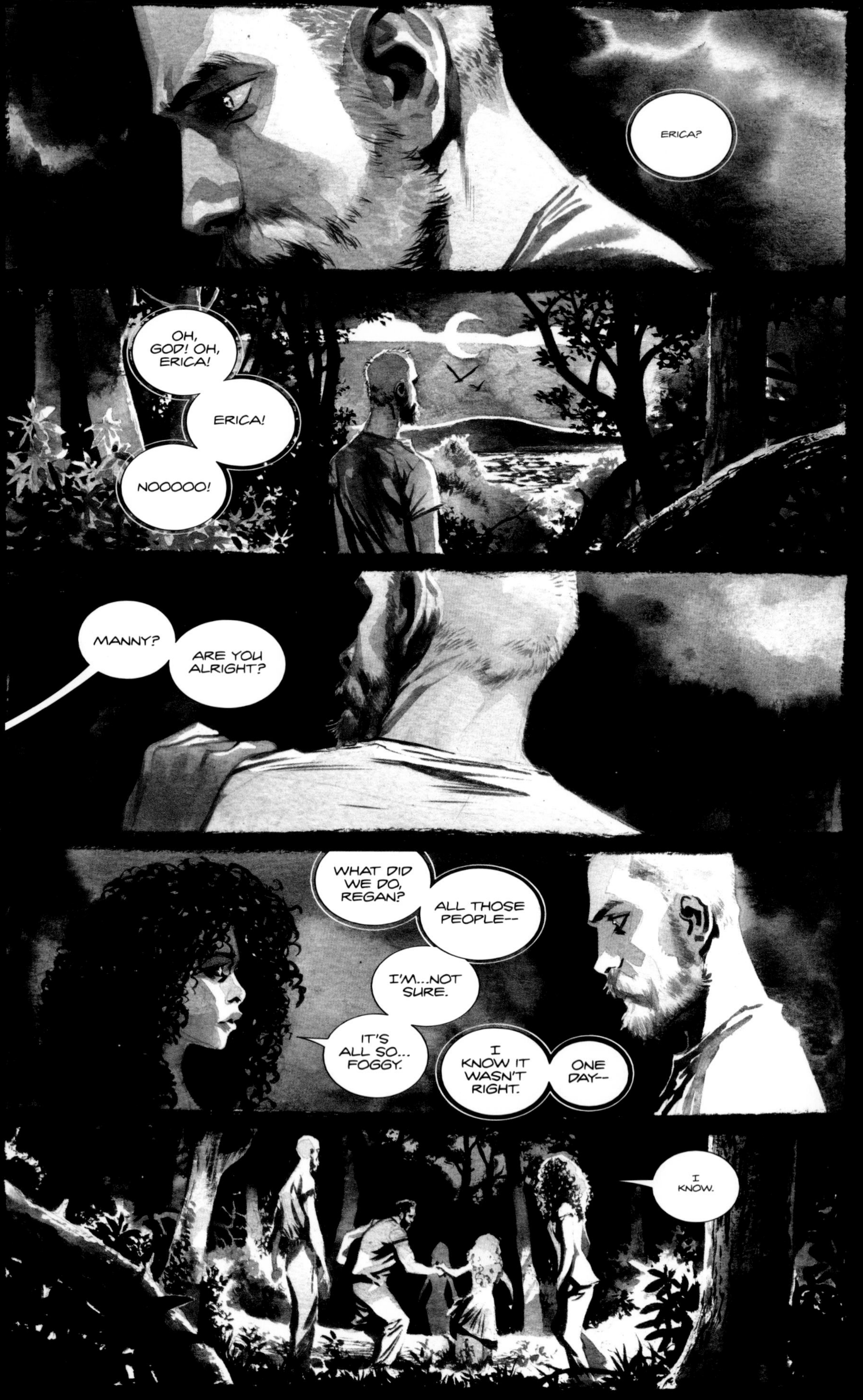
ERICA?
OH, GOD! OH, ERICA!
ERICA!
NOOOOO!
MANNY?
ARE YOU ALRIGHT?
WHAT DID WE DO, REGAN?
ALL THOSE PEOPLE--
I'M...NOT SURE.
IT'S ALL SO... FOGGY.
I KNOW IT WASN'T RIGHT.
ONE DAY--
I KNOW.

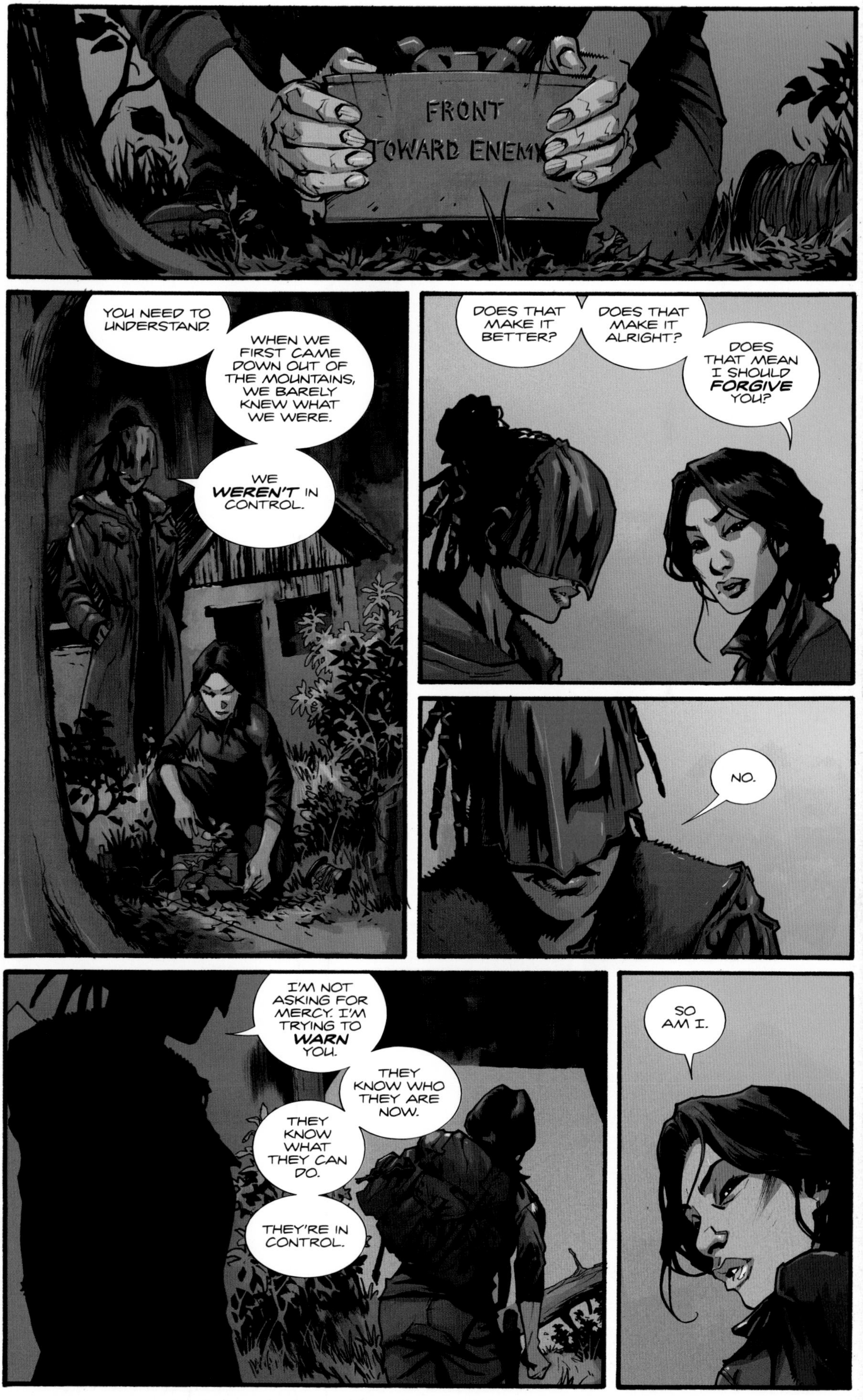
FRONT
TOWARD ENEMY
YOU NEED TO UNDERSTAND.
WHEN WE FIRST CAME DOWN OUT OF THE MOUNTAINS, WE BARELY KNEW WHAT WE WERE.
WE **WEREN'T** IN CONTROL.
DOES THAT MAKE IT BETTER?
DOES THAT MAKE IT ALRIGHT?
DOES THAT MEAN I SHOULD **FORGIVE** YOU?
NO.
I'M NOT ASKING FOR MERCY. I'M TRYING TO **WARN** YOU.
THEY KNOW WHO THEY ARE NOW.
THEY KNOW WHAT THEY CAN DO.
THEY'RE IN CONTROL.
SO AM I.

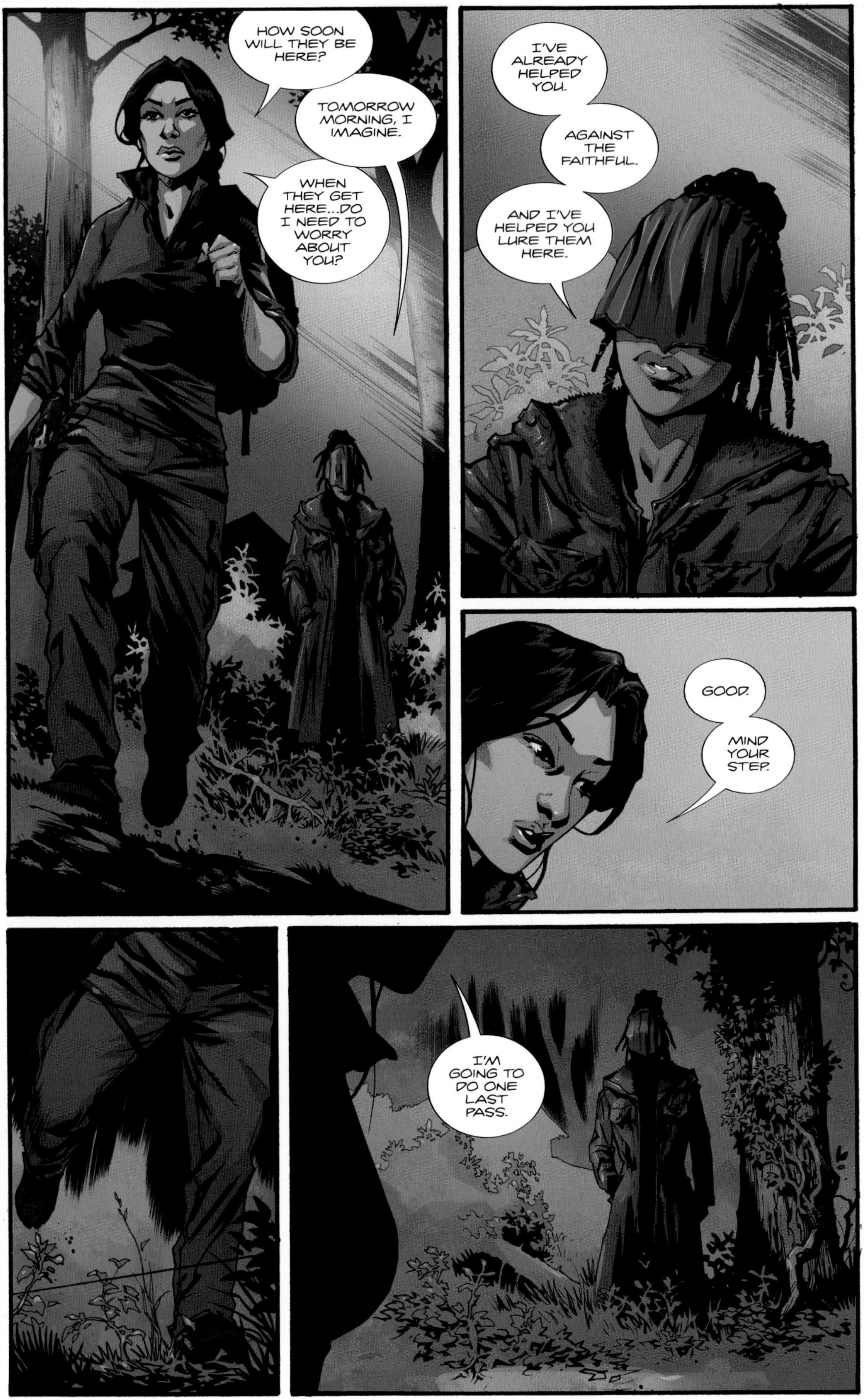
HOW SOON WILL THEY BE HERE?
TOMORROW MORNING, I IMAGINE.
WHEN THEY GET HERE...DO I NEED TO WORRY ABOUT YOU?
I'VE ALREADY HELPED YOU.
AGAINST THE FAITHFUL.
AND I'VE HELPED YOU LURE THEM HERE.
GOOD.
MIND YOUR STEP.
I'M GOING TO DO ONE LAST PASS.

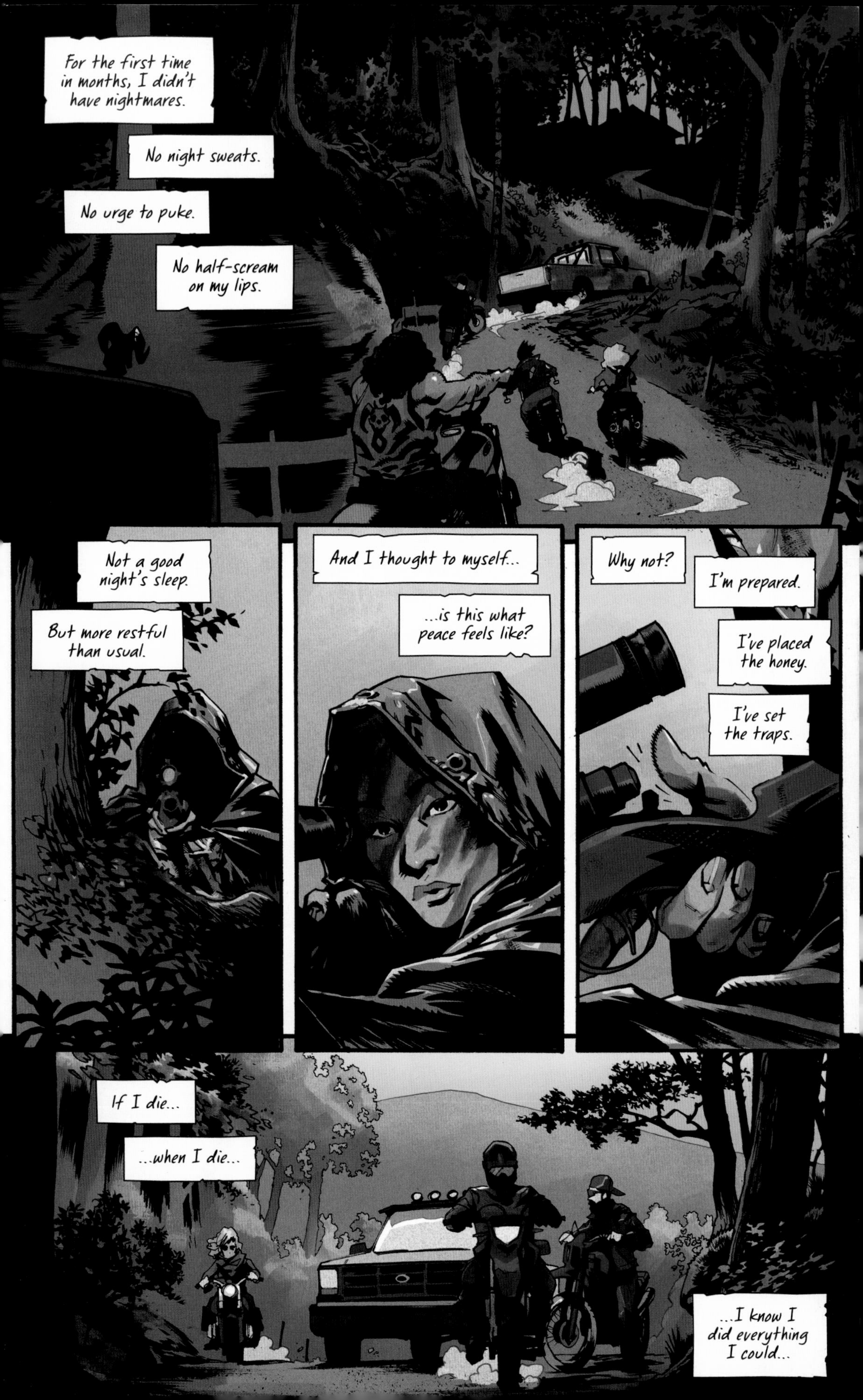

For the first time in months, I didn't have nightmares.
No night sweats.
No urge to puke.
No half-scream on my lips.
Not a good night's sleep.
But more restful than usual.
And I thought to myself...
...is this what peace feels like?
Why not?
I'm prepared.
I've placed the honey.
I've set the traps.
If I die...
...when I die...
...I know I did everything I could...

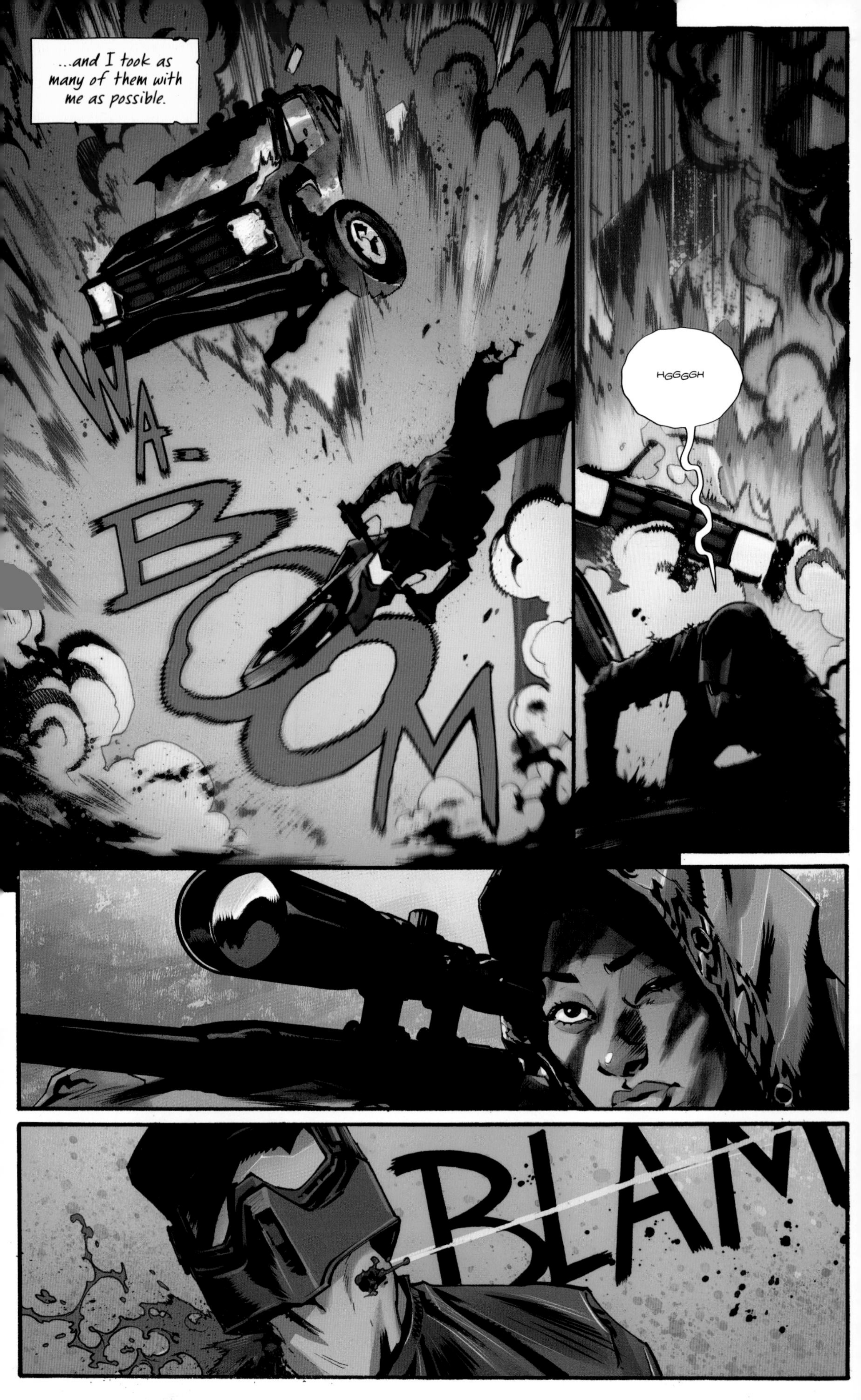

...and I took as many of them with me as possible.
WA-BOOM
HGGGGH
BLAM

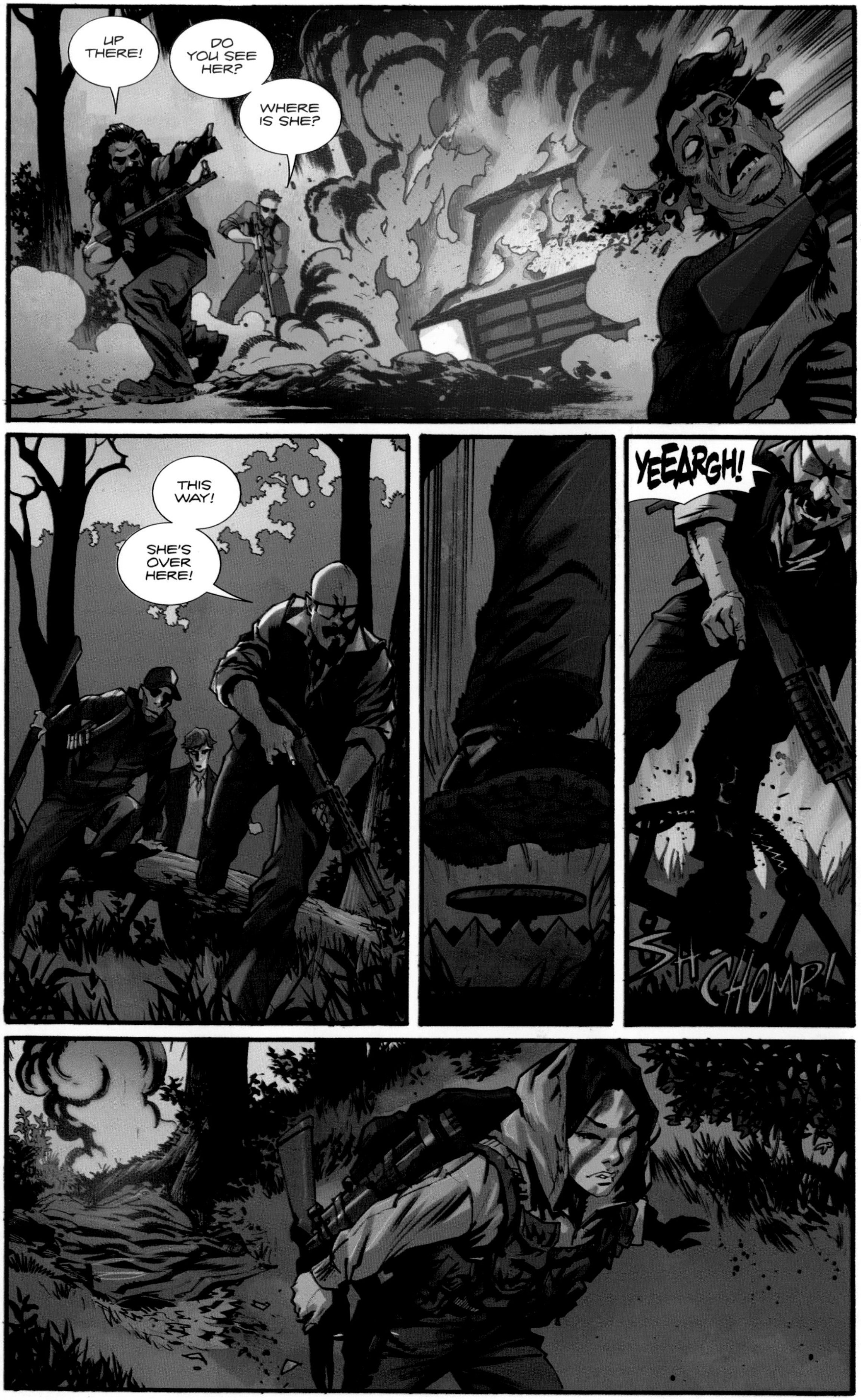
UP THERE!
DO YOU SEE HER?
WHERE IS SHE?
THIS WAY!
SHE'S OVER HERE!
YEEARGH!
SHCHOMP!

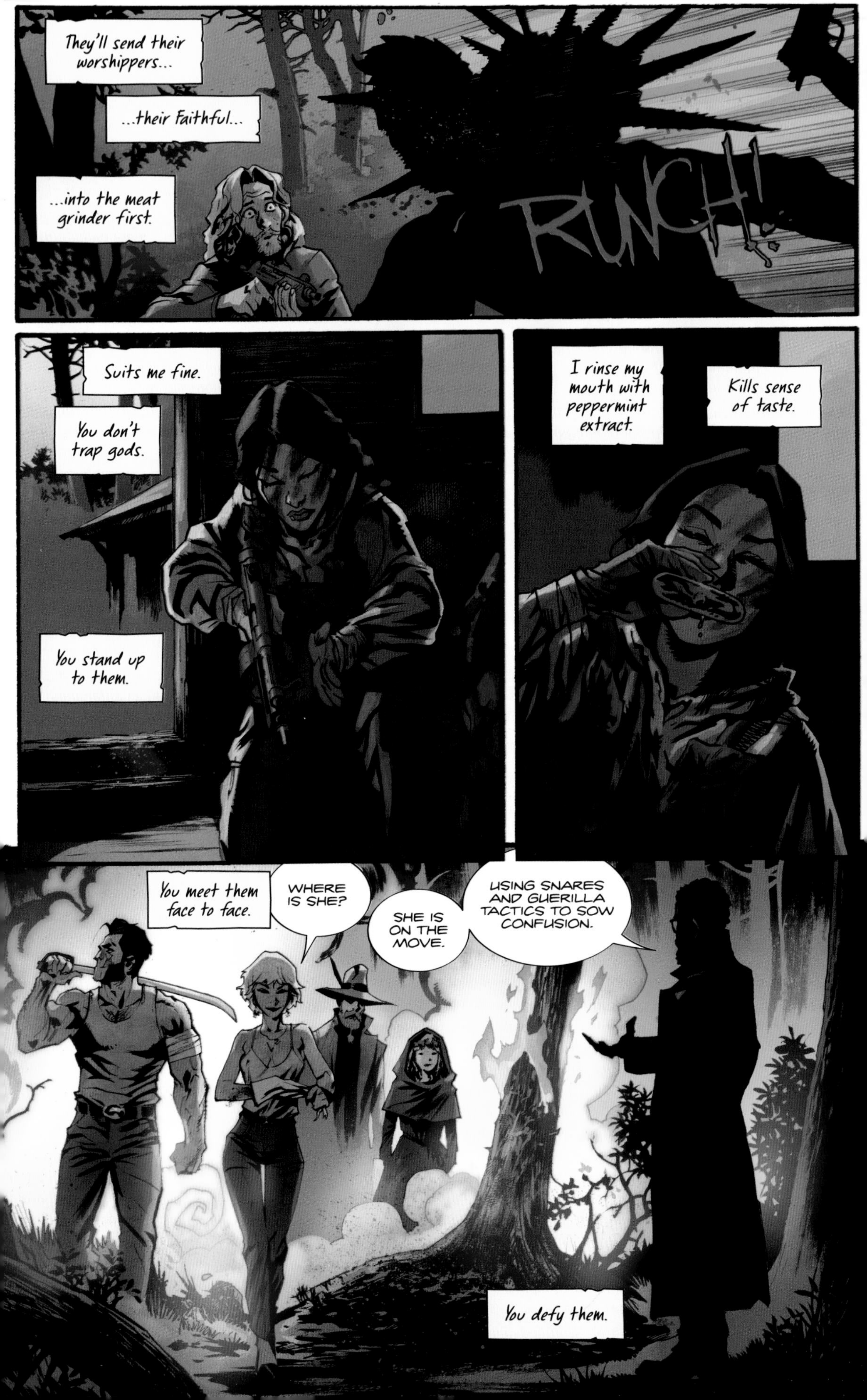
They'll send their worshippers...
...their Faithful...
...into the meat grinder first.
RUNCH!
Suits me fine.
You don't trap gods.
You stand up to them.
I rinse my mouth with peppermint extract.
Kills sense of taste.
You meet them face to face.
WHERE IS SHE?
SHE IS ON THE MOVE.
USING SNARES AND GUERILLA TACTICS TO SOW CONFUSION.
You defy them.

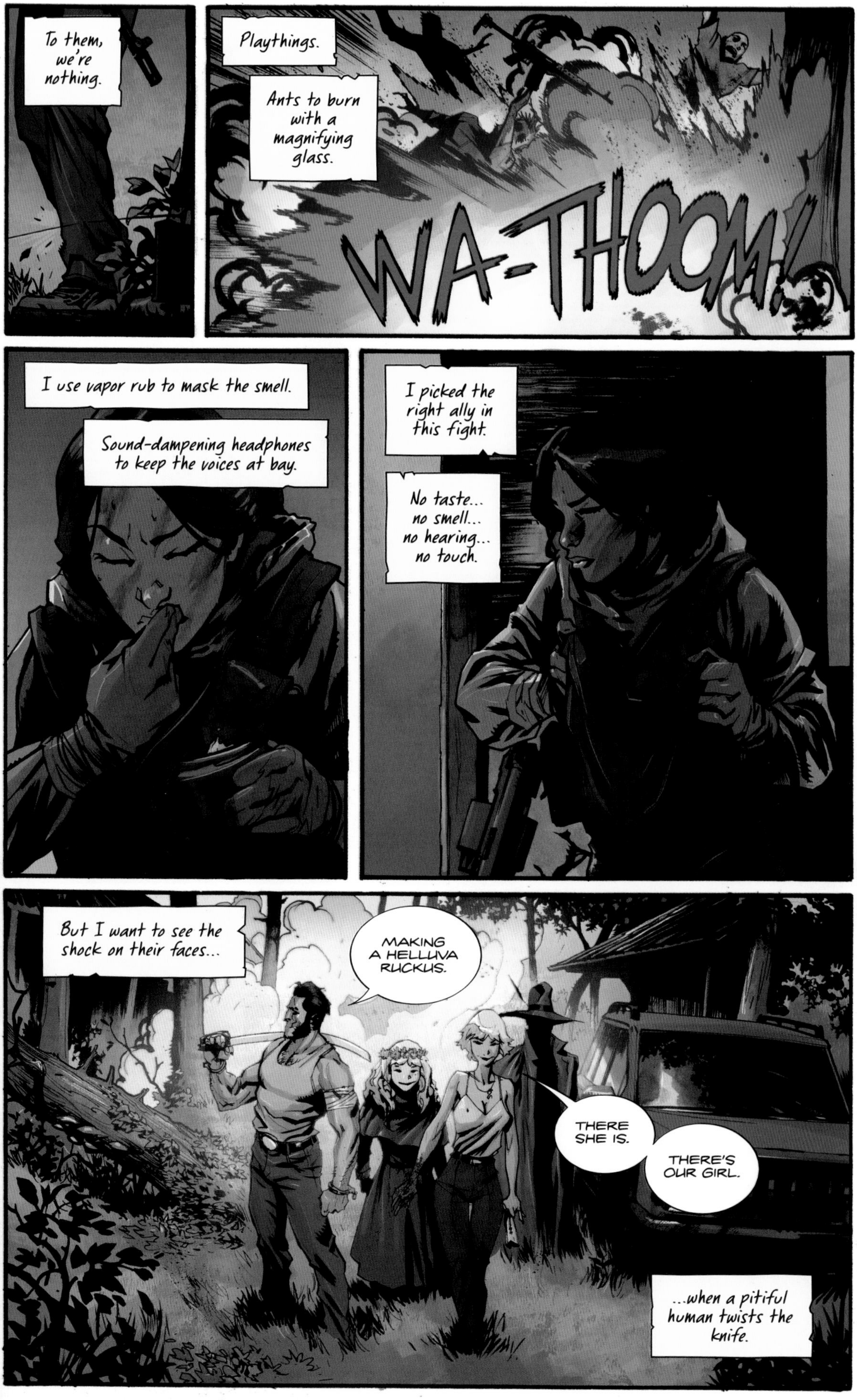
To them, we're nothing.
Playthings.
Ants to burn with a magnifying glass.
WA-THOOM!
I use vapor rub to mask the smell.
Sound-dampening headphones to keep the voices at bay.
I picked the right ally in this fight.
No taste... no smell... no hearing... no touch.
But I want to see the shock on their faces...
MAKING A HELLUVA RUCKUS.
THERE SHE IS.
THERE'S OUR GIRL.
...when a pitiful human twists the knife.

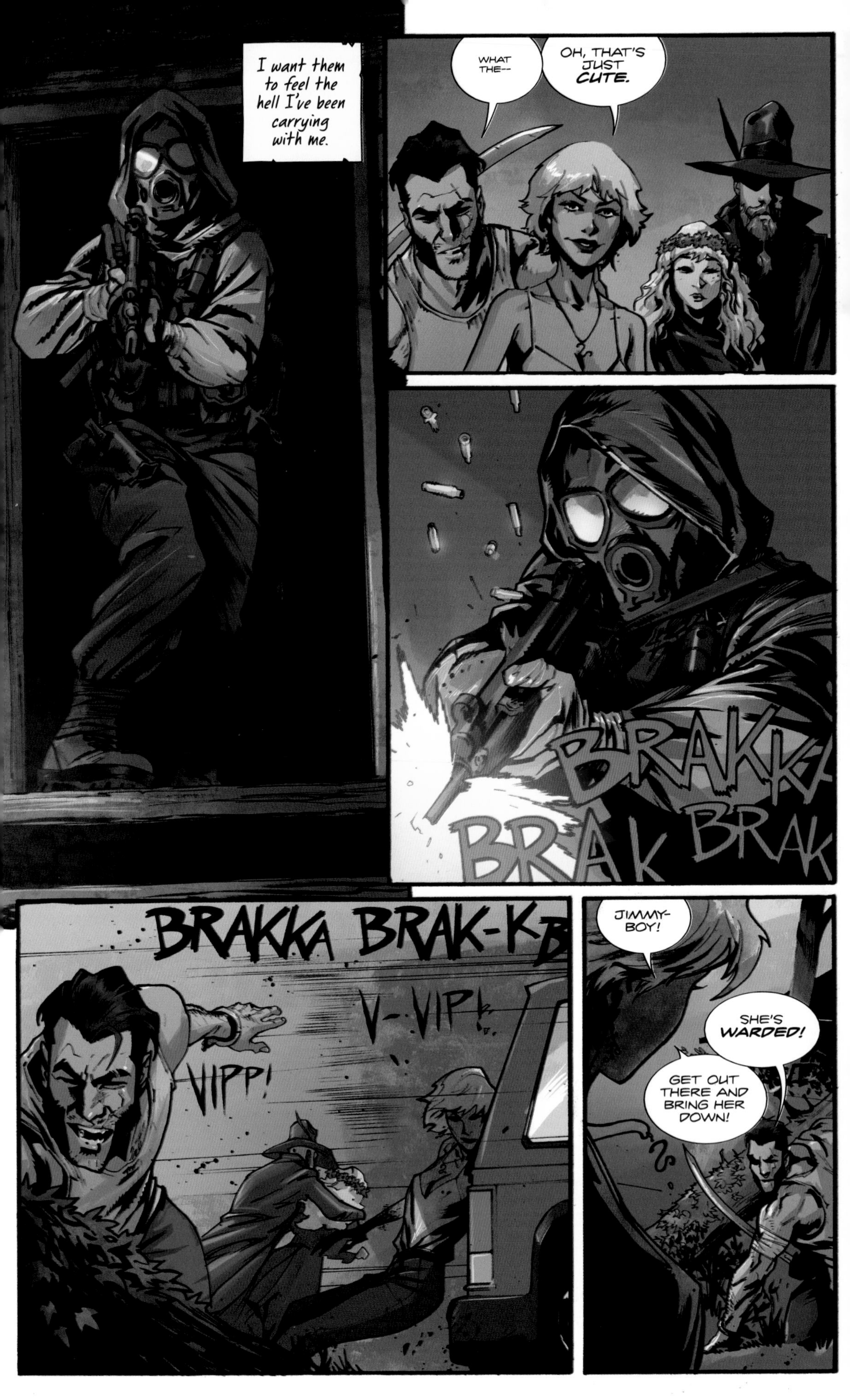
I want them to feel the hell I've been carrying with me.
WHAT THE--
OH, THAT'S JUST CUTE.
BRAKKA
BRAK BRAK
BRAKKA BRAK-K-B
V-VIP!
VIPP!
JIMMY-BOY!
SHE'S WARDED!
GET OUT THERE AND BRING HER DOWN!

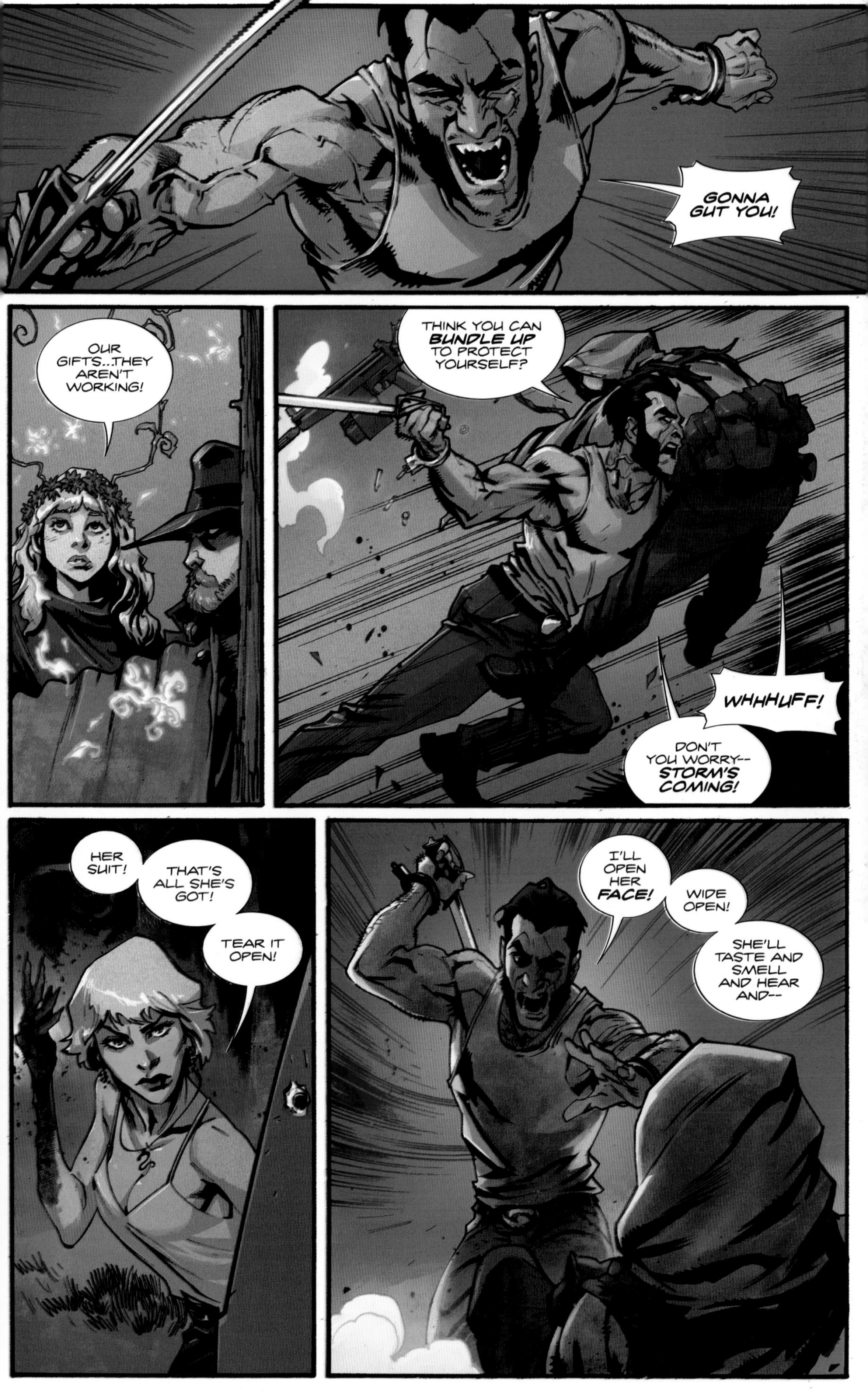
GONNA GUT YOU!
OUR GIFTS...THEY AREN'T WORKING!
THINK YOU CAN BUNDLE UP TO PROTECT YOURSELF?
WHHHUFF!
DON'T YOU WORRY-- STORM'S COMING!
HER SUIT!
THAT'S ALL SHE'S GOT!
TEAR IT OPEN!
I'LL OPEN HER FACE!
WIDE OPEN!
SHE'LL TASTE AND SMELL AND HEAR AND--

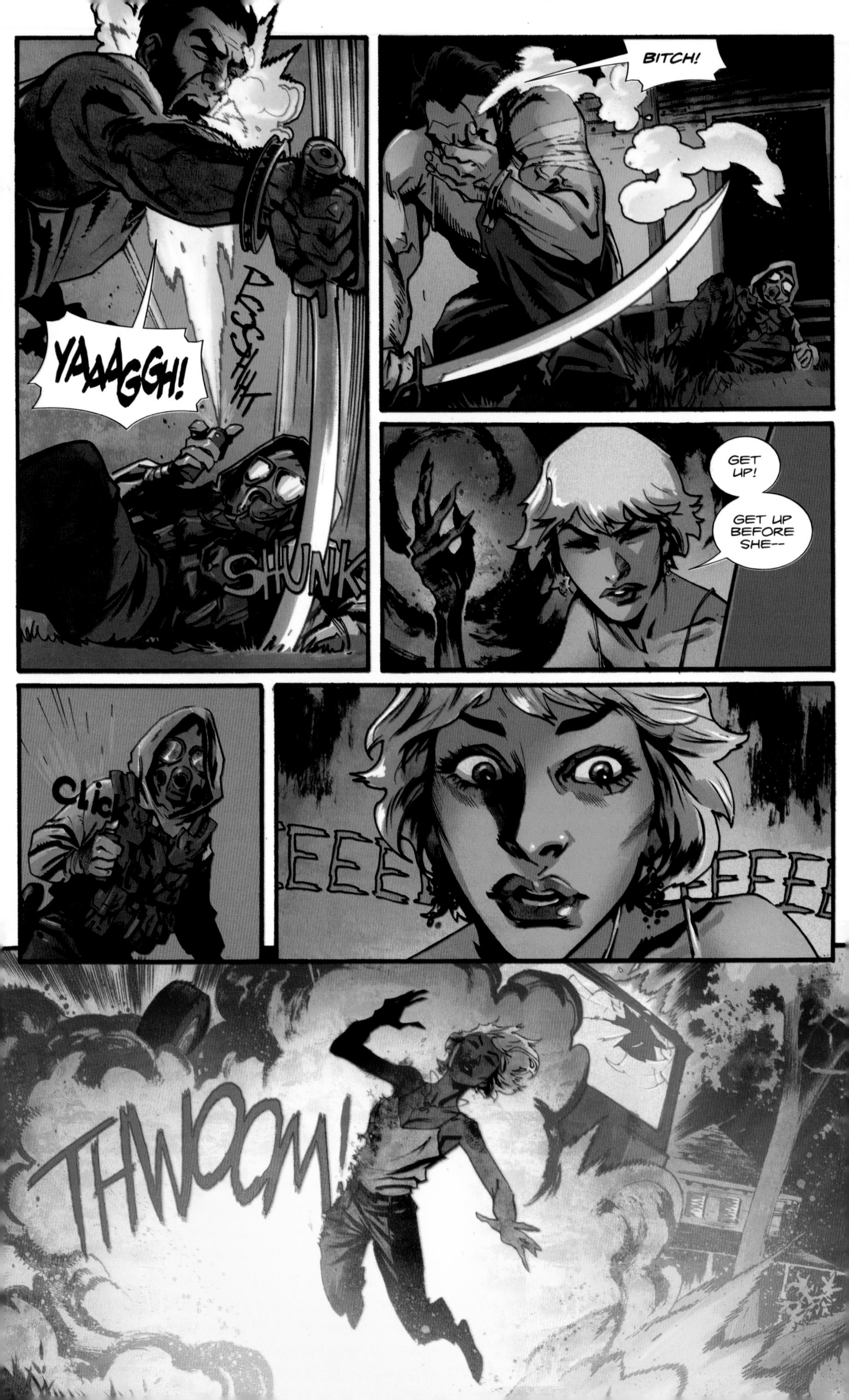
PSSSHHHT
YAAAGGH!
SHUNK
BITCH!
GET UP!
GET UP BEFORE SHE--
CLICK
THWOOM!

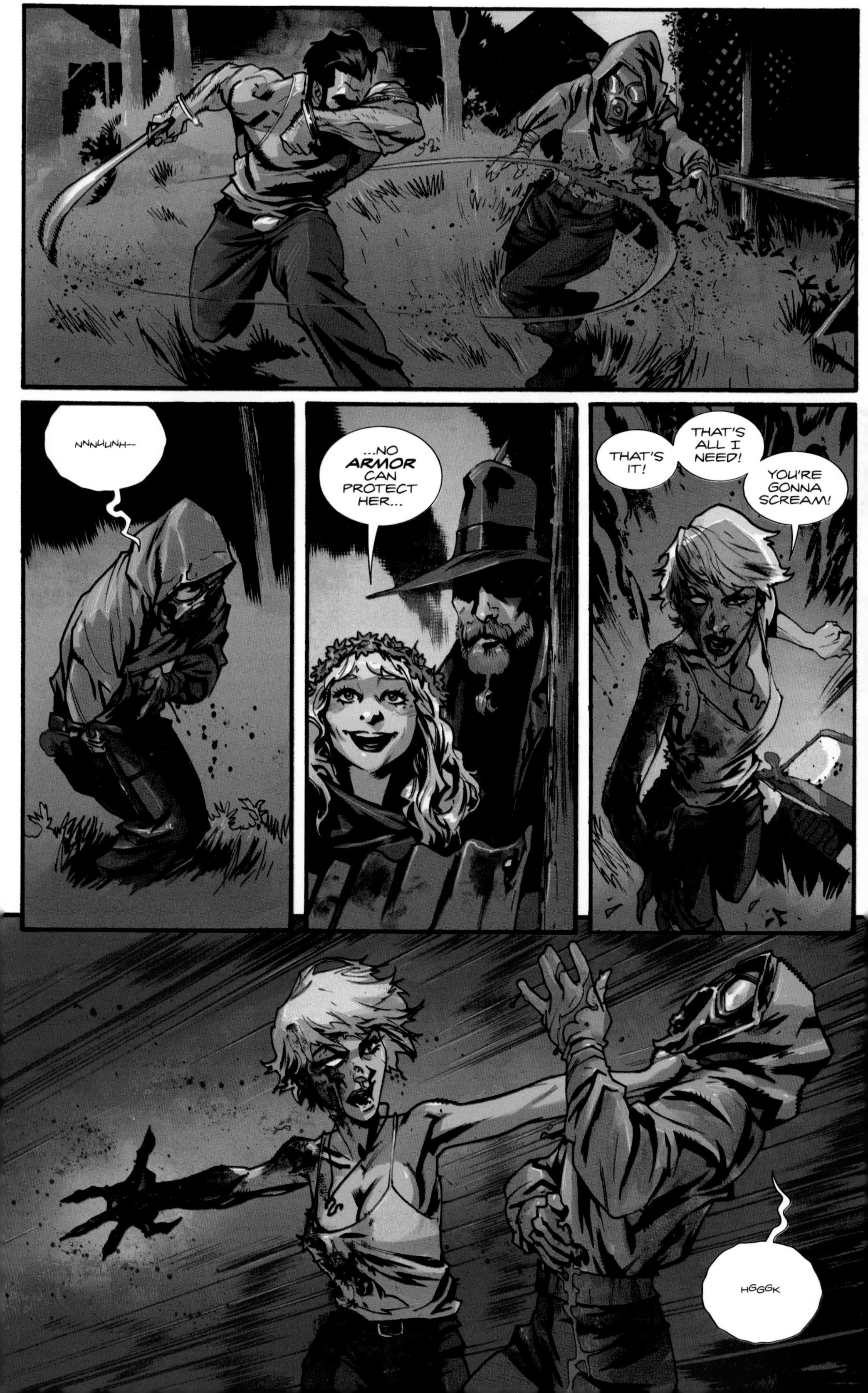
NNNUUNH--
...NO ARMOR CAN PROTECT HER...
THAT'S IT!
THAT'S ALL I NEED!
YOU'RE GONNA SCREAM!
HGGGK

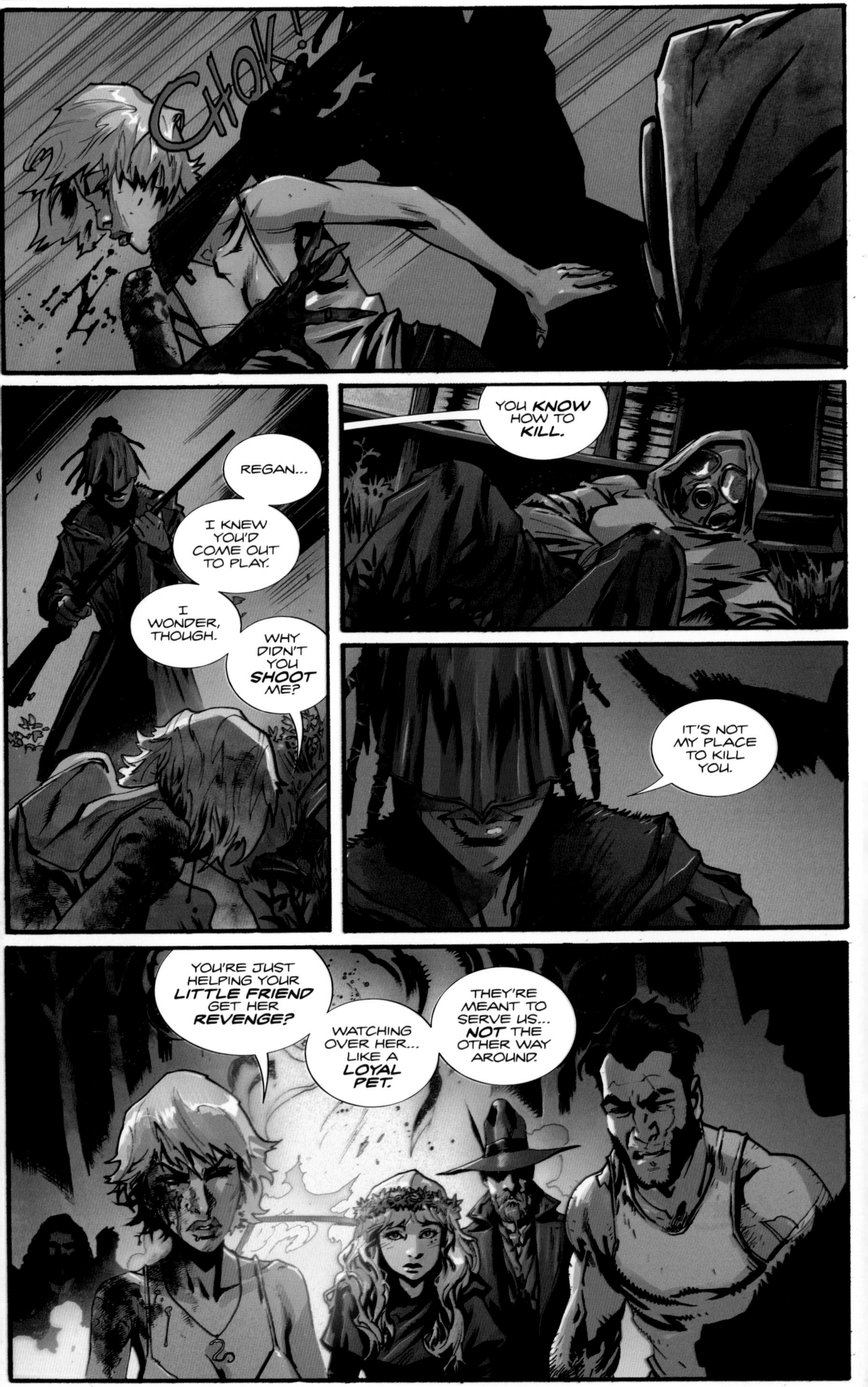
CHOK!
REGAN...
I KNEW YOU'D COME OUT TO PLAY.
I WONDER, THOUGH.
WHY DIDN'T YOU SHOOT ME?
YOU KNOW HOW TO KILL.
IT'S NOT MY PLACE TO KILL YOU.
YOU'RE JUST HELPING YOUR LITTLE FRIEND GET HER REVENGE?
WATCHING OVER HER... LIKE A LOYAL PET.
THEY'RE MEANT TO SERVE US... NOT THE OTHER WAY AROUND.

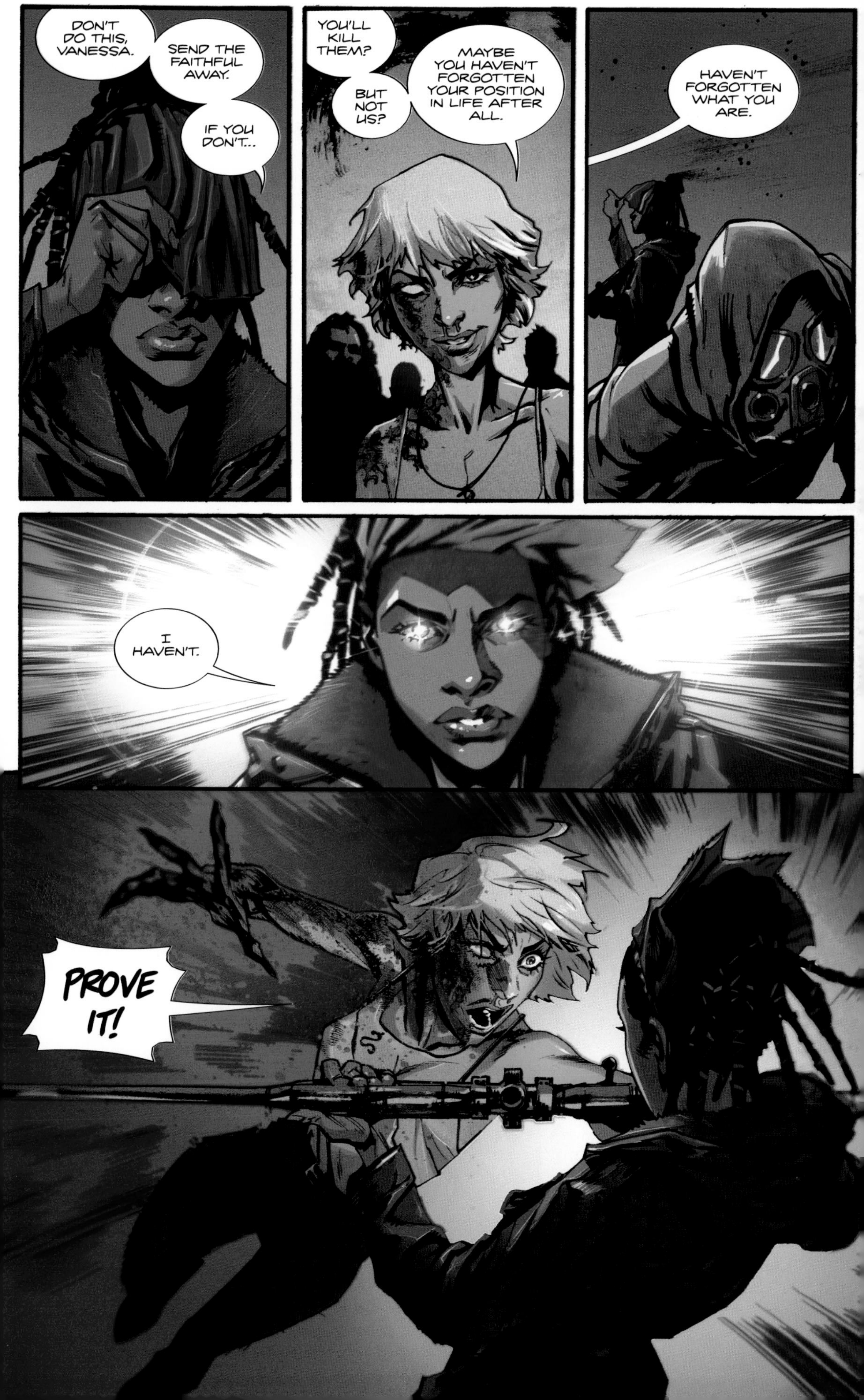
DON'T DO THIS, VANESSA.
SEND THE FAITHFUL AWAY.
IF YOU DON'T...
YOU'LL KILL THEM?
BUT NOT US?
MAYBE YOU HAVEN'T FORGOTTEN YOUR POSITION IN LIFE AFTER ALL.
HAVEN'T FORGOTTEN WHAT YOU ARE.
I HAVEN'T.
PROVE IT!

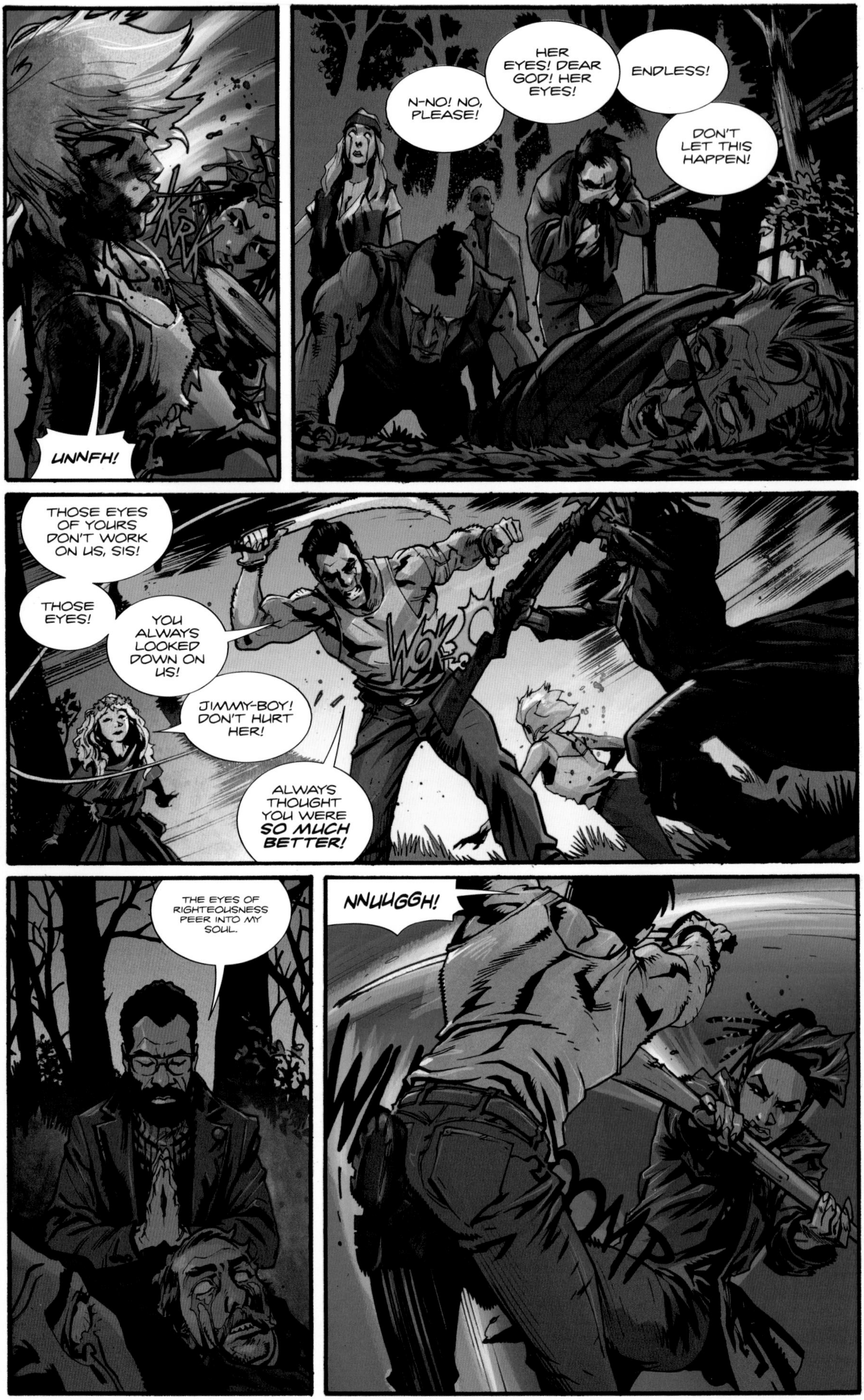
KRK
UNNFH!
N-NO! NO, PLEASE!
HER EYES! DEAR GOD! HER EYES!
ENDLESS!
DON'T LET THIS HAPPEN!
THOSE EYES OF YOURS DON'T WORK ON US, SIS!
THOSE EYES!
YOU ALWAYS LOOKED DOWN ON US!
JIMMY-BOY! DON'T HURT HER!
ALWAYS THOUGHT YOU WERE SO MUCH BETTER!
WOK
THE EYES OF RIGHTEOUSNESS PEER INTO MY SOUL.
NNUUGGH!

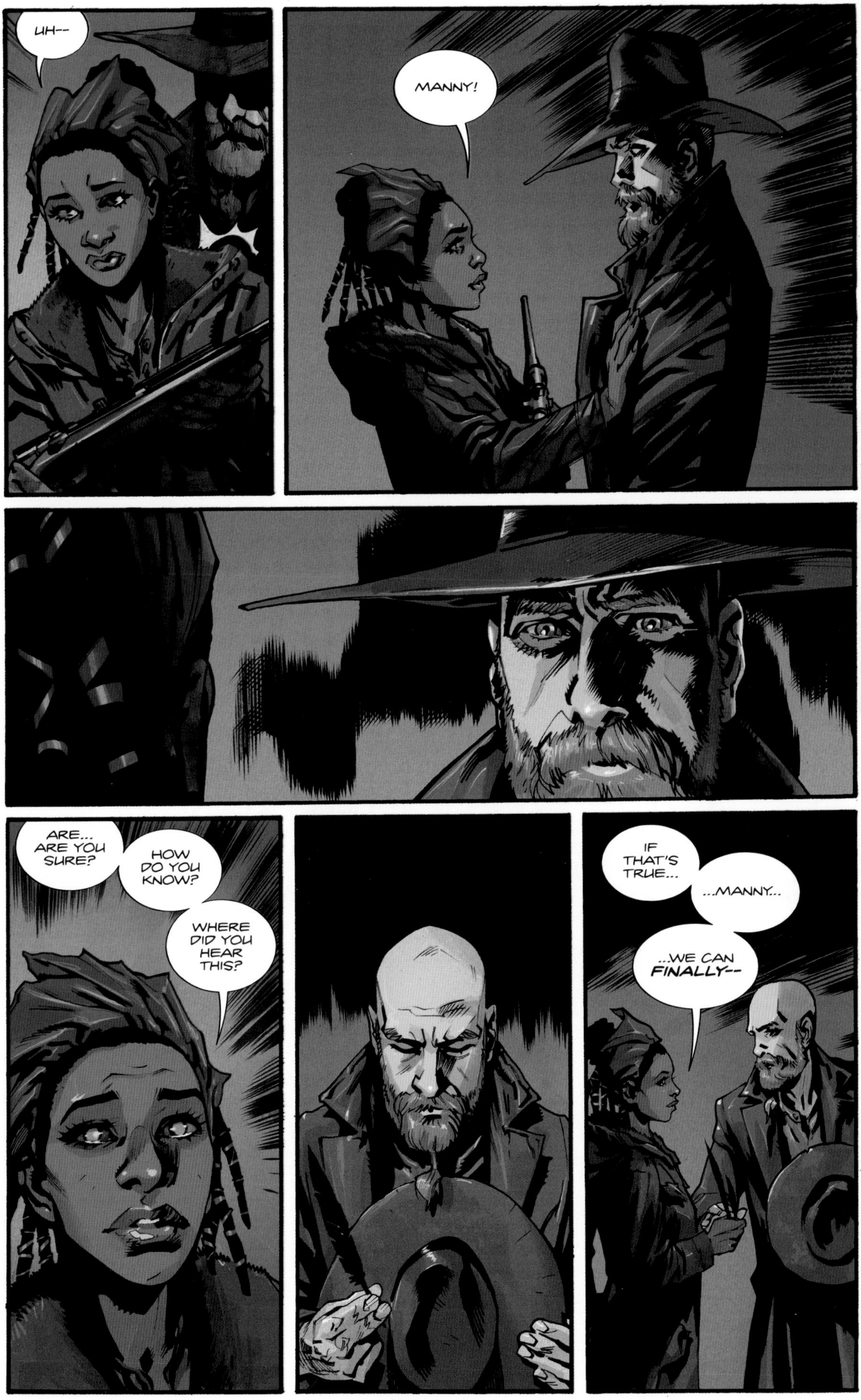
UH--
MANNY!
ARE... ARE YOU SURE?
HOW DO YOU KNOW?
WHERE DID YOU HEAR THIS?
IF THAT'S TRUE...
...MANNY...
...WE CAN *FINALLY*--

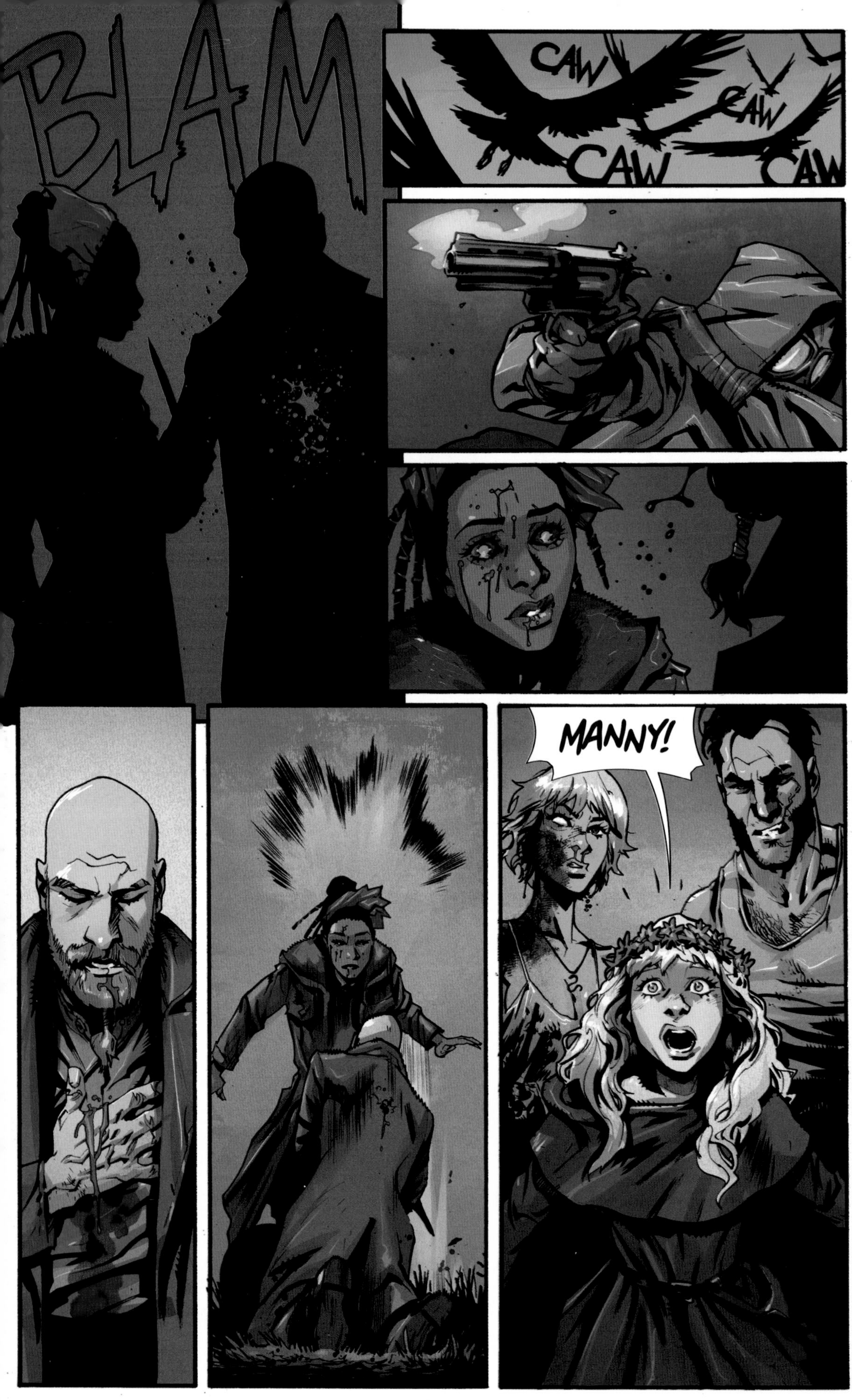
BLAM
CAW
CAW
CAW
CAW
MANNY!

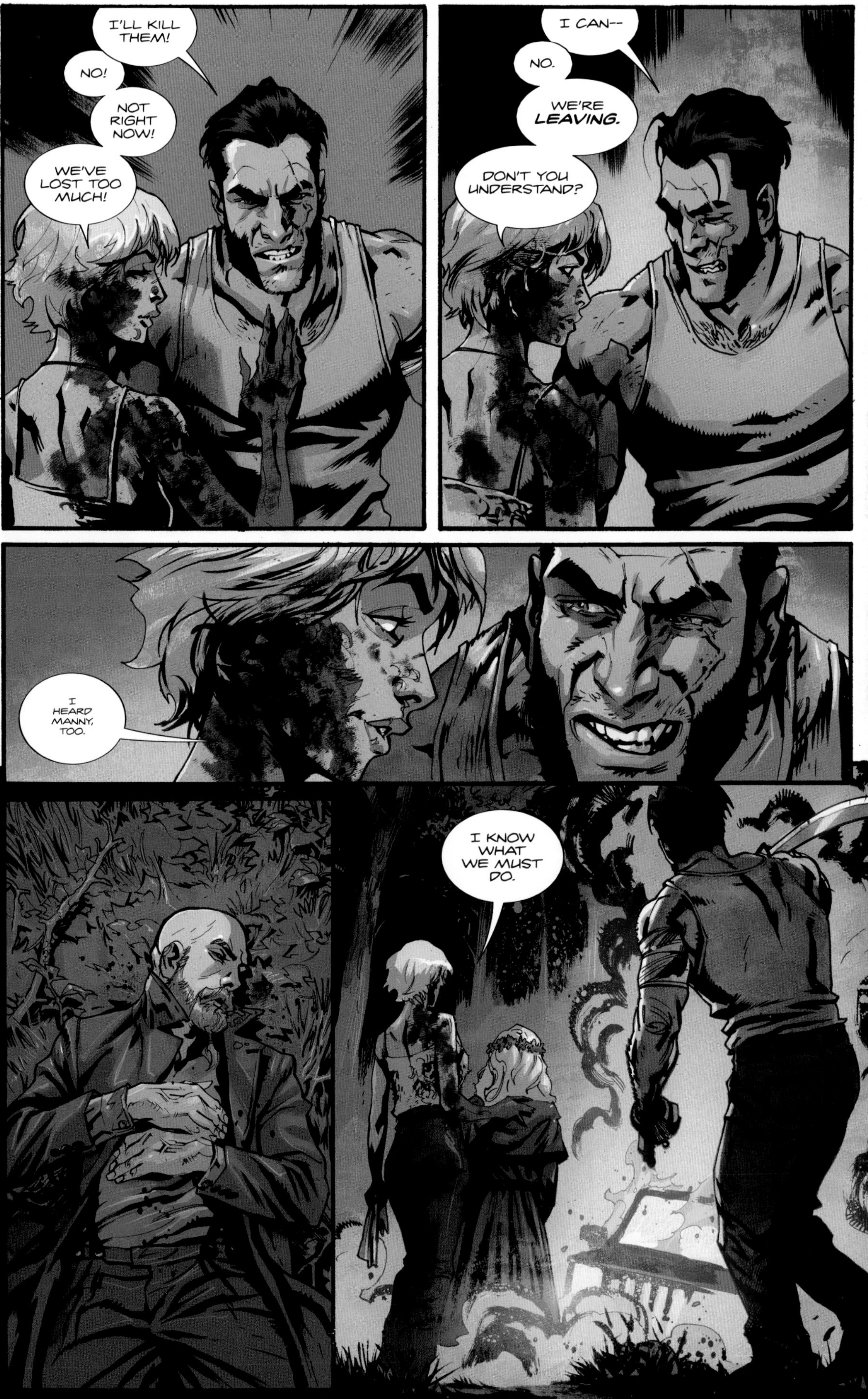
I'LL KILL THEM!
NO!
NOT RIGHT NOW!
WE'VE LOST TOO MUCH!
I CAN--
NO.
WE'RE LEAVING.
DON'T YOU UNDERSTAND?
I HEARD MANNY, TOO.
I KNOW WHAT WE MUST DO.

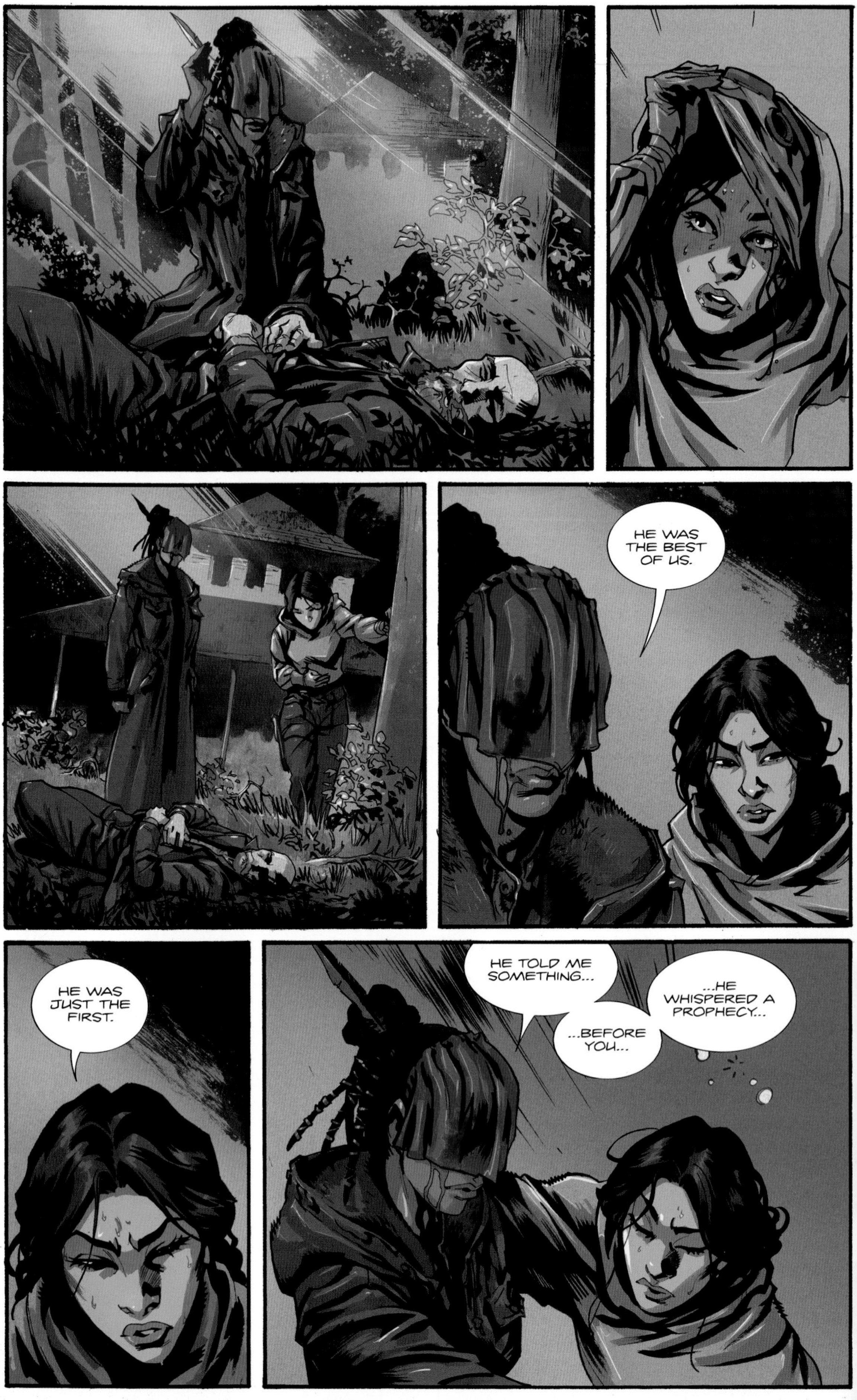
HE WAS
THE BEST
OF US.
HE WAS
JUST THE
FIRST.
HE TOLD ME
SOMETHING...
...BEFORE
YOU...
...HE
WHISPERED A
PROPHECY...

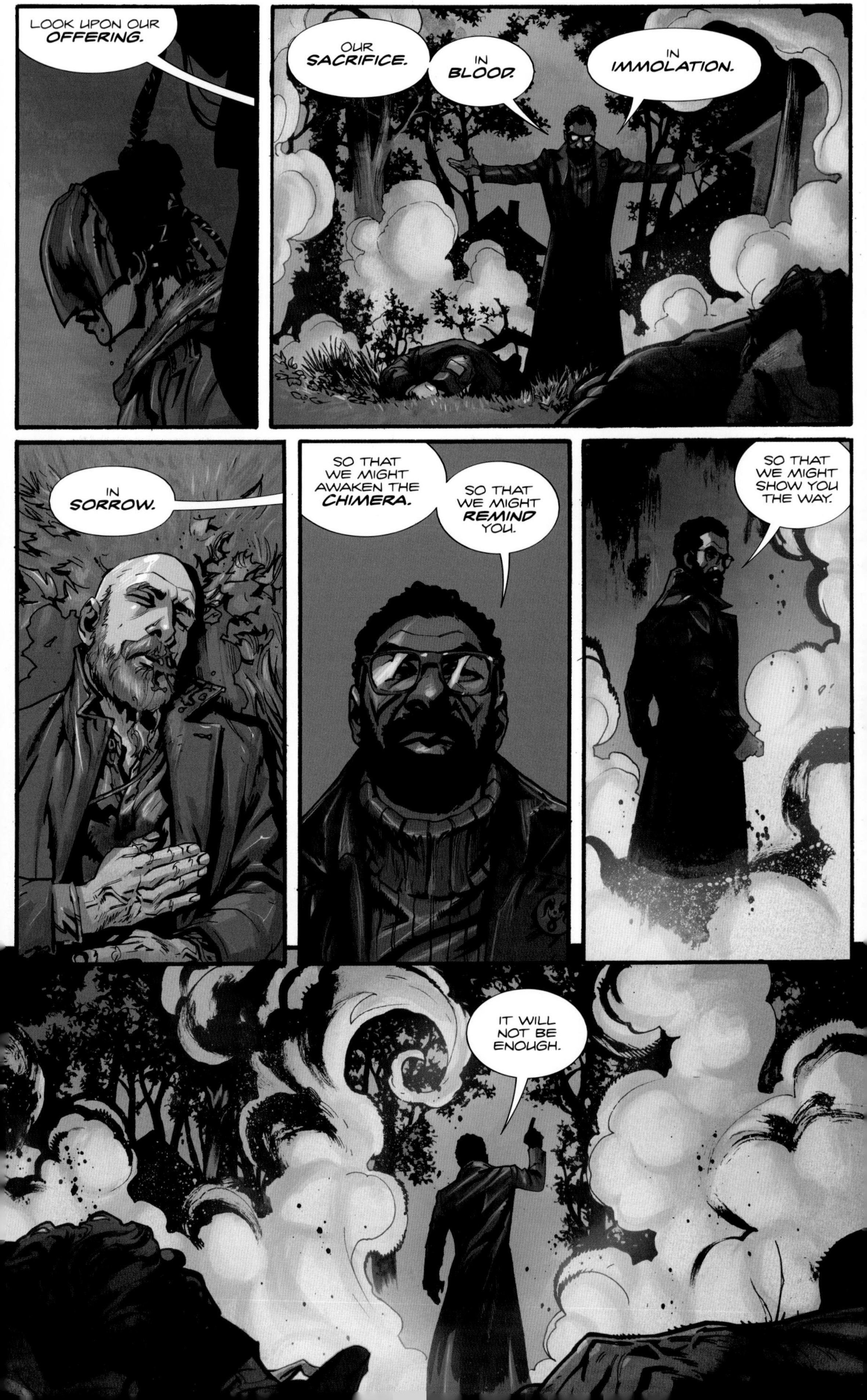
LOOK UPON OUR OFFERING.
OUR SACRIFICE.
IN BLOOD.
IN IMMOLATION.
IN SORROW.
SO THAT WE MIGHT AWAKEN THE CHIMERA.
SO THAT WE MIGHT REMIND YOU.
SO THAT WE MIGHT SHOW YOU THE WAY.
IT WILL NOT BE ENOUGH.

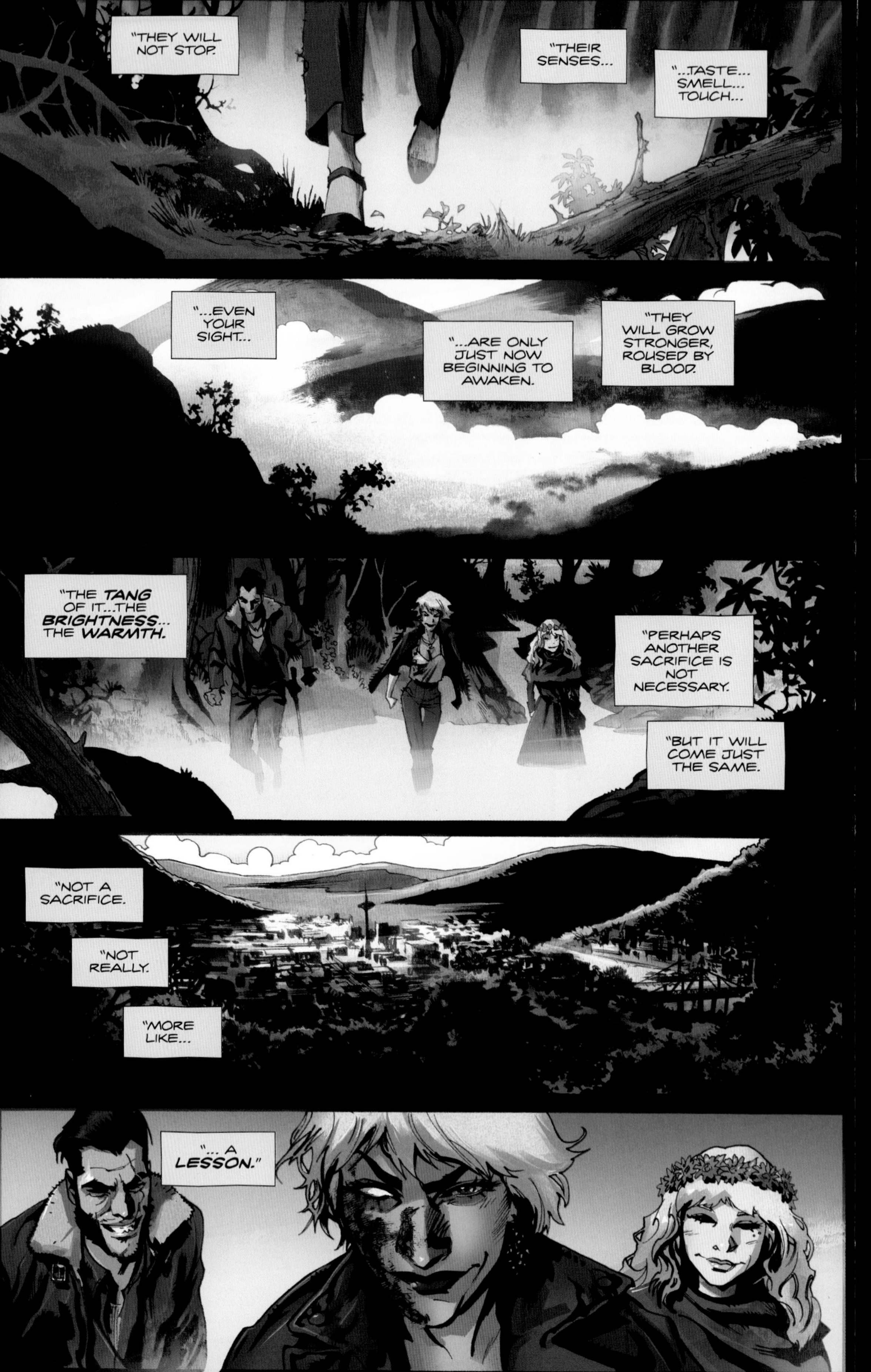
"THEY WILL NOT STOP.
"THEIR SENSES...
"...TASTE... SMELL... TOUCH...
"...EVEN YOUR SIGHT...
"...ARE ONLY JUST NOW BEGINNING TO AWAKEN.
"THEY WILL GROW STRONGER, ROUSED BY BLOOD.
"THE TANG OF IT...THE BRIGHTNESS... THE WARMTH.
"PERHAPS ANOTHER SACRIFICE IS NOT NECESSARY.
"BUT IT WILL COME JUST THE SAME.
"NOT A SACRIFICE.
"NOT REALLY.
"MORE LIKE...
"... A LESSON."

TO BE CONTINUED

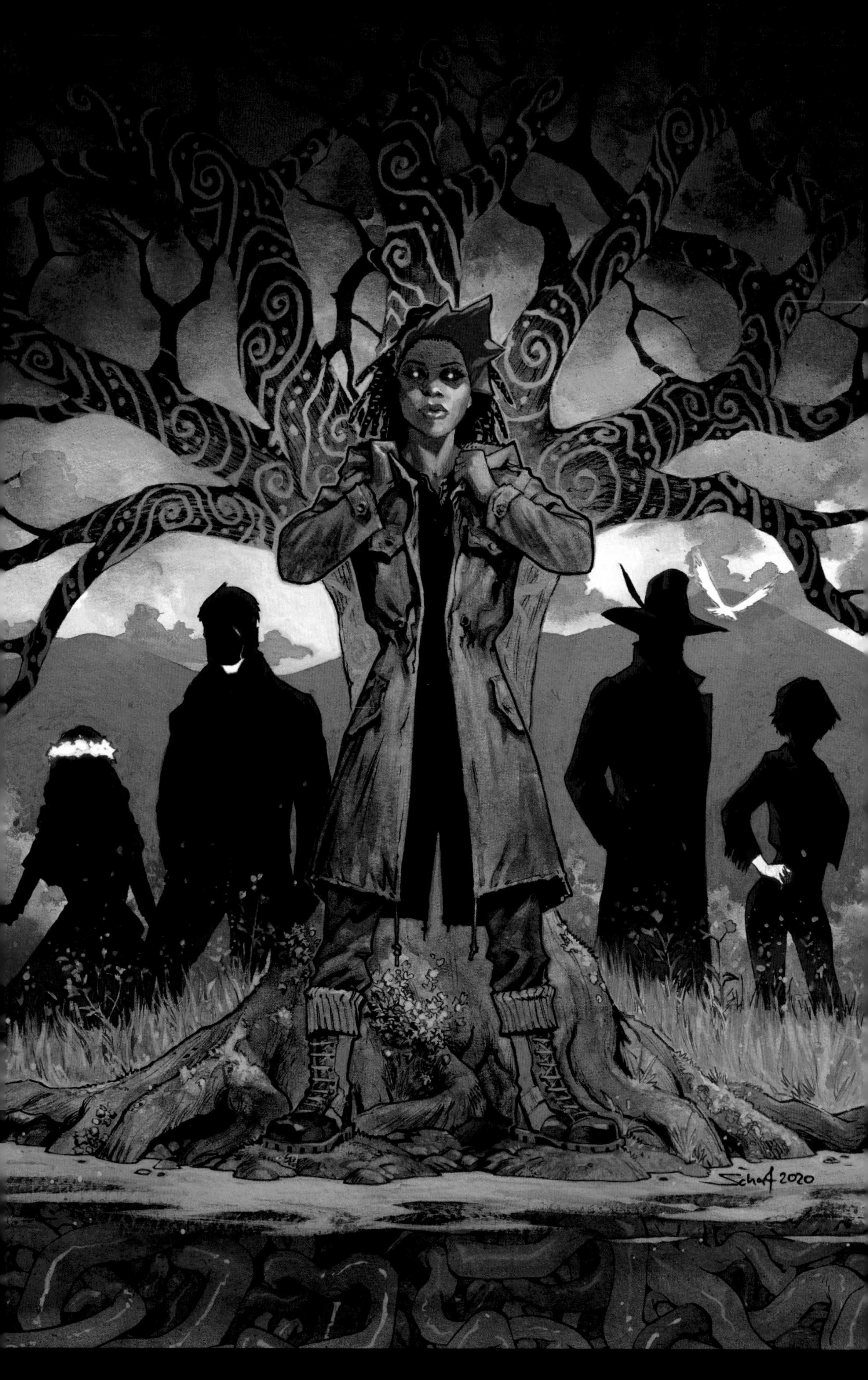
Scharf 2020

Issue One Cover by **JONAS SCHARF**

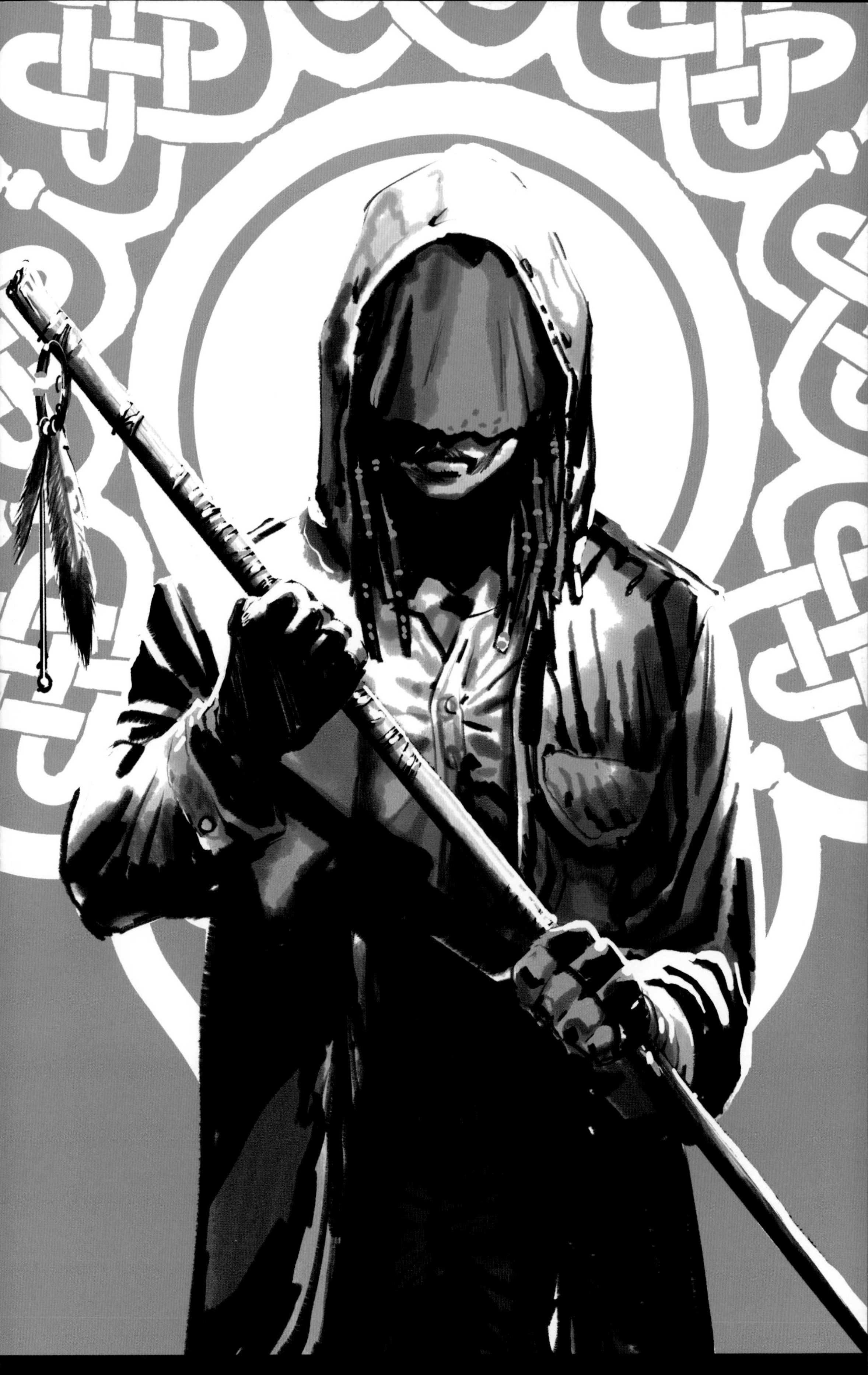

Issue One Cover by **RAFAEL ALBUQUERQUE**

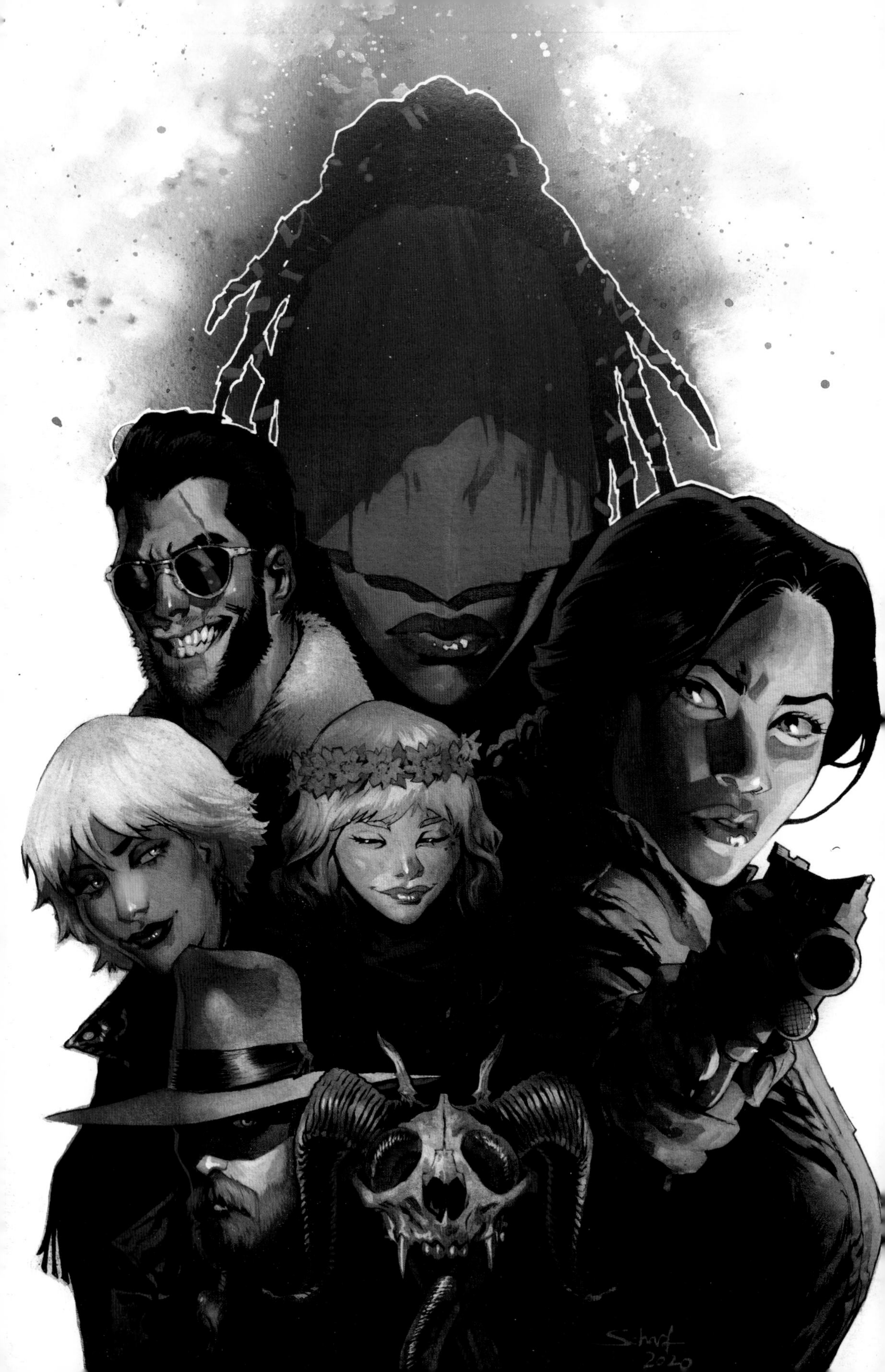

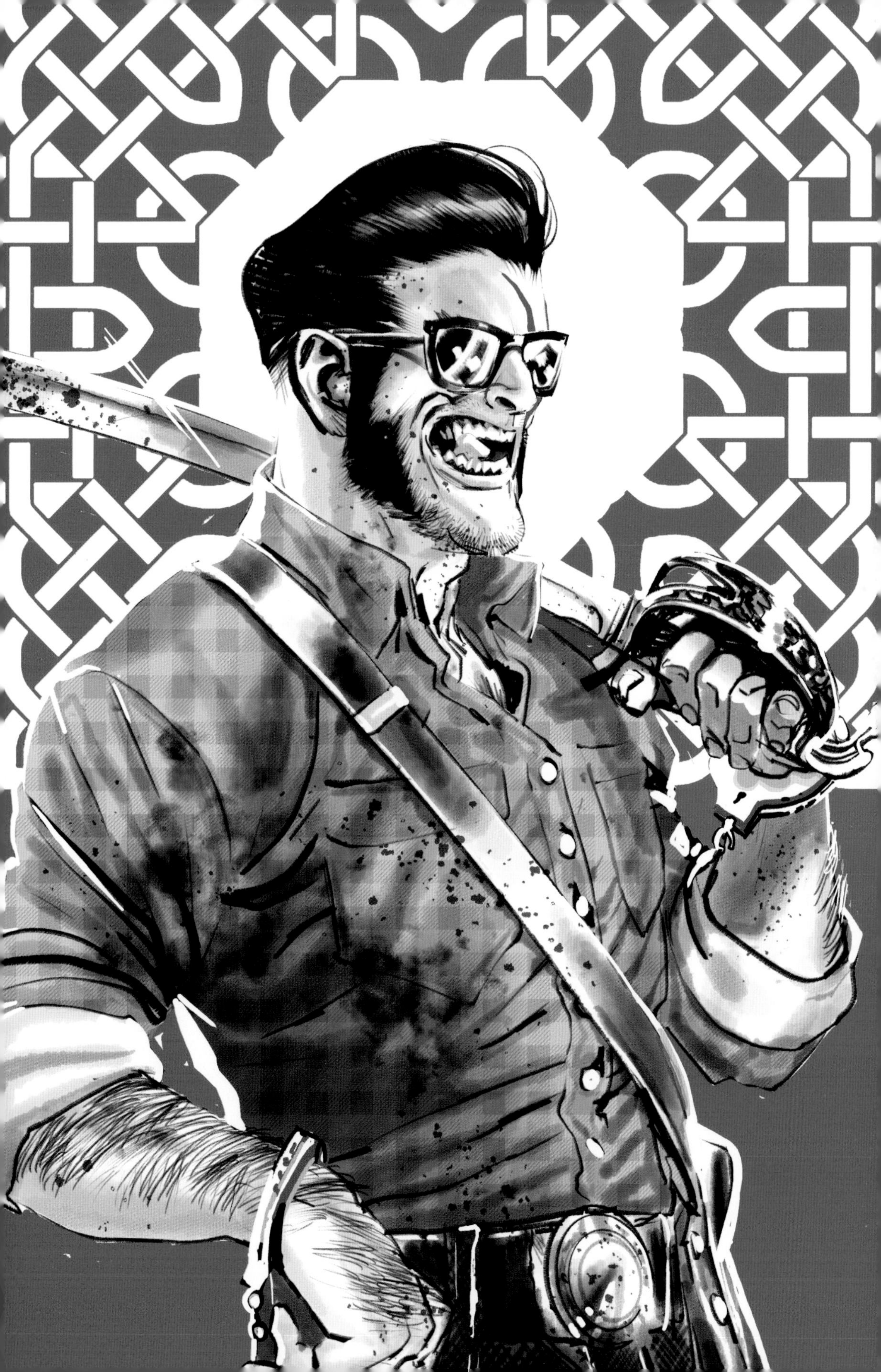

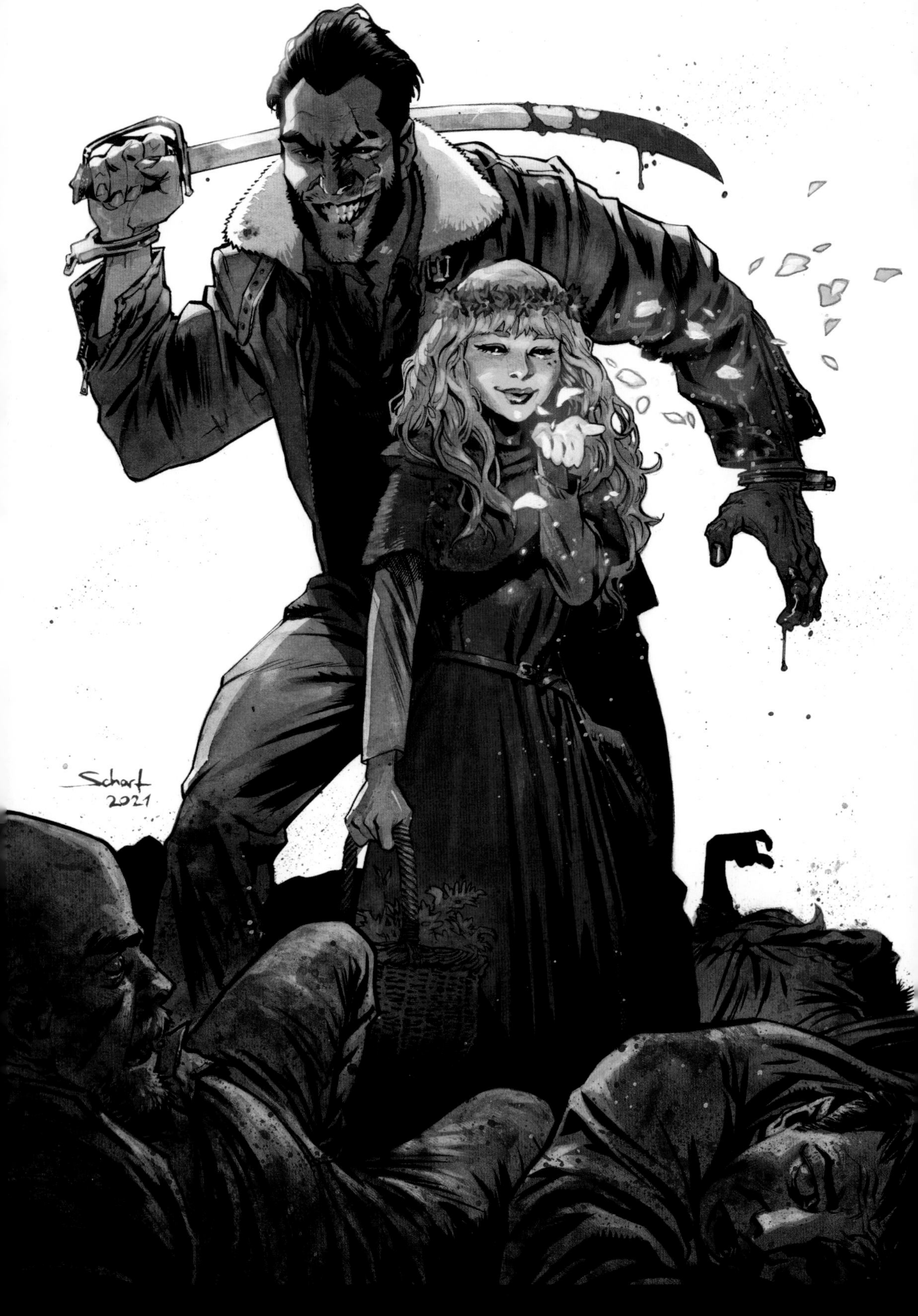
Scharf
2021

Issue Three Cover by **JONAS SCHARF**

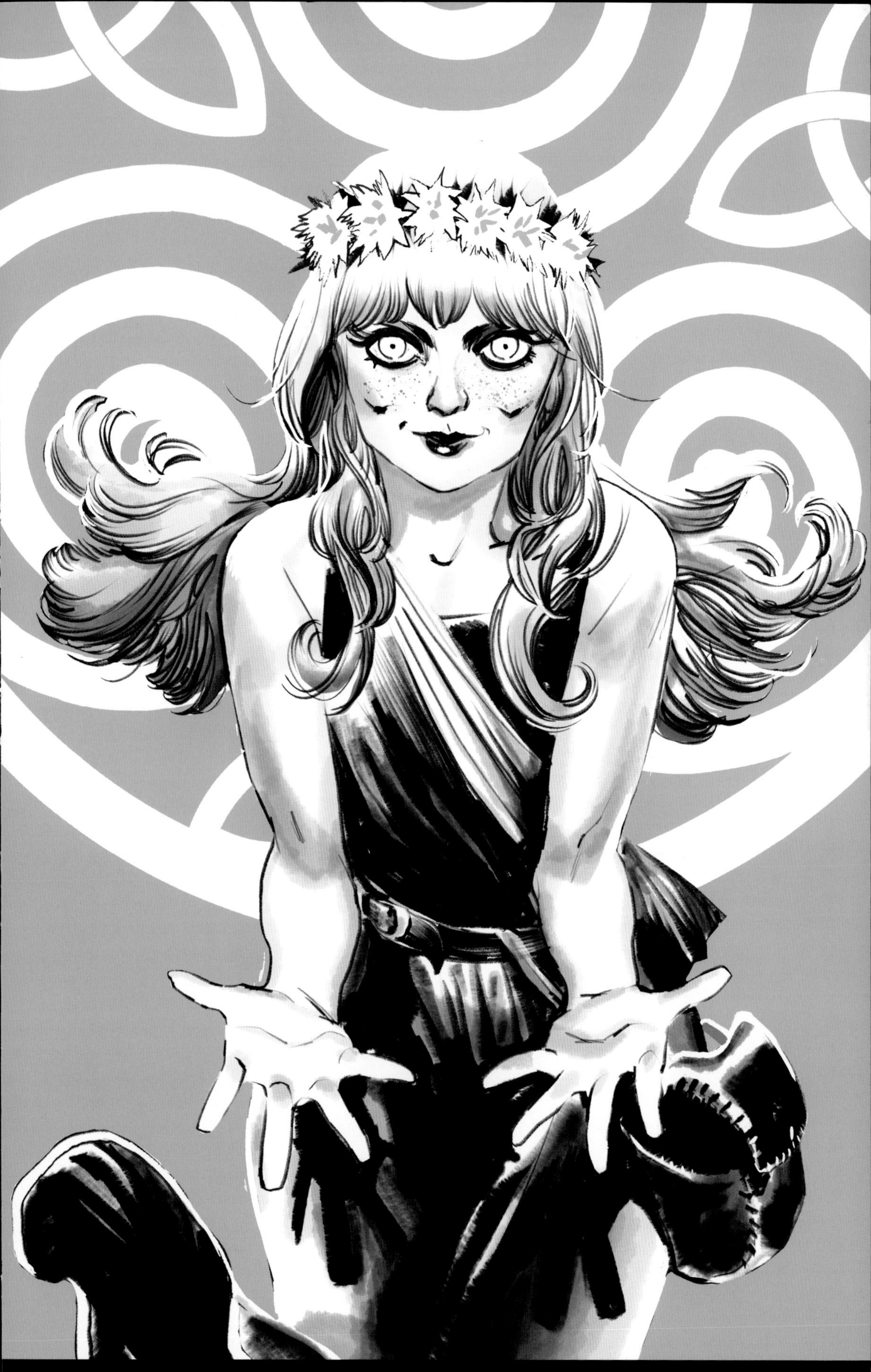

Issue Three Cover by **RAFAEL ALBUQUERQUE**

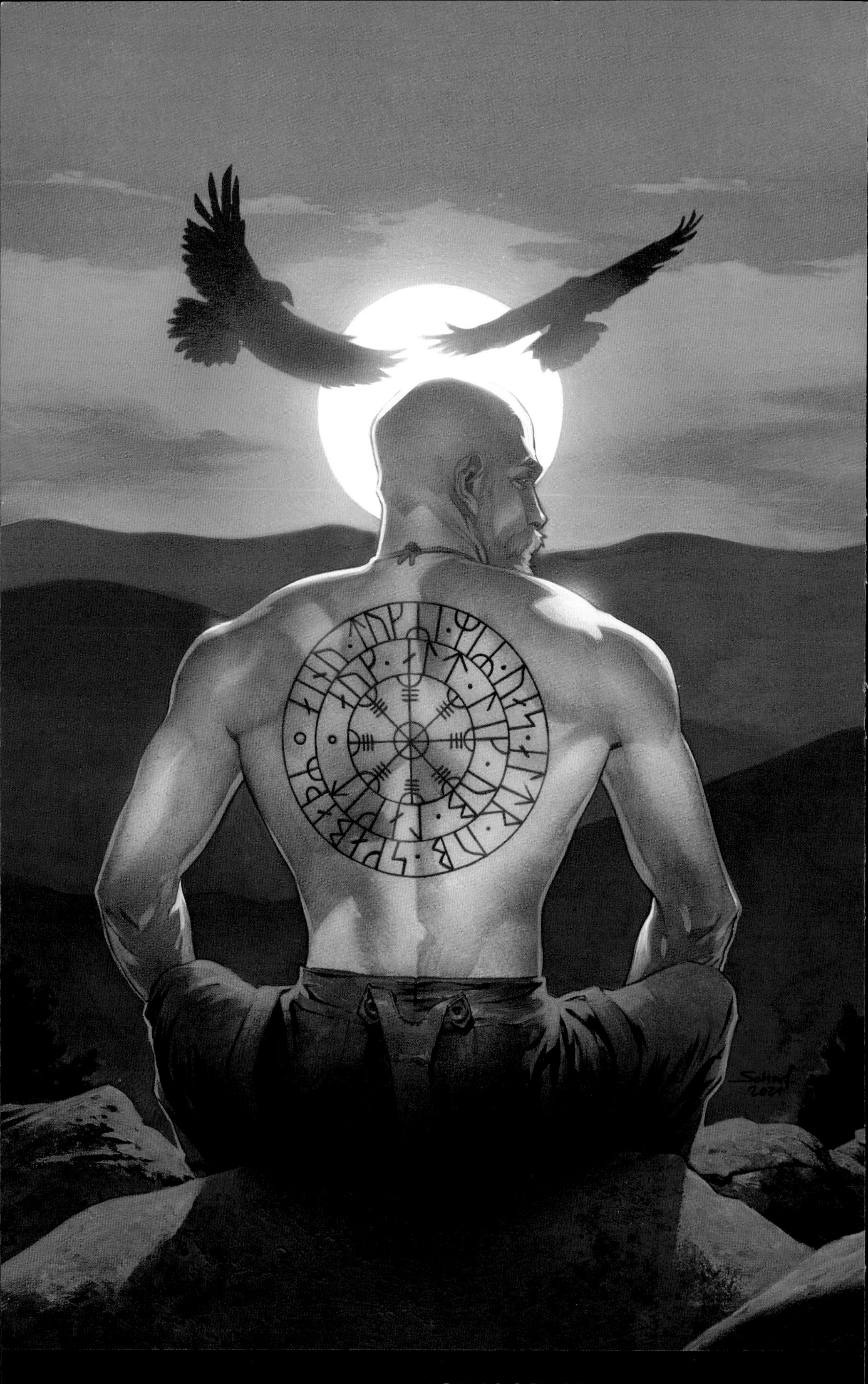

Issue Four Cover by **JONAS SCHARF**

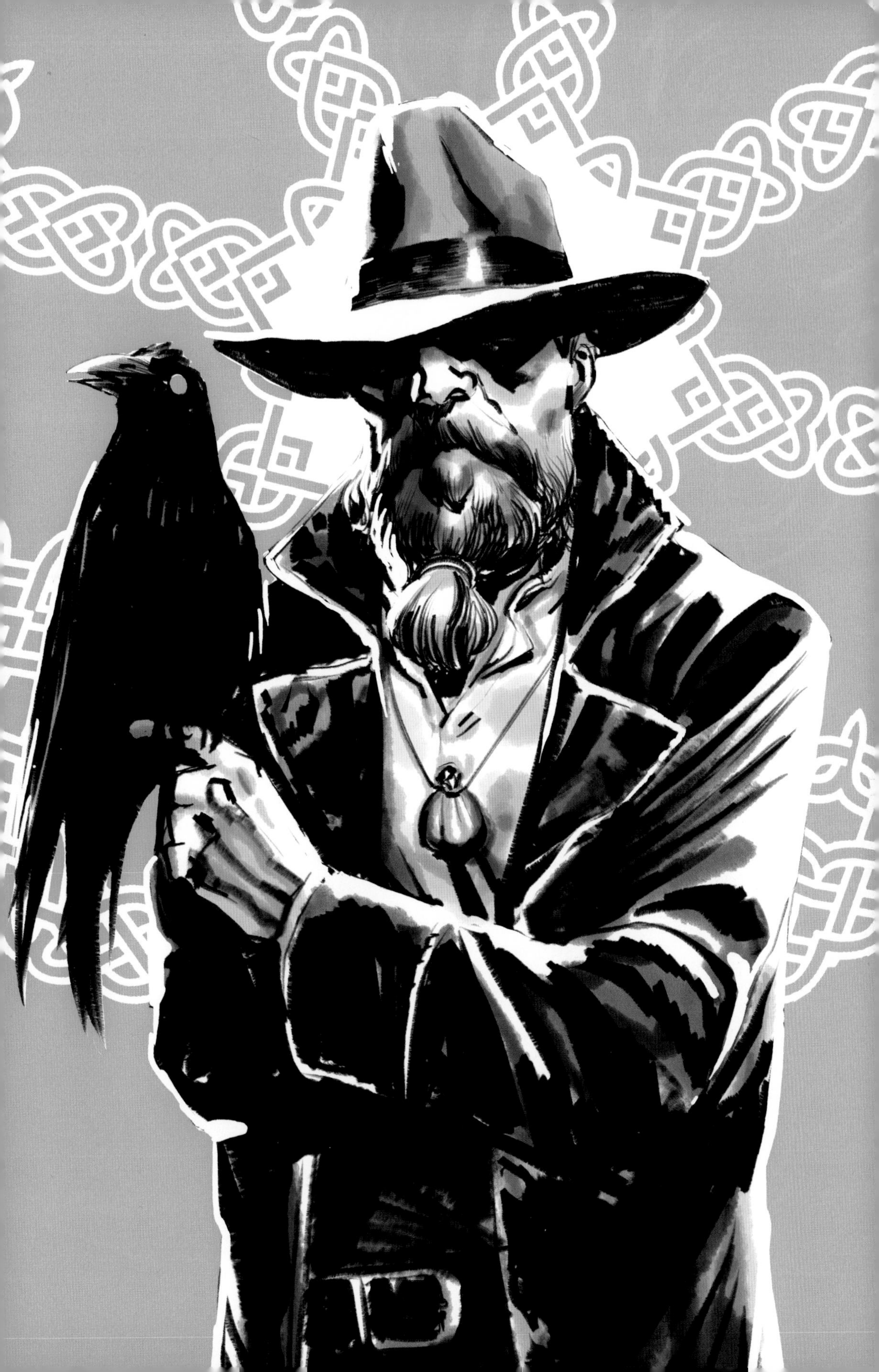

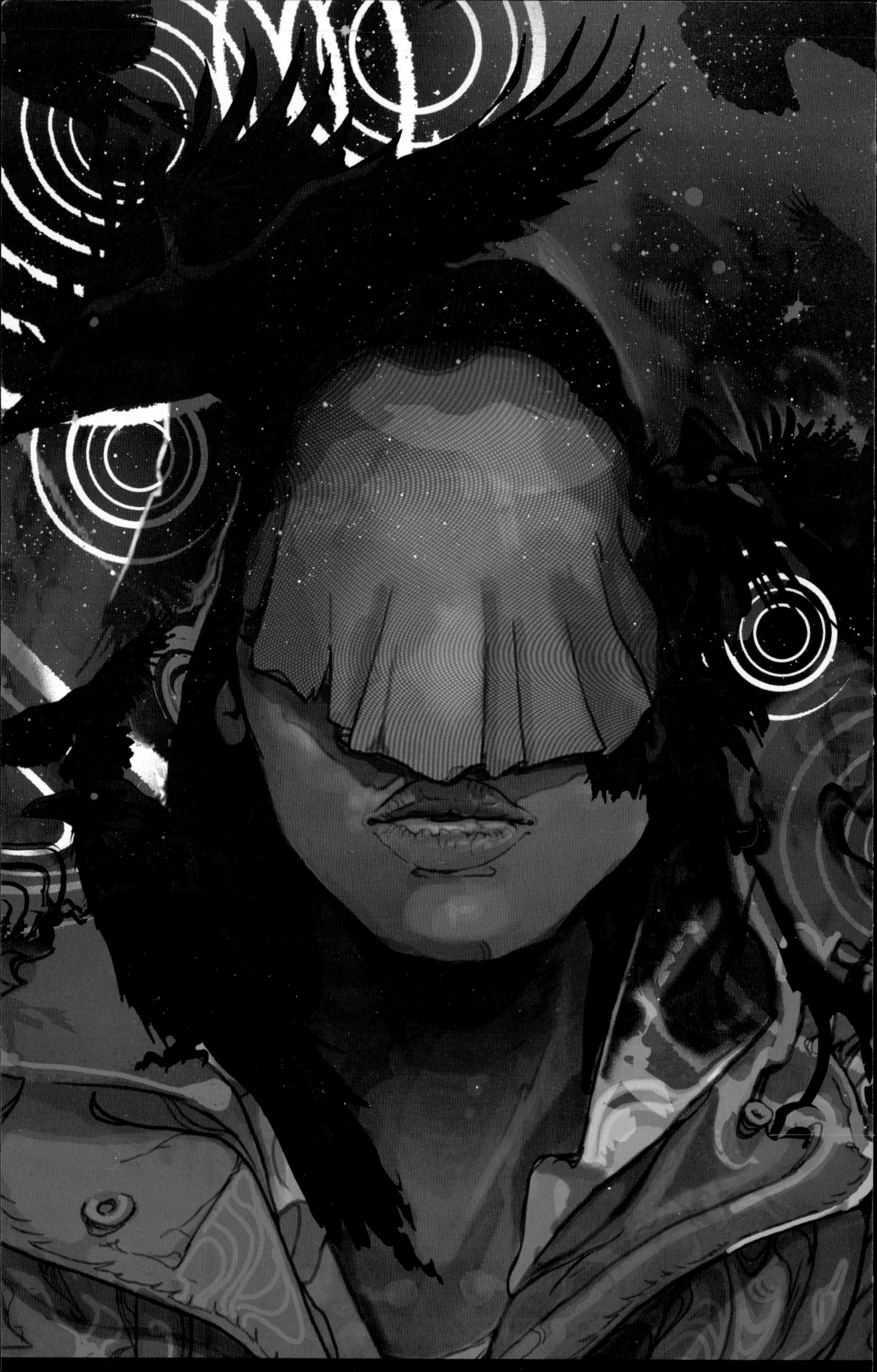

Issue One Cover by **CHRISTIAN WARD**